Contents

Preface ....

Region Index Map 5

Introduction to Britain's Heritage Railway Movement
and Recent Developments 6

Layout of Information 10

Heritage Railway Listings
Region 1. Scotland 13
Region 2. Northern England 27
Region 3. Wales 62
Region 4. West Midlands 70
Region 5. East Midlands....................................... 88
Region 6. Eastern.. 111
Region 7. South-East... 127
Region 8. South-West 148

Proposed Heritage Railway Listings 176

Appendices
Appendix I. Locomotive and Multiple Unit Builders................... 187
Appendix II. Abbreviations 190
Appendix III. Index of Heritage Railways........................... 190

Front Cover Top: The Dartmouth Steam Railway's BR Standard Class 4 4-6-0 75014 "BRAVEHEART" passes Waterside as it climbs towards Churston with the 14.00 Paignton–Kingswear on 26 September 2020.
Stephen Ginn

Front Cover Bottom: 50035 "Ark Royal" powers away from Blue Anchor with the 13.57 Bishops Lydeard–Minehead on 10 June 2018. The locomotive is visiting the West Somerset Railway for the summer Diesel Gala; its usual home is the Severn Valley Railway.
Steve Donald

Back Cover: On 6 July 2019, main line locomotives 20132 & 20096 visited the East Lancashire Railway to participate in its Diesel Gala. The pair have just brought the 17.56 Rawtenstall–Heywood over Duckworth Lane crossing; 56091 is just visible on the rear. The distant signal is notification that Townsend Fold box is around the corner.
Ken Davies

Preface to the Second Edition

A great deal has changed since the first edition of Britain's Heritage Railways was published. Consequently, not only have all the listings for the 100+ railways been updated, with revised stocklists, contact details, opening times and event information, but the sites themselves have changed. Four new railways have been included; the Invergarry & Fort Augustus Railway, the Anglesey Central Railway and the North Dorset Railway have been added to the Proposed Heritage Railways section, as they have reached a sufficiently advanced stage, and the Tamar Belle Heritage Centre is now in the South West section. For a variety of reasons, four sites are no longer included; Manchester's Science and Industry Museum has stopped providing passenger rides, Finmere Railway Station has been cleared of all rolling stock ahead of its redevelopment for HS2, trains no longer operate on the Kingfisher Line and passengers are not carried at Swindon's GWR Steam museum.

One of the strengths of the heritage railway movement is that it keeps growing, with new track continually being laid throughout the country. Despite facing some unprecedented challenges during 2020, several railways have increased their length during the last two years. The Aln Valley, Llangollen and Cambrian Heritage Railways have all extended their lines to newly built stations. Further new lines are under construction at the Royal Deeside, Yorkshire Wolds, Llanelli & Mynedd Mawr, Churnet Valley, Telford Steam, Lincolnshire Wolds, Northampton & Lamport, Mid Norfolk, Mid Suffolk and Swindon & Cricklade Railways. In addition to these active extension projects, many other sites plan to extend in the future. This not only provides plenty of updated content for a second edition, but new interest for enthusiasts and the public alike.

The greatest amount of change has been in the rolling stock found at heritage railways. Hundreds of preserved locomotives or multiple units have moved to, or away from, particular sites since the first edition was published. In many cases it was a transfer from one railway to another, but some preserved locomotives have been returned to main line service and are therefore no longer listed. There has also been an influx of new types that even two years ago were not seen at heritage railways. Production Class 43 High Speed Train powercars now reside at the National Railway Museum in York and at Crewe Heritage Centre. Similarly, the first two Class 60s entered the preservation scene when 60050 and 60086 moved to the Wensleydale Railway in early 2020. A year on, they are now in the process of being moved to a private site in Yorkshire.

Dozens of Class 142 and 144 Pacers have been snapped up by heritage railways as far apart as the Keith & Dufftown and East Kent Railways, after they were retired recently by the main line operator Northern. Preserved Pacers generated what at best could be described as mixed interest from enthusiasts, but this new (or should we say less old!) type of rolling stock came with benefits that heritage railways couldn't ignore; they were in operational condition, available at a low price and have lower operating costs than their alternatives. 142028 & 142060 became the first Pacers to carry passengers in preservation when the two units worked on the Wensleydale Railway in February 2020, not long after they last ran on the national network. Whatever one's particular preference may be, new train types provide preserved railways with fresh publicity and curious new visitors.

Heritage railways have had to contend with some unprecedented financial and logistical challenges recently and these are considered in the updated introduction below. Some serious cracks have begun to appear over the last couple of years and for some railways it has become a financial challenge to keep operating. Consequently, these well-loved sites now need visitors more than ever. Many projects or railway extensions are on hold until sufficient funds have been raised, such as restoring the rope-hauled system designed by George Stephenson at Bowes Railway, or reuniting the two halves of the Great Central Railway. All the sites listed need as much publicity and support as possible and every pound spent on tickets, in gift shops and cafés helps cover their large operating costs. Readers are therefore encouraged to visit sooner rather than later, as it is entirely possible that some of the railways on the pages that follow may not survive these challenging times.

Andy Chard
Manchester, Spring 2021

Maps used in this book
The maps in this book have been derived from a Creative Commons original and are reproduced by permission of the Creative Commons Attribution-ShareAlike 4.0 International Public License. The original map has been modified by addition of the heritage railways.

BRITAIN'S HERITAGE RAILWAYS

SECOND EDITION

Andy Chard

Published by Platform 5 Publishing Ltd,
52 Broadfield Road, Sheffield, S8 0XJ, England.
Printed in England by The Lavenham Press, Lavenham, Suffolk.
ISBN 978 1 909431 87 4

▲ With snow still on the ground from a fall the previous day, GWR 0-6-0 Pannier Tank 1501 heads along the Severn Valley Railway's Tenbury Wall on 30 December 2020. **Martyn Tattam**

SCOTLAND (page 13)
NORTHERN ENGLAND (page 27)
WALES (page 62)
WEST MIDLANDS (page 70)
EAST MIDLANDS (page 88)
EASTERN (page 111)
SOUTH-EAST (page 127)
SOUTH-WEST (page 148)

Introduction to Britain's Heritage Railway Movement and Recent Developments

Two monumental changes took place on Britain's railways during the 1950s and 1960s, which triggered the creation of the heritage railway movement and accelerated its growth; the mass withdrawal of steam locomotives and the closure of thousands of miles of railway lines. These roused many to form railway preservation groups. Some worked to save routes, such as the pioneers of the Keighley and Worth Valley Railway, which was reopened only a few years after it was closed by British Rail in 1962. Other groups wanted to save steam locomotives from being scrapped and find new homes for them to operate at. The two aims of saving railways and saving locomotives married well and were the objectives of many early heritage railways. Whilst the speed with which BR closed lines, lifted track, demolished stations and sold land for development has been well rued over the years, if BR had not acted so fast, the early preservationists may not have been galvanised to act so quickly either and some of today's well-established heritage railways may not otherwise be with us today.

Heritage railways have been evolving since the early days of preservation. As well as preserving steam locomotives, which remain popular with enthusiasts and the public alike, diversification and innovation have brought new sights and sounds. During the early years of the 1960s, heritage railways didn't look much different to the main line network. That began to change once British Rail eradicated steam locomotives and banned them from working on the main line in 1968. As the national operator gradually modernised its stations, trains and infrastructure through the 1960s, 1970s and 1980s, the distinction between the main line network and heritage railways began to become more apparent. The next generation of enthusiasts then saw some of their favourite types eliminated sooner than expected and in response, groups formed to save diesel-hydraulic locomotives during the 1970s and types such as the Class 55 "Deltics" and Class 40 "Whistlers" during the 1980s. These began to arrive at heritage railways, increasing the variety of traction in operation.

▲ Whilst most changes to the length of heritage railways are extensions, some occasionally contract. On 22 April 2011, GWR 2-6-2T 5199 passes Laund Farm crossing with the 14.35 Cauldon Lowe–Froghall; 33021 is just visible on the rear. This section of the Churnet Valley Railway only saw limited use between 2010 and 2014, after which the track between Ipstones and Cauldon Lowe was lifted. 5199 was on loan from Llangollen Railway at the time and is now located at the West Somerset Railway. **Ken Davies**

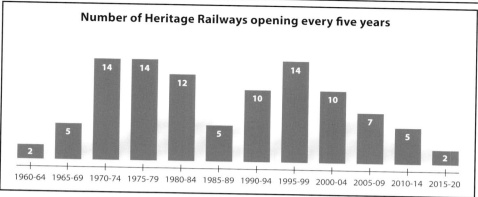

Number of Heritage Railways opening every five years

1960-64	1965-69	1970-74	1975-79	1980-84	1985-89	1990-94	1995-99	2000-04	2005-09	2010-14	2015-20
2	5	14	14	12	5	10	14	10	7	5	2

The adaptation and progress continued, such that standard gauge heritage railways now have equal numbers of steam and diesel locomotives, with almost 1000 examples of each listed in the pages that follow. Diesel multiple unit vehicles are fast catching up; there are now several hundred of these alongside the locomotives, and railcar-themed events are a regular fixture at several railways. Some sites have no steam locomotives and others have lines built at locations with no railway history, neither of which undermine their viability. There are enterprising groups which have restored coaching stock, steam or diesel locomotives to main line standards, so that they can be hired to commercial operators, generating invaluable income to plough back into the heritage scene. In some cases, the members' expertise has been utilised to create specialist subsidiaries or businesses, such as South Devon Railway Engineering at its namesake home, or the Scottish Railway Preservation Society at the Bo'ness & Kinneil Railway, which operates main line charter trains and hires its coaching stock to other operators.

After Britain's railways were privatised in the 1990s, the rate of change on the national network accelerated and wholesale replacement of trains left very few locomotive-hauled services. Passenger numbers grew to unprecedented highs, which required the network to be further modernised, so it could be run as efficiently as possible. Network Rail carries out massive infrastructure upgrades every year, which involve the demolition of signal boxes and the removal of many semaphore signals. Major stations such as Birmingham New Street, Derby, Liverpool Lime Street and Reading have been modernised or completely rebuilt. Together, all of these changes mean that what the public have now become used to when travelling by train is completely different to what they find at a heritage railway. Practises such as exchanging tokens, pulling leavers to move signals and punching holes in Edmondson tickets were the norm little more than a generation ago, as they had been since Victorian times. Nowadays though, they are almost exclusively confined to heritage railways. Consequently, the importance of these living and moving museums has increased. They not only preserve heritage trains, but the Victorian architecture and practises that put them in context. Heritage railways give a unique view of some of Britain's historical achievements, which at one point were the latest technology, while allowing visitors to enjoy some beautiful scenery from the comfort of their seats.

During the last few years, after more than half a century of steady growth, the heritage railway movement has begun to creak under the strain of some new pressures. As the table above shows, the number of new railways opening has been in steady decline over the last two decades. This could be due to the sector reaching maturity, or it could be because it is becoming increasingly difficult to get new projects off the ground. Railways have had to contend with a rising regulatory and legislative burden, at a time when financial and volunteer resources are in shorter supply.

Several heritage railways have already come and gone, but even some of the larger and well-established players have recently encountered difficulties that have jeopardised their future. The West Somerset Railway had to close for an extended period in 2019 while safety concerns were addressed. The passenger line at the Rushden Transport Museum has been out of use since 2018 and the Aln Valley Railway had to temporarily close in late 2020, both also due to safety concerns. Other railways have had to close while costly unbudgeted repairs were carried out, remedying damages caused by factors outside of their control. When the River Churnet flooded in 2019, it washed away a section of the Churnet Valley Railway, which had to be rebuilt.

Flood damage also forced the Tanat Valley Railway to close in 2019 and the necessary repairs aren't expected to be completed until at least 2022. Multiple landslips damaged the Bo'ness & Kinneil Railway in August 2020, requiring repairs which costed in excess of £100 000 and subsidence damage has reduced the operational length of the Bristol Harbour Railway.

To add insult to injury, several railways have suffered malicious attacks. The East Kent Railway incurred significant damage during an arson attack in 2019 and the Border Union Railway was damaged by vandals in August 2020. Tens of thousands of pounds worth of signalling equipment was stolen from the Churnet Valley Railway in September 2020, some of which was to be used on the railway's extension to Leek, and the Derwent Valley Railway had three break-ins and thefts in as many months during 2020. Each of these attacks are costly to rectify and require finances that the railways either don't have, or are earmarked for a different project. They also have a less visible effect, damaging volunteers' morale and motivation, although some generous responses from the public and funding bodies have helped to overcome this.

Even before the game-changing events of 2020 fully unfolded, some railways were encountering significant financial difficulties. The Llangollen Railway for example accrued serious debts which threatened its viability, until a benefactor assisted in 2020. Sadly it seems that that only bought it a bit of time, as the railway had to request the appointment of a receiver in March 2021, leaving the heritage line in a very precarious position. Similarly, the Elsecar Railway had to surrender its lease to Barnsley council in 2020, leaving its future uncertain and efforts to save it are ongoing. In addition, the owner of the Weardale and Dartmoor Railways went into administration in 2020 and whilst the Weardale Railway has since been acquired by a new owner, the situation for the Dartmoor Railway is currently unclear.

Just as the annual heritage railway season was about to begin in March 2020, the coronavirus pandemic hit. This brought so much devastation to the main line operators that the franchising system in place since British Rail was privatised at the end of the last century was abandoned. Heritage railways are completely dependent on visitor income and volunteer labour, both of which ceased immediately, while their fixed costs continued to add up. Practically every heritage railway launched an emergency appeal and it has been estimated that the public

▲ Some heritage railways showcase an area's industrial past very effectively. On 25 May 2019, the Chasewater Railway's No. 2 (works number 2842) has just left Norton Lakeside and heads for Chasetown Church Street during the railway's 2019 Coal Train Weekend. **Alistair Grieve**

generously donated more than £6m in response. It soon became clear that this wouldn't be enough though, and in what might just have saved the heritage railway sector from collapse, a series of government grant schemes were quickly created. Firstly, the National Lottery Heritage Fund established the Heritage Emergency Fund in April 2020, where applications for up to £250 000 could be made. Many railways responded and the table below lists some of the awards made from the fund during 2020.

Site	Sum Awarded	Site	Sum Awarded
Bluebell Railway	£250 000	Foxfield Railway	£81 500
Severn Valley Railway	£250 000	Bressingham	£55 000
Mid Hants Railway	£250 000	Strathspey Railway	£55 500
Great Central Railway	£250 000	Isle of Wight Railway	£49 200
Mid Norfolk Railway	£190 000	North Norfolk Railway	£46 500
East Lancashire Railway	£194 300	Bucks Railway Centre	£40 000
Llangollen Railway	£161 700	Middleton Railway	£39 500
Keith & Dufftown Railway	£127 200	Stainmore Railway	£33 500
South Devon Railway	£124 800	Colne Valley Railway	£34 200
Caledonian Railway	£115 500	West Somerset Railway	£28 700
Midland Railway Butterley	£104 000	Bowes Railway	£27 000
Wensleydale Railway	£60 000	Gwili Railway	£22 400
Keighley & Worth Valley	£60 000	Didcot Railway Centre	£9 900
Nene Valley Railway	£56 500		

Then in Autumn 2020 news of the first round of "lifesaving" grants from the government's £1.57m Culture Recovery Fund started arriving. These were for potentially larger sums, with awards of up to £1m being available. The heritage railway sector has since benefited from millions of pounds from the fund, helping it survive the effects of the Covid-19 pandemic. Recipients of some of the larger sums included the Severn Valley Railway (£906 000), West Somerset Railway (£865 000), East Lancashire Railway (£641 600), Mid Hants Railway (£600 000), North Norfolk Railway (£360 000), South Devon Railway (£332 300), Gloucestershire Warwickshire Railway (£318 000), Kent & East Sussex Railway (£301 500), Bodmin & Wenford Railway (£260 000), Tanfield Railway (£245 500), Keighley & Worth Valley Railway (£231 000), Swanage Railway (£223 200) and Ribble Steam Railway (£207 200). More good news came in late 2020 when the government made a small number of even larger grants of between £1m and £3m from the Culture Recovery Fund, with a massive £1.94m going to the North Yorkshire Moors Railway. These sums illustrate something of the size of the running costs that heritage railways face and perhaps what good value their ticket prices represent.

While the effects of the pandemic were playing out during 2020, heritage railways were dealt another potentially catastrophic blow. Steam locomotives require washed bituminous lump coal and the last domestic mine to produce this closed in August 2020. Two new mines, either of which would have secured the necessary coal supply for Britain's heritage railways, were planned for north-eastern England; one at Highthorn in Northumberland and another at Dewley Hill near Newcastle. Despite lobbying in favour of these from the Heritage Railway Association and other organisations, in mid-2020 the government refused permission for the Highthorn mine to open. In December 2020, Newcastle City Council then refused planning permission for the Dewley Hill mine. The decisions are believed to be motivated by the desire to reduce carbon emissions, however, without a new British mine, coal will have to be imported from countries such as the USA or Russia, the transport of which would generate between five and six times more carbon dioxide than domestically sourced coal! The government has said that it has no wish to see the end of heritage steam trains in Britain, yet it appears to be taking a macro "not in my back yard" position, which will create one of two unsatisfactory outcomes. Either carbon dioxide emissions will see a net increase, as heritage railways are forced to transport coal from another continent, or the increased cost of importing coal will be beyond the means of heritage railways, putting the operation of steam trains in doubt. With no domestic coal extraction now taking place, current supplies are expected to last until 2021 or 2022. It remains to be seen whether imported coal will be affordable.

The Situation Today

Heritage railways now make a significant contribution to Britain's leisure activities, tourism and culture. According to the Heritage Railway Association, they attract millions of annual visitors, provide 4000 jobs nationally, and are major contributors to local and regional finances, adding some £400m to the nation's visitor economy. There are now more than 100 sites operating standard gauge trains and substantially more when narrow gauge railways and tramways are included.

These railways are comprised of people, as much as they are of infrastructure and rolling stock. Committed and tenacious pioneers fundraised and negotiated the purchase of railway trackbeds, locomotives and carriages from BR and its successors. They restored, and in many cases rebuilt, the rolling stock, depots and station buildings, before any trains could run. The backbone of what has been achieved to date is a legion of volunteers, who now form the vast majority of the workforce on today's heritage railways. This brings valuable social benefits that aren't obvious to visitors or easy to quantify; the volunteers form communities where friendships are made, and where engineering and customer facing skills are developed. New volunteers are continually sought and the railways will be delighted to hear from any readers who may want to help!

This book lists the heritage railways and museums within Great Britain and the Channel Islands, where trains carry passengers on a standard gauge line (4 foot 8½ inches). It introduces some fascinating corners of Great Britain, with quintessential rural branch lines and attractions that bring Britain's industrial or military history to life, such as the Northampton Ironstone, Tanfield and Chatham Dockyard Railways. Some sites don't fit into any obvious category and are better seen than described; Appleby Froddingham, Bressingham and Fawley Hill, for example. There is a diverse geographical spread, with routes which traverse the Scottish Highlands (Strathspey, Keith & Dufftown), the rugged North of England (Wensleydale, Eden Valley, Stainmore, Lakeside & Haverthwaite), rural Wales (Llangollen and others), urban areas (Bristol Harbour, Ribble and Epping Ongar) and offer dramatic coastal views (North Norfolk, Dartmouth and West Somerset). Each site has its own merit and therefore reasons to be visited.

Layout of Information

The heritage railway listings have been split into nine regions. The first eight are arranged in geographical order from north to south and the final section lists heritage railways which are nearing the point of operating passenger trains. Within each region, the railways are in alphabetical order and each listing follows the same format.

1. Introduction and History

The history of each site is summarised, including key dates and landmark events from the time the railway was created, through its evolution to heritage status today. Many sites make the journey of ascension, decline and restoration; however, some have taken a different route or become a heritage railway after an entirely different history. The focus on how the site came to be a heritage railway briefly gives credit to many years of hard work and persistence by its founders. As heritage railways are a fluid and developing movement, future extension plans have been researched and are included. Some are long-term aspirations and for others, track is being laid as this book is being read.

2. Contact Details

Contact details follow the same format and if necessary the railway's website can be consulted for the latest timetable information, locomotive rosters or special event details.

3. Transport Links

Where there is a main line rail connection, this is stated, otherwise the nearest main line railway station and its distance from the site is given, as it may be possible to walk or travel by taxi. Car parking facilities are listed, with postcodes for satnav systems and where there is no charge for parking, this is mentioned. If a railway can be reached by another mode of transport, details are given. For example, several railway lines share their route with cycle paths or walkways and some of these have cycle hire facilities adjacent to stations. Others can be reached by boat, including the Battlefield Line (by canal) or the Swanage, Lakeside & Haverthwaite and Dartmouth Railways which all have connecting waterborne services.

4. Opening Times

The dates and times on which the railway operates are summarised. These vary greatly across sites, with some operating almost every day of the year, through to those which do so on a select few dates. Most railways have a set pattern of running dates and times, however, these can be subject to change. The coronavirus pandemic caused most railways to close for extended periods during 2020. Consequently, whilst it is hoped that the effects of this will be comparatively minimal during 2021 and beyond, actual opening times may still be affected and differ from those stated. Due to the uncertainty this creates, readers are advised to check railways' websites or social media outlets for the latest information before travelling.

5. Line Mileage and Journey Time

The line mileage figures provide information on the length of each railway and the distance between stations and termini. Mileages are given to the nearest quarter of a mile, in line with those in national rail network timetables. Where the operational section is short (generally less than one mile) or there is only one station or boarding point, mileage figures are not always shown in list format. The journey times are the minimum needed to make a round trip and can vary depending on the starting point. Further time should be allowed where journeys are broken to explore the attractions and facilities along the route.

6. Stock List

All standard or broad gauge main line locomotives, industrial locomotives and multiple units based at each site are listed. The lists do not include coaches, wagons, London Underground and narrow gauge vehicles. Steam locomotives are shown first, followed by diesel and electric locomotives and then multiple units. The lists are arranged in approximate increasing size order, within each type. See 6.1 for details of types. Stock lists show vehicles based at the railway in 2021, some of which may not be present on a given date, such as when a locomotive visits another heritage railway, is on short-term hire to a main line operator or elsewhere for repairs. Further technical information and details of the names and former numbers carried by main line locomotives and multiple units can be found in Platform 5 Publishing's 'Preserved Locomotives of British Railways' and 'Diesel and Electric Loco Register'.

6.1 Rolling Stock Type

The vast majority of rolling stock listed is comprised of steam locomotives, diesel locomotives and multiple units, with a small number of more unusual vehicles. Each item listed falls into one of the following categories.
Steam: Steam locomotives, with all main line and industrial examples at each railway listed.
Diesel: Locomotives with diesel engines. All main line, shunting and industrial examples are given.
Electric: Locomotives powered by electricity, supplied by AC overhead, DC overhead or DC third rail systems.
Electro-Diesel: Locomotives with diesel engines, which are also capable of drawing electric power.
Battery: Battery-powered locomotives.
Gas Turbine: Locomotives powered by gas turbines (only two are listed).
Petrol: Locomotives powered by a petrol engine (only two are listed).
Steam Railcar: Steam powered single car (only two are listed).
DMU: Diesel Multiple Units; single or multiple carriages powered by self-contained diesel engines.
DEMU: Electric Multiple Units fitted with a diesel engine, enabling power from either source.
EMU: Electric Multiple Units; self-contained carriages powered by overhead or third rail electric power supplies.
Battery EMU: Battery-powered multiple units.

6.2 Number

This lists the number carried, or in some cases the name, by which the vehicle can be identified. Industrial locomotives which have not been given a number or name are listed by their works number, which was assigned by the locomotive builder. Where a locomotive's name is visible and the identifying number is not, for clarity both the name and number are given. Where the number is a low and commonly held value, such as a one or two digit number, the works number is also shown in brackets if this is known. In some cases, a second previously carried number has been added in brackets, where this may be helpful in identifying or distinguishing the vehicle from another. The number currently carried is listed, irrespective of whether that was the most recently carried number in main line service, which in some cases means that locomotives of the same class are listed with very different numbers. For example, steam locomotive 21C123 at the

Bluebell Railway (BR number 34023) carries its Southern Railway number, whereas classmate 34059 at the same location carries its BR number (its previous Southern Railway number was 21C159). For multiple units, individual vehicle numbers are given, as the partners to which they are attached can be changed. As Pacer set formations rarely change, the individual vehicle numbers and the set numbers to which they are more commonly referred are both given.

6.3 Builder

The builder that constructed the locomotive or multiple unit is shown. These are a combination of commercial builders, railway companies including British Rail/Railways and modern organisations that have constructed replica or new-build locomotives. Some of the builders have been abbreviated and a complete list, including their full names is given in Appendix I.

6.4 Details

For all steam locomotives and some smaller diesel locomotives with driving wheels connected by coupling rods, the Whyte notation is used. The three numbers separated by dashes consist of the leading (non-driving) wheels, followed by the number of driving wheels and then the number of trailing (non-driving) wheels. Many steam locomotives have one of the following suffixes: T – side tank, PT – pannier tank, ST – saddle tank, WT – well tank, CT – crane tank, F – fireless, VBT – vertical boiler tank, VBGT – vertical boiler geared tank. For example, 2-4-0ST would be a saddle tank locomotive with 2 leading wheels, 4 driving wheels and no trailing wheels. For locomotives where driving wheels are connected by means other than coupling rods, w is used to indicate powered axles. For example, 4w indicates a four-wheeled bogie with all four wheels powered. The suffixes DE, DM and DH denote diesel-electric, diesel-mechanical and diesel-hydraulic respectively. For some main line diesel and electric locomotives, the number of driven axles is represented by a letter (A = 1, B = 2, C = 3), followed by a number which states the number of non-powered axles. When the letter o is used, this indicates that each axle is individually powered. The majority of multiple units and the remaining diesel and electric locomotives are listed by their TOPS class. This is a classification system introduced by British Railways in 1968 which classified locomotives by a two digit class number and multiple units by a three digit class number.

7. Attractions

This lists attractions at the site, particularly those which are railway related, such as museums, restored signal boxes and miniature railways, as well as any other facilities or services which may be of interest. Some of the more well-known attractions in the surrounding area are also given, including nearby heritage railways, to give ideas for combined visits.

8. Special Events

Heritage railways hold a rich variety of events every year, including beer festivals, live music, transport themed events, family activities and Santa Specials. Many of these attract thousands of visitors and can be a good opportunity to explore something new, inspire children, or something to avoid depending on one's priorities! The information on special events has either been provided by the railways or is based on previous years' calendars of activities. Readers are advised to check the latest information before travelling for particular events.

9. Appendices

Appendix I gives the abbreviations and the full names of all locomotive and multiple unit builders found in the individual railway listings.

Appendix II lists the general abbreviations used in this book.

Appendix III lists all the heritage railways in alphabetical order, with their region and the page number on which they can be found. This acts as a useful index to find the entry for each railway in this book.

Updates and Contact Details

Every effort has been made to ensure the information given is correct, with each of the railways and a large variety of reference sources having been consulted. The content has been updated to April 2021 and the author would be pleased to hear from any reader with information about any inaccuracies or suggestions for enhancements to future editions. Please send any comments to the publisher's address on the title page of this book, or by email to: updates@ platform5.com. The author and publisher cannot take responsibility for any errors, changes or cancellations that may take place.

SCOTLAND

Keith & Dufftown Railway ●

Strathspey Railway ●

Invergarry & Fort Augustus ● Railway (proposed)

Royal Deeside Railway ●

Caledonian Railway ●

Fife Heritage Railway ●

Lathalmond Railway Museum ●

Bo'ness & Kinneil Railway ●

● Doon Valley Railway

Border Union Railway ●

Region 1 – Scotland

Bo'ness & Kinneil Railway

Introduction and History
The branch line from Manuel to Bo'ness Harbour on the Firth of Forth opened in 1848 and was initially only used for carrying minerals and other freight. Passenger services did not commence until 1856 and were withdrawn a century later in 1956, when Bo'ness station was closed. The branch line continued to be used for carrying freight; however, the station was demolished and its original site is now a car park. The Scottish Railway Preservation Society (SRPS) formed in 1961 and started a collection of steam locomotives, which was initially housed at a base in Falkirk, until 1979 when the society acquired the Bo'ness site. The first preserved trains ran in 1981 after a new station was constructed at Bo'ness on the site of former sidings, near where the original station stood. All the buildings at Bo'ness have been brought from other stations or railway sites. The running line was extended to Kinneil Halt in 1987, Birkhill in 1989 and it reached Manuel in 2010, although the station at Manuel was not opened until 2013. The railway museum at the Bo'ness site opened in 1995, was extended in 2002 and a new engineering facility to house the locomotive collection is expected to be completed in 2021.

Contact Details
Website: www.bkrailway.co.uk
Tel: 01506 825855
Email: enquiries.railway@srps.org.uk
Address: Bo'ness & Kinneil Railway, Bo'ness Station, Union Street, Bo'ness, EH51 9AQ.

Transport Links
By Rail: The nearest railway station is Linlithgow, which is four miles away.
By Road: Free car parking is available at Bo'ness (EH51 9AQ).

Opening Times
The railway operates on Saturdays, Sundays and Tuesdays and selected other weekdays from late March until late October. Trains run between approximately 10.45–16.30, depending on which timetable is in operation. The museum at Bo'ness is open 11.00–16.30 every day from April to October.

Line Mileage and Journey Time
0.00   Bo'ness
1.00   Kinneil Halt
3.50   Birkhill
4.75   Manuel

A return journey takes about one hour.

Stock List

Type	Number	Builder	Details
Steam	6 (2127)	Andrew Barclay	0-4-0CT
Steam	3 (1937)	Andrew Barclay	0-4-0ST
Steam	6 (2043)	Andrew Barclay	0-4-0ST
Steam	CITY OF ABERDEEN (912)	Black Hawthorn	0-4-0ST
Steam	3640	Hawthorn Leslie	0-4-0ST
Steam	13 (2203)	Neilson Reid	0-4-0ST
Steam	68095	North British	0-4-0ST
Steam	419	Caledonian Railway	0-4-4T
Steam	65243	Neilson & Co	0-6-0
Steam	LORD ASHFIELD (1989)	Andrew Barclay	0-6-0F
Steam	3 LADY VICTORIA	Andrew Barclay	0-6-0ST
Steam	68007	Bagnall	0-6-0ST
Steam	17 (2880)	Hunslet	0-6-0ST
Steam	19 (3818)	Hunslet	0-6-0ST
Steam	5 (3837)	Hunslet	0-6-0ST
Steam	20 (2068)	Andrew Barclay	0-6-0T

Steam	24 (2335)	Andrew Barclay	0-6-0T
Steam	1 (5710)	Neilson & Co	0-6-0T
Steam	61994	LNER	2-6-0
Steam	80105	British Railways	2-6-4T
Steam	45170	North British	2-8-0
Steam	49 (62277)	North British	4-4-0
Steam	9561	Sentinel	4wVBT
Steam	9627	Sentinel	4wVBT
Steam	9631	Sentinel	4wVBT
Electric	1131	Fairfield Shipbuilding & Engine Co.	0-4-0
Electric	84001	North British	Class 84
Diesel	FGF (552)	Andrew Barclay	0-4-0DH
Diesel	D2767	North British	0-4-0
Diesel	Tiger (27415)	North British	0-4-0
Diesel	262998	Ruston & Hornsby	0-4-0
Diesel	321733	Ruston & Hornsby	0-4-0
Diesel	1 (421439)	Ruston & Hornsby	0-4-0
Diesel	7 (275883)	Ruston & Hornsby	0-4-0
Diesel	P6687	Ruston & Hornsby	0-4-0
Diesel	802 (457299)	Ruston & Hornsby	0-4-0
Diesel	1 (343)	Andrew Barclay	0-6-0
Diesel	D3558	British Railways	Class 08
Diesel	20020	English Electric	Class 20
Diesel	25235	British Railways	Class 25
Diesel	26024	BRCW	Class 26
Diesel	26038	BRCW	Class 26
Diesel	27001	BRCW	Class 27
Diesel	27005	BRCW	Class 27
Diesel	37214	English Electric	Class 37
Diesel	37261	English Electric	Class 37
Diesel	37067/37703	English Electric	Class 37
Diesel	37403	English Electric	Class 37
Diesel	47643	British Railways	Class 47
DMU	51017, 51043, 59404 & 79443	British Railways	Class 126
EMU	61503, 75597 & 75632	Pressed Steel	Class 303

Attractions

The Museum of Scottish Railways at Bo'ness is Scotland's second largest railway museum. There is also a Brass Rubbing Trail, an 'O' gauge model railway and a picnic area at Bo'ness. Steam and diesel footplate experiences are available on the railway. Other attractions in the area include the Kinneil Estate and Museum, Kinneil Nature Reserve, Bo'ness Motor Museum, the Linlithgow Museum, Linlithgow Palace and the city of Edinburgh.

Special Events

Events that usually take place on the railway include:

Easter Egg Specials.
Day Out with Thomas.
Father's Day Event in June.
Afternoon Tea and Evening Fish & Chip Specials.
1950s themed events.
Steam and Diesel Galas.
Santa Specials and Hogmanay trains during December.

▲ North British 0-4-0 diesel-hydraulic shunter D2767 transfers a rake of coaches into Bo'ness yard during the Bo'ness & Kinneil Railway's Diesel Gala on 27 July 2013. **Keith Sanders**

▼ The Bo'ness & Kinneil Railway's Class 126 DMU, which consists of vehicles 51043, 59404 & 51017, approaches Kinneil Halt during the railway's diesel gala on 27 July 2013. **Keith Sanders**

Border Union Railway

Introduction and History

The Border Union Railway, which was marketed as the Waverley Route, ran from Edinburgh to Carlisle via Hawick. It opened in 1862, providing an alternative route from Scotland to England across tough terrain, which required many curves and steep gradients. It was earmarked for closure in Dr Beeching's 1963 report and, despite fierce opposition, was closed in 1969. Between 2012 and 2015, the northern section of the railway was relaid between Edinburgh and Tweedbank and now forms the well-used Borders Railway. In 2002 the Waverley Route Heritage Association obtained a lease for a section of trackbed south of Whitrope Tunnel and its base at Whitrope Heritage Centre is on this. The centre formally opened in 2012 and has an operational section of running track. The railway hopes to extend south by a further two miles in the near future, taking it to Riccarton Junction.

Contact Details

Website: wrha.org.uk
Telephone: 07366 260584
Email: info@wrha.org.uk
Address: Border Union Railway, Whitrope, Hawick, Roxburghshire, TD9 9TY.

Transport Links

By Rail: The site is in a remote location and the nearest stations are Tweedbank (29 miles) and Carlisle (34 miles).
By Road: Car parking is available at Whitrope Heritage Centre (TD9 9TY), which is on the B6399, immediately south of Whitrope Tunnel.

Opening Times

The usual operating times are 10.00 to 16.00 on the first Saturday and Sunday of the month between May and October, with trains running at 40-minute intervals, plus occasional special events during bank holiday weekends.

Line Mileage and Journey Time

0.00	Whitrope Tunnel
0.25	Whitrope Halt
0.50	Golden Bridge

A round trip takes about 30 minutes.

Stock List

Type	Number	Builder	Details
Diesel	3777	Hibberd	4wDM
Diesel	411319	Ruston & Hornsby	4wDM
Diesel	D5340	BRCW	Class 26
DMU	RB004	BREL/Leyland	Prototype Railbus
DMU	142019 (55560 & 55610)	BREL/Leyland	Class 142
DMU	142020 (55561 & 55611)	BREL/Leyland	Class 142
EMU	69316	BREL	Class 422

Attractions

The railway has a collection of second generation diesel multiple units, with a Class 141 prototype railbus and two recently acquired Class 142 "Pacers". These, along with the diesel shunter and restored brake van, are used to carry passengers. The exhibition showing the history and operations of the railway, which includes a signalling experience and various artefacts, is due to be updated for the 2021 season. The buffet coach provides refreshments and contains further railway exhibits. Other attractions in the region include Hermitage Castle to the south, the village of Newcastleton with a Stane from the Seven Stanes Walk and a nearby golf course. To the north, Hawick is the home of cashmere, with textile outlets, a whisky distillery and the annual common riding.

Caledonian Railway

Introduction and History

The railway between Brechin and Bridge of Dun opened in 1848 and later became part of the original Caledonian Railway. The line closed to passenger services in 1952 but continued to be used for freight traffic for almost 30 years until this ended in 1981. Two groups formed in 1979, the Caledonian Railway (Brechin) and the Brechin Railway Preservation Society, to preserve the line. The first locomotive arrived in 1979; however, it wasn't until 1993 when a Light Railway Order was obtained, that passenger services could begin between Brechin and Bridge of Dun. Initially there were aspirations to extend the railway a further three and a half miles from Bridge of Dun to Dubton where the trackbed has been built upon, but this is no longer being pursued.

Contact Details

Website: www.caledonianrailway.com
Tel: 01356 622992
Email: enquiries@caledonianrailway.com
Address: Caledonian Railway, The Station, Park Road, Brechin, DD9 7AF.

Transport Links

By Rail: The nearest railway station is Montrose, which is eight miles away.
By Road: Free car parking is available at both Brechin (DD9 7AF) and Bridge of Dun (DD10 9LH).

Opening Times

The railway is open most Saturdays and Sundays from June to September, with selected other running dates for special events. In addition, the Whistle Stop Coffee Shop at Brechin station opens Wednesdays to Saturdays.

Line Mileage and Journey Time

0.00   Brechin
4.00   Bridge of Dun

A return journey takes about one hour.

Stock List

Type	Number	Builder	Details
Steam	1863	Andrew Barclay	0-4-0ST
Steam	1376 Patricia	Peckett	0-4-0ST
Steam	16 (2759)	Bagnall	0-6-0ST
Steam	6 (2749)	Bagnall	0-6-0ST
Steam	2879	Hunslet	0-6-0ST
Steam	2153	Peckett	0-6-0ST
Steam	MENELAUS	Peckett	0-6-0ST
Steam	2107	Andrew Barclay	0-6-0T
Diesel	3747	Hibberd	0-4-0
Diesel	421700	Ruston & Hornsby	0-4-0
Diesel	458957	Ruston & Hornsby	0-4-0
Diesel	211 ROLLS	Yorkshire Engine Co.	0-4-0
Diesel	212 ROYCE	Yorkshire Engine Co.	0-4-0
Diesel	D3059	British Railways	Class 08
Diesel	12052	British Railways	Class 11
Diesel	12093	British Railways	Class 11
Diesel	20016	English Electric	Class 20
Diesel	20081	English Electric	Class 20
Diesel	20088	English Electric	Class 20
Diesel	25072	British Railways	Class 25
Diesel	25083	British Railways	Class 25
Diesel	26035	BRCW	Class 26
Diesel	D5301	BRCW	Class 26
Diesel	D5314	BRCW	Class 26
Diesel	D5353	BRCW	Class 27
Diesel	D5370	BRCW	Class 27
Diesel	37097	English Electric	Class 37

Attractions

The railway has a large collection of steam and diesel locomotives comparative to its size; the original railway station and railway yard can be seen at Brechin. Nearby attractions include Brechin Castle and Gardens (open on selected dates), Lunan Bay, Montrose Basin Nature Reserve and the coastal town of Montrose.

Special Events

Events that usually take place on the railway include:

Easter Eggspress event.
Food and drink themed events including "Take the Sloe Train" and "Whisky Whistler".
Days Out With Thomas.
Murder on the Brechin Express.
Diesel Weekends.
Santa Specials during December.

▲ Having just arrived on the 10.30 from Dufftown, Class 108 DMU vehicles 53628 & 56224 "Spirit of Speyside" stand at Keith Town, the eastern terminus of the Keith & Dufftown Railway, on 14 September 2019. **Ian Beardsley**

Doon Valley Railway

Introduction and History
The railway between Ayr and Dalmellington opened in 1856, carrying passengers and freight from the iron and coal pits at Dalmellington. Passenger services were withdrawn in 1964 and regular freight traffic continued to use the branch until 1978, when many of the collieries closed. The Ayrshire Railway Preservation Group (ARPG) formed in 1974, with the aim of preserving the area's railway heritage. The group were initially based at the former Minnivey Colliery in Ayrshire from 1980 and moved to the current site at Dunaskin, on the former Dalmellington branch, in 2002. To better reflect the primary purpose of operating heritage trains, the organisation's name was changed from the Scottish Industrial Railway Centre to the Doon Valley Railway in 2019. The railway has a collection of industrial steam and diesel locomotives, many of which were built by Andrew Barclay & Sons at nearby Kilmarnock.

Contact Details
Website: www.doonvalleyrailway.co.uk
Tel: 01292 269260
Email: info@doonvalleyrailway.co.uk
Address: Doon Valley Railway, Dunaskin, Ayr, KA6 7JH.

Transport Links
By Rail: The nearest stations to the Dunaskin site are Maybole (11 miles) and Ayr (12 miles).
By Road: Free parking is available at Dunaskin.

Opening Times
The usual opening times are 11.00–16.30 on selected Sundays between April and September. Trains operate during these times and are usually steam-hauled.

Line Mileage and Journey Time
0.00   Dunaskin
2.50   Minnivey

A return journey takes about 30 minutes.

Stock List

Type	Number	Builder	Details
Steam	8 (1952)	Andrew Barclay	0-4-0F
Steam	1 (2368)	Andrew Barclay	0-4-0ST
Steam	10 (2244)	Andrew Barclay	0-4-0ST
Steam	16 (1116)	Andrew Barclay	0-4-0ST
Steam	19 (1614)	Andrew Barclay	0-4-0ST
Steam	23 (2260)	Andrew Barclay	0-4-0ST
Steam	25 (2358)	Andrew Barclay	0-6-0ST
Diesel	7	Andrew Barclay	0-4-0
Diesel	AC118 M3571	Andrew Barclay	0-4-0
Diesel	Powfoot No. 1	Andrew Barclay	0-4-0
Diesel	Lily of the Valley	Fowler	0-4-0
Diesel	107	Hunslet	0-4-0
Diesel	27644 (ARMY 409)	North British	0-4-0
Diesel	421697	Ruston & Hornsby	0-4-0
Diesel	324 Blinkin Bees (284239)	Ruston & Hornsby	0-4-0
Diesel	417890 Johnnie Walker	Ruston & Hornsby	0-4-0
Diesel	BE116 DY322	Ruston & Hornsby	0-4-0
Diesel	10012	Sentinel	0-4-0

Attractions
Steam or diesel locomotives give brake van rides on the former industrial railway line which runs east from the Dunaskin site. There are a variety of steam and diesel locomotives to see, with standard and narrow gauge exhibits, plus a model railway and photographic archives to explore. Nearby attractions include the Galloway Forest Park, the Scottish Dark Sky Observatory, the village of Straiton and the coast and beaches on the southern Firth of Clyde.

Fife Heritage Railway

Introduction and History

The Lochty Private Railway ran on a former mineral railway in Fife from 1967 until it closed in 1992. The Kingdom of Fife Railway Preservation Society then formed in 1992 to find a new home for the remaining railway stock, which was initially moved to the closed railway site at Methil Power Station. In 2001 the society acquired the nearby former marshalling yard at Kirkland, near Leven, and in 2003 after laying track and landscaping the site, the rolling stock was moved there. It opened to the public in 2008; the first steam train ran in 2016 and the railway now has half a mile of track, an engine shed and several sidings. The heritage railway had hoped to gain access to the disused Leven branch and run towards Cameron Bridge, however this may not be possible as the main line connection from Thornton to Cameron Bridge and Leven is due to be reinstated as part of the national network.

Contact Details

Website: www.fifeheritagerailway.co.uk
Email: enquiries@fifeheritagerailway.com
Address: Fife Heritage Railway, Kirkland Sidings, Leven, Fife, KY8 4RB.

Transport Links

By Rail: The nearest railway station is Markinch, which is six miles from the railway.
By Road: On-site parking is available (KY8 4RB).

Opening Times

Open days are on the last Sunday of the month from April to October, when trains provide passenger rides.

Line Mileage and Journey Time

The railway currently runs for half a mile and the journey time is relatively short.

Stock List

Type	Number	Builder	Details
Steam	17	Andrew Barclay	0-4-0ST
Steam	10 FORTH	Andrew Barclay	0-4-0ST
Steam	3 (2046)	Andrew Barclay	0-4-0ST
Diesel	400 RIVER EDEN	North British	0-4-0
Diesel	1	Ruston & Hornsby	0-4-0
Diesel	7	Ruston & Hornsby	0-4-0
Diesel	2 The Garvie Flyer	Ruston & Hornsby	0-4-0
Diesel	4	Ruston & Hornsby	0-4-0
Diesel	10	North British	0-6-0

Attractions

A café has recently been added and this is open on railway operating days. Other nearby attractions include Methil Heritage Centre, Leven Beach and Riverside Park in Glenrothes. The Lathalmond Railway Museum is 23 miles away and the Bo'ness & Kinneil Railway is 35 miles away.

Special Events

Events that usually take place on the railway include:

Easter Bunny event.
Steam and diesel Galas.
Halloween event in October and Santa Specials during December.

Keith & Dufftown Railway

Introduction and History

The three railway lines which converge at Keith were constructed in stages. The route from Aberdeen reached Keith in 1856 and the line from Inverness in 1858, creating a through route. The branch from Keith to Dufftown opened in 1862 and this was extended from Dufftown to Nethy Bridge in 1863 and forward to Boat of Garten in 1866, allowing through running to Aviemore. The line had rail connections at many of the distilleries along the route, allowing whisky to be transported by rail. Through passenger services from Keith to Aviemore via Dufftown ceased in 1965, followed by freight in 1968. Whisky trains ran from Aberlour to Keith until 1971 and from Dufftown until 1985. Occasional charter services continued to visit Dufftown until the last of these ran in 1991. The Keith and Dufftown Railway acquired the line in 1998 and the first trains in preservation ran in 2000. The railway is no longer connected to the national network, as a short section of track in Keith has been lifted; however, it is hoped that this can be reinstated in the future.

Contact Details

Website: www.keith-dufftown-railway.co.uk
Tel: 01542 882123
Email: info@keith-dufftown-railway.co.uk
Address: Keith Town Station, Keith, Banffshire, AB55 5BR.

Transport Links

By Rail: The nearest station is Keith, which is less than one mile from Keith Town station.
By Road: Free parking is available at Dufftown (AB55 4BA) and Keith Town station (AB55 5BR).

Opening Times

Trains operate every Saturday and Sunday from April to September, plus most Fridays and on selected other dates.

Line Mileage and Journey Time

0.00	Dufftown
4.50	Drummuir
10.25	Keith Town

A return journey takes about 1 hour 40 minutes from Dufftown (longer if starting from Keith).

Stock List

Type	Number	Builder	Details
Diesel	415	Andrew Barclay	0-4-0
Diesel	The Wee Mac	Clayton	0-4-0
Diesel	Spirit O Fife	English Electric	0-6-0
DMU	50628, 51568, 52053, 56224 & 56491	British Railways	Class 108
DMU	140001 (55500 & 55501)	BREL/Leyland	Class 140
DMU	144022 (55822, 55858 & 55845)	Alexander/BREL	Class 144

Attractions

Keith Town station has a shop, which includes various railway books and model railway items. The railway offers a diesel shunter driving experience, which is unusual among heritage railways, as driving experiences tend to use main line steam or diesel locomotives. At Dufftown visitors can look around the locomotive shed and heritage centre by arrangement, plus the shop and Sidings Café which are housed inside converted carriages. The station is less than one mile from the centre of historic Dufftown, which is known as the whisky capital of the world and has seven working distilleries. Other attractions in the region include the 13th Century Balvenie Castle and the Speyside Way, which is a traffic-free path along much of the railway trackbed to Grantown-on-Spey near the Strathspey Railway, which is approximately 33 miles away.

Special Events

Events that usually take place on the railway include:

Children's Easter Bunny Challenge.
Food and drink related events include the Spirit of Speyside Whisky Festival, Pie & Pint Specials and Fish & Chip specials.

1940s Weekend.
Teddy Bears' Weekend.
Halloween Ghost Train.
Santa Specials during December.

Lathalmond Railway Museum

Introduction and History

This region of Fife was home to a number of railways and narrow gauge tramways built to carry minerals, the first of which opened in 1864. During the Second World War, the Royal Navy built a stores and transit depot on the Lathalmond site, for the nearby Rosyth Dockyard and this facility used the extensive railway network until 1971. The Royal Navy site closed in 1993 and in 1995 part of the grounds were acquired by the Scottish Vintage Bus Museum to house its exhibits. In 1997 the Shed47 Railway Restoration Group was formed, with the aim of re-establishing some of the vast railway network that occupied the site, which the group share with the bus museum.

Contact Details

Website: www.shed47.org
Tel: 07379 914801
Email: mail@shed47.org
Address: Shed47 Railway Restoration Group at SVBM, M90 Commerce Park, Lathalmond, KY12 OSJ.

Transport Links

By Rail: The nearest station is Dunfermline Town, which is three miles away.
By Road: Car parking is available on site (KY12 OSJ).

Opening Times

The railway museum opens each Sunday from April to October inclusive. Standard gauge trains run on selected Sundays.

Line Mileage and Journey Time

The standard gauge railway line is 400 metres long and the journey time is relatively short.

Stock List

Type	Number	Builder	Details
Steam	17	Andrew Barclay	0-4-0ST
Steam	29	Andrew Barclay	0-4-0ST
Diesel	236 (372)	Andrew Barclay	0-4-0DM
Diesel	385	Andrew Barclay	0-4-0DM
Diesel	4210140	Fowler	0-4-0
Diesel	D2650	Hunslet	0-4-0
Diesel	251	Hunslet	0-4-0

Attractions

The site is shared with the Scottish Vintage Bus Museum, which opens simultaneously. It is the home of the 1942-built locomotive shed, a working weighbridge and a 2-foot gauge railway, which runs for 300 metres. The Knockhill Racing Circuit is nearby; to the east is the Fife Heritage Railway and to the south is the Forth Bridge, across which is the Bo'ness & Kinniel Railway and the city of Edinburgh.

Special Events

The vintage bus museum has special events on particular dates. These are subject to a charge by the bus museum and standard and narrow gauge trains usually run on these dates from 11.00. Other events may be added during 2021 – please check the website.

Royal Deeside Railway

Introduction and History

When the railway from Aberdeen to Banchory was completed in 1853, Crathes Castle station on the route opened as a private station for the Laird of Crathes. The line was extended to Aboyne in 1859 and to its final terminus Ballater in 1866. In 1863 Crathes Castle became a public railway station, being renamed Crathes and until the route's closure in 1966, it was regularly used by the Royal Family to reach Balmoral Castle. The Royal Deeside Railway Preservation Society formed in 2003 and began restoring the line in 2003. A base was established at Crathes and as the previous station had become a private residence, the new Milton of Crathes station was built at a more accessible location. The railway currently runs for one mile and is gradually being extended westwards along the original trackbed. Once a new bridge to carry the Deeside Way footpath over the Burn of Bennie has been installed, the railway will be reinstated on the original bridge, allowing the line to continue west. The long-term aim is to reach Banchory, which will give the line a running length of over 2 miles.

Contact Details

Website: www.deeside-railway.co.uk
Tel: 01330 844416
Email: opsdir@deeside-railway.co.uk
Address: The Royal Deeside Railway, Milton of Crathes, Banchory, Aberdeenshire, AB31 5QH.

Transport Links

By Rail: The nearest railway stations are Portlethen (14 miles) and Aberdeen (16 miles).
By Road: Parking for the railway is available at the Milton of Crathes art & craft village (AB31 5QH).

Opening Times

Trains depart on the hour 11.00–16.00 each Sunday from April to October and on selected Wednesdays and Saturdays during April, July and August. Services are hauled by a steam or Class 03 diesel locomotive on alternate dates.

Line Mileage and Journey Time

From Milton of Crathes the railway operates for one mile. A return journey takes about 20 minutes.

Stock List

Type	Number	Builder	Details
Steam	BON ACCORD	Andrew Barclay	0-4-0ST
Steam	6 (2110)	Peckett	0-4-0ST
Steam	SALMON	Andrew Barclay	0-6-0ST
Diesel	D2037	British Railways	Class 03
Diesel	D2094	British Railways	Class 03
Diesel	D2134	British Railways	Class 03
Battery EMU	79998 & 79999	British Railways	Derby Lightweight

Attractions

The railway is situated within the Milton of Crathes complex which includes craft shops, galleries, a children's play area and a restaurant. There is a Victorian station, a railway carriage tearoom, a shop and great views of the surrounding hills as the line follows the River Dee. Steam driving experiences are available. The region is home to Crathes Castle garden and estate, the city of Aberdeen, Balmoral Castle, Craigievar Castle and Grampian Transport Museum.

Special Events

Events that usually take place on the railway include:

Mother's Day event with Cream Teas.
End of Season Gala.
Santa Specials and Mince Pie Specials during December.

Strathspey Railway

Introduction and History

The railway from Aviemore to Forres, which includes the route of today's Strathspey Railway, opened in 1863. The route from Dufftown to Nethy Bridge (see Keith & Dufftown Railway) also opened in 1863 and was extended south to Boat of Garten in 1866. The Aviemore to Forres via Boat of Garten route was the original Highland Main Line, until the direct route from Aviemore to Inverness was completed in 1898. This led to the line via Boat of Garten becoming a secondary route and passenger services eventually ceased in 1965. Freight traffic, which mainly consisted of locally produced whisky, ended in 1968 when the line was closed. The first preservation group formed in 1971, buying the trackbed from British Rail and the first trains ran from a site north of Aviemore to Boat of Garten in 1978. The railway was extended into the main line station at Aviemore in 1998; in 2002 a further extension north to Broomhill opened and there are long-term plans for the railway to continue north to Grantown-on-Spey.

Contact Details

Website: www.strathspeyrailway.co.uk
Tel: 01479 810725
Email: Written enquiries can be made via the website.
Address: Strathspey Railway, Aviemore Station, Dalfaber Road, Aviemore, PH22 1PY.

Transport Links

By Rail: Main line rail connection at Aviemore; just cross the footbridge to Platform 3.
By Road: Car parking is available at Aviemore (PH22 1PD – use the main line station postcode), Boat of Garten (PH24 3BH) and Broomhill (PH26 3LX).

Opening Times

The operating season usually starts at the end of March, with trains running on Saturdays, Sundays and some weekdays until late October. Santa Specials also run during weekends in December. Trains usually operate between 10.30 and approximately 16.30, although this may differ during special events.

Line Mileage and Journey Time

0.00	Aviemore
5.25	Boat of Garten
9.25	Broomhill

A return journey takes about 1 hour 45 minutes.

Stock List

Type	Number	Builder	Details
Steam	2 (2020)	Andrew Barclay	0-4-0ST
Steam	828	Caledonian Railway	0-6-0
Steam	9	Robert Stephenson & Hawthorns	0-6-0ST
Steam	WPR17 (2017)	Andrew Barclay	0-6-0T
Steam	46512	British Railways	2-6-0
Steam	46464	British Railways	2-6-0
Steam	45025	Vulcan Foundry	4-6-0
Diesel	517	Andrew Barclay	0-4-0
Diesel	27549	North British	0-4-0
Diesel	260756	Ruston & Hornsby	0-4-0
Diesel	265618	Ruston & Hornsby	0-4-0
Diesel	277V	Thomas Hill	4wDH
Diesel	D2774	North British	D2/10
Diesel	D3605	British Railways	Class 08
Diesel	D5302	BRCW	Class 26
Diesel	D5325	BRCW	Class 26
Diesel	D5394	BRCW	Class 27
Diesel	D5862	Brush Traction	Class 31
DMU	51990, 52008 & 52030	British Railways	Class 107
DMU	56047	British Railways	Class 114
DMU	51367, 51402 & 59511	Pressed Steel	Class 117

Attractions

The railway has a variety of heritage rolling stock and travels through the spectacular Scottish highland scenery. The shops at the railway's three stations include a selection of second-hand railway books and magazines. Aviemore is in the Monadhliath and Cairngorm mountain region and Boat of Garten has a golf and tennis club. The RSPB observation hide at the Osprey Centre is 1.5 miles from the station. There are many walks and cycle routes in the area, most notably the Speyside Way which follows much of the former railway line and the Keith & Dufftown Railway is at the northern end of this, approximately 33 miles away.

Special Events

Events that usually take place on the railway include:

Afternoon tea, traditional lunch and evening dining trains.
Summer Event during July.
Halloween Event.
Santa Express and Mince Pie Specials during December.

▲ The Strathspey Railway has a varied locomotive fleet which includes several diesels. On 17 October 2018, Class 08 D3605, Class 27 D5394 and Class 31 D5862 are stabled at the railway's Aviemore depot. **Tony Christie**

NORTHERN ENGLAND

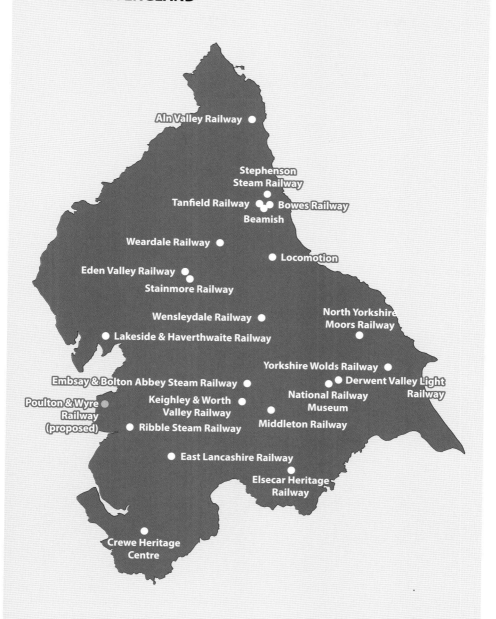

Aln Valley Railway

Stephenson Steam Railway

Tanfield Railway

Bowes Railway

Beamish

Weardale Railway

Locomotion

Eden Valley Railway

Stainmore Railway

Wensleydale Railway

North Yorkshire Moors Railway

Lakeside & Haverthwaite Railway

Yorkshire Wolds Railway

Embsay & Bolton Abbey Steam Railway

Derwent Valley Light Railway

Poulton & Wyre Railway (proposed)

Keighley & Worth Valley Railway

National Railway Museum

Ribble Steam Railway

Middleton Railway

East Lancashire Railway

Elsecar Heritage Railway

Crewe Heritage Centre

Region 2 – Northern England

Aln Valley Railway

Introduction and History

The 2.75-mile branch line from Alnmouth to Alnwick opened in 1850 and remained in use for well over a century, until it closed to both passenger and freight traffic in 1968. The Aln Valley Railway was established during the 1990s and built a new station and base at the Lionheart site. This is on the outskirts of Alnwick, as the trackbed nearer the town centre has been built upon. The first passenger trains operated on a short stretch of track in 2013, which was then increased to a length of three quarters of a mile. In 2019 it was further extended by another half mile to a new eastern terminus called Greenrigg Halt, which was due to open in April 2020, but the coronavirus restrictions caused this to be postponed until 2021. More than half of the branch has now been reinstated and works to extend it further are ongoing.

Contact Details

Website: www.alnvalleyrailway.co.uk
Tel: 0300 030 3311
Email: getintouch@alnvalleyrailway.co.uk
Address: Lionheart Railway Station, Lionheart Enterprise Park, Alnwick, NE66 2EZ.

Transport Links

By Rail: Alnmouth Railway Station is four and a half miles from Lionheart by road.
By Road: Ample parking is available at the Lionheart site (NE66 2HT), which is close to the A1 and Alnwick town centre. Parking is free, although a voluntary contribution may be requested during special events.
By Bike: There is a cycle route from the centre of Alnwick to the nearby Lionheart Enterprise Park.

Opening Times

The railway usually operates on Saturdays, Sundays and Bank Holidays from April to September, with occasional exceptions, plus selected weekdays and weekends during October and December.

▲ 26020 is the sole surviving Class 76 DC electric locomotive and can be found on display at the National Railway Museum in York, where is it seen on 14 April 2019. **Alisdair Anderson**

Line Mileage and Journey Time

0.00   Alnwick Lionheart
1.25   Greenrigg Halt

A round trip on the line takes about half an hour.

Stock List

Type	Number	Builder	Details
Steam	3799 PENICUIK	Hawthorn Leslie	0-4-0ST
Steam	48 (WD 75015)	Hunslet	0-6-0ST
Steam	60 (3686)	Hunslet	0-6-0ST
Steam	9 RICHBORO	Hudswell Clarke	0-6-0T
Diesel	265617	Ruston & Hornsby	4wDM
Diesel	L2 (312989)	Ruston & Hornsby	0-4-0DE
Diesel	20/110/711 (615)	Andrew Barclay	0-6-0
Diesel	8199	Drewry	0-6-0
Diesel	12088	British Railways	Class 11
DMU	144004 (55804 & 55827)	Alexander/BREL	Class 144
DMU	144016 (55816, 55852 & 55839)	Alexander/BREL	Class 144

Attractions

The Alnwick site has a museum with photographs and artefacts from the branch line's history. There is also a café, shop, children's playground, model railway which has several layouts and some restored vintage carriages. Driving Experiences are available using diesel locomotives. Alnwick has a number of attractions including Alnwick Castle and other nearby destinations include Holy Island, Dunstanburgh Castle and Craster, home of the kipper.

Special Events

Events that usually take place on the railway include:

Easter Steam Weekend and Easter Bunny Hunt.
Music Festival during May.
Classic & Vintage Vehicles Weekend during June.
1940s Weekend during July.
Teddy Bears' Picnic during August.
Model Rail Exhibition during September.
Halloween Ghost Trains.
Santa Specials and Mince Pie Specials during December.

Beamish: The Living Museum of the North

Introduction and History

Beamish is a 350-acre site, housing a number of interactive displays of industrial life through Georgian, Victorian, Edwardian and 20th Century England. The museum opened on its current site in 1972 and has a variety of original and replica buildings, a working tramway and standard and narrow gauge railways. The standard gauge line has a railway station, which was relocated from Rowley, County Durham and this was reopened by poet Sir John Betjeman in 1976. After more than four decades of operation, the railway track is in need of renewal works and these are due to be completed during 2021. Consequently, the standard gauge line will not operate during 2021 and it is hoped that trains will return in 2022. The narrow gauge railway will continue to run during 2021.

Contact Details

Website: www.beamish.org.uk
Tel: 0191 370 4000
Email: museum@beamish.org.uk
Address: Beamish Museum, Regional Resource Centre, Beamish, County Durham, DH9 0RG.

Transport Links

By Rail: Chester-le-Street is the nearest railway station and is five miles away.
By Road: Ample car parking is available at the museum.

Opening Times

The Museum usually opens 10.00-16.00 every day except Christmas Day and Boxing Day. Trains usually operate during weekends, bank holidays and school holidays only.

Line Mileage and Journey Time

The standard gauge railway from Rowley station is approximately one sixth of a mile and the journey time is relatively short.

Stock List

Type	Number	Builder	Details
Steam	"Puffing Billy" (replica)	Alan Keef	0-4-0
Steam	7006	Robert Stephenson & Hawthorns	0-4-0CT
Steam	1370	Peckett	0-4-0ST
Steam	5 MALLEABLE	South Durham Steel & Iron	0-4-0ST
Steam	18	Stephen Lewin	0-4-0ST
Steam	1	Head Wrightson	0-4-0VBGT
Steam	17	Head Wrightson	0-4-0VBT
Steam	"Steam Elephant" (replica)	Alan Keef	0-6-0
Steam	1532 NEWCASTLE	Manning Wardle	0-6-0ST
Steam	1	Black Hawthorn	2-4-0CT

Attractions

The museum includes an 1820s landscape and wagonway, a 1900s town, a pit village, colliery and 1940s farm. There is a one and a half mile working tramway and an operational railway with an 1850 goods shed, an 1896 signal box, a wrought iron footbridge and a coal drop. There are extensive collections of domestic, rural, industrial and transport related exhibits. At certain times, themed visitor experiences are available for an additional charge and these include the Tram Driving Experience. Nearby heritage railways include Tanfield Railway (three miles away), Bowes Railway (eight miles) and Stephenson Steam Railway (16 miles). The cities of Newcastle and Sunderland are ten and 14 miles from Beamish respectively.

Special Events

Events that usually take place on the railway include:

Seasonal events take place at Easter, Halloween and Christmas.

▲ On 8 April 2018, during its Steam Fair, Beamish Museum's replica of 0-4-0 Puffy Billy is seen in action on the site's Colliery Line. **Alisdair Anderson**

Bowes Railway

Introduction and History

The first incarnation of what became Bowes Railway was a wooden horse-drawn wagonway built during the 1720s to carry coal from the Durham Coalfield to the River Wear. When the standard gauge railway opened in 1826, it was one of the world's first railways. It was 15 miles long and carried coal to the River Tyne at Jarrow. Trains were locomotive-hauled at each end of the railway and the six-mile middle section was rope-worked, as this included some very steep gradients. Most of the line was closed between 1968 and 1974 and the final 3.5-mile section was operated by the National Coal Board until 1974. The original part of the railway which dates from 1826 was acquired for preservation in 1976. In 2002 Bowes Railway was granted museum status and the site is now registered with Historic England as a Scheduled Ancient Monument. Two other parts of the original Bowes Railway have been preserved; Springwell Bankfoot Loco Shed, which is the home of North East Bus Preservation Society and Marley Hill Shed and Yard, which are part of nearby Tanfield Railway. Bowes Railway is now the only remaining standard gauge rope hauled railway in the world.

Contact Details

Website: www.bowesrailway.uk
Tel: 0191 416 1847
Email: amandacuskin@communityopportunities.co.uk
Address: Bowes Railway, Springwell Road, Gateshead, NE9 7QJ.

Transport Links

By Rail: Bowes Railway is 2.5 miles from Heworth Metro station and 4 miles from Newcastle Central.
By Road: Car parking is available at Bowes Railway (NE9 7QJ).

Opening Times

The usual opening times are 10.00–15.00 on Thursdays, Fridays and Saturdays, plus the first Sunday of the month. Guided tours are available on request.

Line Mileage and Journey Time

0.00   Springwell Halt
1.00   Wrekenton

The Springwell to Wrekenton section is used to carry passengers and a return journey takes about 30 minutes. The railway line also continues north to the start of Springwell Incline and south to the rope hauling house at Blackham's Hill.

Stock List

Type	Number	Builder	Details
Steam	22	Andrew Barclay	0-4-0ST
Steam	WST	Andrew Barclay	0-4-0ST
Diesel	PINKY	Robert Stephenson & Hawthorns	0-4-0DH
Diesel	PERKY	Robert Stephenson & Hawthorns	0-4-0DH
Diesel	101	Hibberd	0-4-0DM
Diesel	6263	Hunslet	0-4-0
Diesel	476140	Ruston & Hornsby	0-4-0

Attractions

The standard gauge rope-hauled railway is unique. It has some well-preserved early features designed by George Stephenson, including the "Kip and Dish" and brake cabin at the top of Springwell Bank. The colliery yard has a varied collection of more than 40 railway wagons built between the 1880s and 1960s, including the restored wagon in which the Queen Mother travelled in 1976. The restored colliery workshops, which have been in use since 1826, house a museum with many exhibits, including narrow gauge mining locomotives, historic machines including an operational Fairbairn Naylor MacPherson & Co wheel lathe and an operational blacksmith's workshop. The Bowes Model Railway Club operate the model railway on selected dates and there is a tea room and gift shop. Passengers can't currently be carried and services will be reinstated once the Office of Rail and Road (ORR) has carried out an inspection of the line. Nearby transport-themed attractions include the Tanfield Railway, Beamish and the North-East Land, Sea & Air Museum. Newcastle, Sunderland and the coast are all only a few miles away.

Crewe Heritage Centre

Introduction and History

Crewe Heritage Centre opened in 1987 and is located on the site of the railway yard immediately north of Crewe station, between the Chester line and West Coast Main Line, at the point where they split. The site includes Crewe North Junction signal box, which was preserved after it was decommissioned in 1985, complete with a viewing balcony which is ideal for watching passing trains. A main line rail connection allows visiting steam and diesel locomotives and some of the home-based locomotives to travel to other sites.

Contact Details

Website: www.crewehc.org
Tel: 01270 212130
Email: Written enquiries can be made via the website.
Address: The Crewe Heritage Centre Trust Ltd, Vernon Way, Crewe, Cheshire, CW1 2DB.

Transport Links

By Rail: The Heritage Centre is less than a mile from Crewe railway station.
By Road: Car parking is available on site (CW1 2DB).

Opening Times

The Centre opens 10.00–16.30 (last admission 15.30) on Saturdays, Sundays and Bank Holidays from April to October inclusive.

Line Mileage and Journey Time

There are various standard gauge lines and sidings at the centre, a short stretch of which is sometimes used for giving brake van rides using diesel locomotives 03073 or 47192.

Stock List

Type	Number	Builder	Details
Diesel	10007	Sentinel	0-4-0
Diesel	132C	Thomas Hill	0-4-0DH
Diesel	03073	British Railways	Class 03
Diesel	37108	English Electric	Class 37
Diesel	43018	British Railways	Class 43
Diesel	47192	British Railways	Class 47
Electric	87035	BREL	Class 87
EMU	48103, 48106, 48404, 48602, 48603, 49002, 49006	BREL	Class 370

Attractions

The centre is home to one of the two remaining Advanced Passenger Trains (APT). Rolling stock to recently be added to the site's collection includes a Class 86 cab, a Mark 3 DVT and Metrolink T-68 tram number 1023. There are three complete signal boxes, with information on how they were used and the viewing platform gives direct views of trains travelling through Crewe. There is also a selection of locomotives and a 7¼ in gauge miniature railway which visitors can ride on. The region is also home to Crewe's Lyceum Theatre, Crewe Hall, Nantwich, Tatton Park and Jodrell Bank.

Special Events

Events that usually take place on the railway include a diesel gala and signalling gala. In addition, third party organised events are held and these include a toy & train collectors fair, a beer festival and music themed events.

Derwent Valley Light Railway

Introduction and History

The railway from York Layerthorpe to Cliff Common near Selby opened in 1913 as a light railway, with lower speed limits and weight limits from its beginning. Regular passenger services were withdrawn as early as 1926, although passenger specials used the route occasionally. The line continued to carry a variety of local goods, some via the railway connection to the Rowntree factory in York. The DVLR was one of the few to remain in private ownership both after the 1923 Grouping and the formation of British Railways in 1948. The southern section between Wheldrake and Cliff Common was closed in 1964, after the main line connection near Selby had been lost and levels of traffic were declining. Seasonal passenger steam trains returned to the northern section between 1977 and 1979, but after a further decline in use, the remainder of the railway closed in 1981 and the track was later lifted. In 1982 the Yorkshire Farming Museum acquired the Murton Park site, which included part of the railway. In the following years, the DVLR Society relaid a section of track and built the new Murton Park station. The first trains in preservation ran in 1992.

Contact Details

Website: www.dvlr.org.uk
Tel: 01904 489966
Email: info@dvlr.org.uk
Address: Derwent Valley Light Railway, Murton Park, Murton Lane, Murton, York, YO19 5UF.

Transport Links

By Rail: The nearest station is York, which is four miles away.
By Road: Free parking is available at Murton Park (YO19 5UF), chargeable only during occasional special events.

Opening Times

Trains operate from Murton Park station on Sundays and Bank Holidays from April until October, as well as on selected other dates and during December for Santa Specials. Entry to the railway is with a ticket to the Murton Park complex, which comprises of the Derwent Valley Light Railway and Yorkshire Museum of Farming.

Line Mileage and Journey Time

0.00   Murton Park
0.40   Line end

A return journey takes approximately 20 minutes.

Stock List

Type	Number	Builder	Details
Diesel	4100005 CHURCHILL	Fowler	0-4-0
Diesel	2 (421419)	Ruston & Hornsby	4wDM
Diesel	3 KEN COOKE (441934)	Ruston & Hornsby	4wDM
Diesel	JIM (417892)	Ruston & Hornsby	4wDM
Diesel	OCTAVIUS ATKINSON (466630)	Ruston & Hornsby	4wDM
Diesel	327964	Ruston & Hornsby	0-4-0DM
Diesel	03079	British Railways	Class 03
Diesel	D2245	Robert Stephenson & Hawthorns	Class 04
Diesel	08528	British Railways	Class 08

Attractions

The operational signal box at Murton Park was transferred from Muston, near Filey, and the station building was transferred from Wheldrake and rebuilt at Murton Park. There is a museum and shop at the Murton Park base. Railway themed attractions include shunting and freight demonstrations, driving experiences and a signal box experience. The adjacent Yorkshire Museum of Farming has a variety of animals, exhibits, a nature trail and a reconstructed Viking village. The Roman city of York is four miles from Murton Park and has many attractions including the National Railway Museum, the City Walls, The Shambles and York Minster.

Special Events

December: Santa Specials.

East Lancashire Railway

Introduction and History

The railway between Heywood and Bury opened in 1841. The line between Clifton Junction Bury and Rawtenstall then opened in 1846 and was extended north to Bacup in 1852. The line north of Rawtenstall to Bacup closed in 1966; passenger services between Heywood and Bury were withdrawn in 1970 and between Bury and Rawtenstall in 1972. Freight trains from Bury to Rawtenstall continued until 1980, when British Rail closed Bury Bolton Street station and relocated the terminus of the line from Manchester to Bury Interchange. The route from Manchester to Bury used third rail electric multiple units until 1992, when these were superseded by Metrolink trams. In 1972 the ELR Preservation Society took possession of the former Castlecroft Goods Shed immediately north of Bolton Street station. After the main line electric services to Manchester Victoria moved to Bury Interchange in 1980, Bolton Street station became the railway's base Heritage trains to Ramsbottom began in 1987, were extended to Rawtenstall in 1991 and to Heywood in 2003, after a steeply graded line was built across the Metrolink line to Bury. The railway remains connected to the main line network between Heywood and Castleton and the ELR plans to extend to a new station at Castleton, which would increase its length by a further 1.5 miles

Contact Details

Website: www.eastlancsrailway.org.uk
Tel: 0333 320 2830 or 0161 764 7790.
Email: enquiries@eastlancsrailway.org.uk
Address: East Lancashire Railway, Bolton Street Station, Bury, Lancashire, BL9 0EY.

Transport Links

By Rail: Bury Interchange (Metrolink) is less than half a mile away from Bolton Street station Heywood station is three miles from Castleton railway station by road.
By Road: Parking is available at all stations, however this is subject to charges at Bury (BL9 0EY) is limited at Ramsbottom (BL0 9AL) and Rawtenstall (BB4 6AG). There is ample free parking at Heywood (OL10 1NH).

Opening Times

Trains operate on Saturdays and Sundays all year round, plus on a large number of weekdays between April and September and during selected weekdays in winter.

▲ 56006 brings the 10.06 Rawtenstall–Heywood across the East Lancashire Railway's Roch Viaduc on 23 September 2018. **Tom McAtee**

Line Mileage and Journey Time

0.00   Heywood
4.00   Bury Bolton Street
5.25   Burrs Country Park
6.50   Summerseat
8.00   Ramsbottom
10.00   Irwell Vale
12.00   Rawtenstall

A return journey takes up to 2 hours 40 minutes, depending on the starting point.

Stock List

Type	Number	Builder	Details
Steam	7164 (7232)	Sentinel	4wVBGT
Steam	1 (1927)	Andrew Barclay	0-4-0ST
Steam	52322	Lancashire & Yorkshire	0-6-0
Steam	752	Beyer Peacock	0-6-0ST
Steam	32 (680)	Hudswell Clarke	0-6-0T
Steam	47298	Hunslet	0-6-0T
Steam	47324	North British	0-6-0T
Steam	42859	LMS	2-6-0
Steam	46428	British Railways	2-6-0
Steam	13065	LMS	2-6-0
Steam	80097	British Railways	2-6-4T
Steam	3855	GWR	2-8-0
Steam	7229	GWR	2-8-2T
Steam	45212	Armstrong Whitworth	4-6-0
Steam	45337	Armstrong Whitworth	4-6-0
Steam	45407	Armstrong Whitworth	4-6-0
Steam	44871	LMS	4-6-0
Steam	34092	British Railways	4-6-2
Diesel	3438	Hibberd	4wDM
Diesel	9009	Simplex	4wDM
Diesel	4002	Hudswell Clarke	0-6-0
Diesel	D2956	Andrew Barclay	Class 01
Diesel	D2062	British Railways	Class 03
Diesel	07013	Ruston & Hornsby	Class 07
Diesel	08164	British Railways	Class 08
Diesel	08479	British Railways	Class 08
Diesel	08944	British Railways	Class 08
Diesel	09024	British Railways	Class 09
Diesel	D9502	British Railways	Class 14
Diesel	D9531	British Railways	Class 14
Diesel	D8233	British Thomson-Houston	Class 15
Diesel	D5054	British Railways	Class 24
Diesel	D7629	Beyer Peacock	Class 25
Diesel	D5705	Metropolitan Vickers	Class 28
Diesel	31106	Brush Traction	Class 31
Diesel	6536	BRCW	Class 33
Diesel	33046	BRCW	Class 33
Diesel	33109	BRCW	Class 33
Diesel	D7076	Beyer Peacock	Class 35
Diesel	37109	English Electric	Class 37
Diesel	40135	English Electric	Class 40
Diesel	D832	British Railways	Class 42
Diesel	45108	British Railways	Class 45
Diesel	45135	British Railways	Class 45
Diesel	47765	British Railways	Class 47
Diesel	D1501	Brush Traction	Class 47
Diesel	50015	English Electric	Class 50
Diesel	D1041	British Railways	Class 52
Diesel	56006	Electroputere	Class 56
DMU	50437, 50455, 50494, 50517, 59137 & 59228	BRCW	Class 104

DMU	51485 & 56121	Cravens	Class 105
DMU	51813, 51842 & 59701	BRCW	Class 110
DMU	144009 (55809 & 55832)	Alexander/BREL	Class 144
DMU	56289	Pressed Steel	Class 121
DMU	55001	GRCW	Class 122
DEMU	60130 & 60904	British Railways	Class 207
EMU	70549	British Railways	Class 411
EMU	65451 & 77172	British Railways	Class 504

Attractions

Bury Transport Museum is adjacent to Bolton Street station. The railway offers Real Ale Trail guided tours, with information on the history of the area; platform 2 at Bolton Street is home to The Trackside real ale pub and Buffer Stops Bar is part of Rawtenstall station. Photography, steam and diesel driving experiences are available. Attractions in the area include Bury Art Museum, Bury's Fusilier Museum, Helmshore Mills Textile Museum, Irwell Sculpture Trail, Greater Manchester Museum of Transport, The Whitaker Museum & Art Gallery and Ski Rossendale.

Special Events

29–31 May 2021: 1940s Weekend.
1–3 July 2021: Summer Diesel Gala.
17–18 September 2021: Autumn Diesel Gala.
29–30 August 2021 & 3–5 September 2021: Flying Scotsman Returns.
15–17 October 2021: Autumn Steam Gala.
28–30 October 2021: Halloween Ghost Trains.
13–14 November 2021: DMU Gala.

In addition, the following usually take place on the railway:

A variety of dining, wine, gin & whiskey tasting and murder mystery trains run through the year.
Steam and diesel galas with visiting locomotives.
Halloween Ghost Trains during October.
DMU Gala during November.
Santa Specials and Mince Pie Specials during December.

▲ 1916-built Hudswell Clarke 0-6-0ST "ILLINGWORTH" departs from the Embsay & Bolton Abbey Railway's western terminus with one of the first post lockdown services on 25 July 2020. **Mike Heath**

Eden Valley Railway

Introduction and History

The railway between Clifton near Penrith and Kirkby Stephen via Warcop opened in 1862, forming a through route across the Pennines to Bishop Auckland and Darlington. Closure was proposed in 1959 and following a battle resisting this, passenger traffic ended in 1962, when the Appleby to Clifton section closed. The line south of Warcop closed in 1974 when quarry traffic ended and after Ministry of Defence trains ceased in 1989, the line south to Warcop fell into disuse. The Eden Valley Railway Society formed in 1995; the first brake van rides were provided in 2003 and regular services began in 2006. The railway's operational line has gradually been extended north from its Warcop base and there are plans to extend it a further three miles to Appleby, giving a northern terminus near to Appleby's main line station.

Contact Details

Website: www.evr-cumbria.org.uk
Tel: 01768 342309
Email: enquiries@evr-cumbria.org.uk
Address: Eden Valley Railway, Warcop Station, Warcop, Appleby, Cumbria, CA16 6PR.

Transport Links

By Rail: Appleby is the nearest railway station and is six miles from the Warcop site.
By Road: Car parking is available at Warcop (CA16 6PR), which is the only site with public access.

Opening Times

Trains operate on Sundays and Bank Holidays from April to October inclusive, plus on Tuesdays and Wednesdays from mid-July to late-August.

Line Mileage and Journey Time

0.00   Warcop
2.25   Operational line end

A return journey takes less than one hour.

Stock List

Type	Number	Builder	Details
Diesel	2181	Drewry	0-4-0
Diesel	21	Fowler	0-4-0
Diesel	ND3815 (2389)	Hunslet	0-4-0
Diesel	130c	Thomas Hill	0-4-0
Diesel	8343	Robert Stephenson & Hawthorns	0-6-0
Diesel	37042	English Electric	Class 37
Diesel	47799	British Railways	Class 47
DEMU	60108, 60658 & 60808	British Railways	Class 205
EMU	61798, 61799, 70229 & 70354	British Railways	Class 411
EMU	61804, 61805, 70539 & 70607	British Railways	Class 411
EMU	68003, 68005 & 68010	British Railways	Class 419

Attractions

The railway has a varied collection of operational rolling stock, including electric vehicles, main line diesel and shunting locomotives. 'Driver for a Fiver' experiences using a diesel shunter (usually number 21) are available on Sundays during the operating season (subject to staff availability, so please check before travelling for this). The second-hand book shop has an excellent selection of railway books, tickets and many non-railway books. There are two model railways of different gauges ('N' and 'O') and a small museum within the signal box, which has many artefacts from the railway's past. Hot drinks and light snacks are also available. The Stainmore Railway at Kirkby Stephen is eight miles away, making a combined visit possible on a day that both sites are open. The railway is located between the Yorkshire Dales National Park, the Lake District and the North Pennines (an Area of Outstanding Natural Beauty), giving many opportunities to explore the landscape of northern England.

Elsecar Heritage Railway

Introduction and History

The railway is on a branch line which left the Barnsley to Mexborough route at Elsecar Junction. This opened in 1850 and carried iron and coal from several local mines and ironworks. It was not a passenger route, however Earl Fitzwilliam ran private trains from his own station at Elsecar, which is now part of the Heritage Centre. The Elsecar site became known as Elsecar Goods Station and this closed in the early 1970s. The northern section of the branch survived until Cortonwood Colliery closed in 1984 and the track was lifted shortly afterwards. In 1994 Barnsley Council opened the Elsecar Heritage Centre to showcase the area's industrial heritage. The railway was part of this and after the track had been relaid and a platform built, the first trains ran in 1996. Responsibility for the railway passed to Elsecar Heritage Railway in 2006. Track has recently been laid on a further half-mile section to Cortonwood and it is hoped that services will be able to operate on this soon. In August 2020, Barnsley Council, owner of the land on which the railway is sited, confirmed that as the railway was facing a number of challenges, its trustees had surrendered the lease to the council. The future of the railway therefore currently remains unclear.

Contact Details

Website: www.elsecarrailway.co.uk
Tel: 01226 746746
Email: enquiries@elsecarrailway.co.uk
Address: Elsecar Heritage Railway, Wath Road, Elsecar, Barnsley, S74 8HJ.

Transport Links

By Rail: The nearest station is Elsecar which is about half a mile away.
By Road: Free parking is available (S74 8HJ).
By Bike: On the Trans-Pennine Trail.

Opening Times

The railway's usual operating times are 10.00–16.00 on Sundays and on selected other dates. Elsecar Heritage Centre opens 11.00–15.00 every day except between 24 December and 2 January.

Line Mileage and Journey Time

0.00	Elsecar Rockingham
1.00	Hemmingfield
1.50	Cortonwood (not yet operational)

A return journey takes about half an hour.

Stock List

Type	Number	Builder	Details
Steam	7 (9374)	Sentinel	4wVBT
Steam	10 (9376)	Sentinel	4wVBT
Steam	9599	Sentinel	4wVBT
Steam	BIRKENHEAD	Robert Stephenson & Hawthorns	0-4-0ST
Steam	GERVASE	Sentinel	0-4-0VBGT
Steam	EARL FITZWILLIAM	Avonside	0-6-0ST
Steam	15	Hunslet	0-6-0ST
Steam	2150	Peckett	0-6-0ST
Diesel	ELIZABETH	Sentinel	0-4-0
Diesel	Louise (6950)	Hunslet	0-6-0
Diesel	2895	Yorkshire Engine Co.	0-6-0
Diesel	466618	Robert Stephenson & Hawthorns	0-6-0DH

Attractions

The railway is based at Elsecar Heritage Centre, which has various exhibits from the area's industrial past, including the Elsecar New Colliery and the Newcomen Beam Engine which dates from 1795. Driving experiences are available, using both steam and diesel locomotives over the line's steep gradients. Resident Peckett 2150 "Mardy Monster" is the most powerful industrial locomotive built in the UK. The Trans-Pennine Trail follows the route of the line and runs between the railway and the Elsecar Canal. Other attractions in the area include Locke Park, RSPB Old Moor and Worsbrough Mill & Country Park.

Embsay & Bolton Abbey Steam Railway

Introduction and History

The railway between Skipton and Ilkley opened in 1888 and after declining use, it was closed by British Rail in 1965. The first preservation group formed in 1968, initially hoping to preserve the line from Skipton to Grassington, which deviated from the route to Bolton Abbey and Ilkley at Embsay Junction. The majority of the Grassington branch survived and continues to be used today by freight trains to Rylstone; the group instead acquired Embsay station during the early 1970s. The first section of railway from Embsay opened to the public in 1981 and this was extended to Holywell Halt in 1987 and to Bolton Abbey in 1997. There are long-term aims to extend the railway further east to Addingham and to reconnect to the main line network at Embsay Junction, enabling through trains between Bolton Abbey to Skipton.

Contact Details

Website: www.embsayboltonabbeyrailway.org.uk
Tel: 01756 710614
Email: office@ebar.org.uk
Address: Bolton Abbey Station, Skipton, North Yorkshire, BD23 6AF.

Transport Links

By Rail: The nearest station is Skipton, which is two miles from Embsay.
By Road: There is ample parking at Bolton Abbey (BD23 6AF) and Embsay (BD23 6QX) stations.

Opening Times

The railway operates on most Saturdays, Sundays and Bank Holidays through the year, plus Tuesdays from April to October and every day in August, with trains running between 10.30 and 16.30.

Line Mileage and Journey Time

0.00	Bolton Abbey
2.25	Holywell Halt
3.50	Embsay
4.00	Embsay Junction line end (not regularly used)

A return journey takes about one hour.

Stock List

Type	Number	Builder	Details
Steam	22 (2320)	Andrew Barclay	0-4-0ST
Steam	YORK No.1 (2474)	Yorkshire Engine Co.	0-4-0ST
Steam	7661	Robert Stephenson & Hawthorns	0-4-0ST
Steam	1821	Hudswell Clarke	0-6-0ST
Steam	ILLINGWORTH	Hudswell Clarke	0-6-0ST
Steam	SLOUGH ESTATES No. 5	Hudswell Clarke	0-6-0ST
Steam	1440	Hunslet	0-6-0ST
Steam	2414	Hunslet	0-6-0ST
Steam	3788	Hunslet	0-6-0ST
Steam	7 BEATRICE	Hunslet	0-6-0ST
Steam	8 (3776)	Hunslet	0-6-0ST
Steam	PRIMROSE No.2	Hunslet	0-6-0ST
Steam	S134 WHELDALE	Hunslet	0-6-0ST
Steam	7086	Robert Stephenson & Hawthorns	0-6-0ST
Steam	5643	GWR	0-6-2T
Diesel	1 (440)	Andrew Barclay	0-4-0
Diesel	The Bug/Clockwork Orange	Baguley	0-4-0
Diesel	4200003	Fowler	0-4-0
Diesel	H.W. Robinson (4100003)	Fowler	0-4-0
Diesel	887	Ruston & Hornsby	0-4-0
Diesel	36 (D1037)	Hudswell Clarke	0-6-0
Diesel	D2203	Vulcan Foundry	Class 04
Diesel	08054	British Railways	Class 08
Diesel	08773	British Railways	Class 08

Diesel	38	British Railways	Class 14
Diesel	31119	Brush Traction	Class 31
Diesel	D5600	Brush Traction	Class 31
Diesel	37294	English Electric	Class 37
Diesel	D1524	Brush Traction	Class 47
DMU	3170	NER	Autocar

Attractions

The North Eastern Railway Autocar operates on the railway; after being restored, this unique vehicle returned to service during 2019 and is now almost 120 years old. Trains with a variety of food and drink related themes operate (see events below), some of which feature Queen Victoria's Golden Jubilee Saloon and the LNWR Director's saloon. Bolton Abbey station is home to the Hambleton Valley Miniature Railway, a signal box display which can be accessed when staff are present, and a wetland area. Embsay station has a gift shop, a very well-stocked railway bookshop, a coffee shop and picnic area. The site of Bolton Abbey, the priory and River Wharfe are about one and a half miles from Bolton Abbey station. The market town of Skipton is nearby, where Skipton Castle, canal boat trips and Craven Museum and Gallery can be found. The Keighley & Worth Valley Railway (see below) is relatively close and the area is on the edge of the Yorkshire Dales National Park.

Special Events

26 June 2021: A Taste of Faulty Towers.

Further events that usually take place on the railway include:

A variety of dining trains, including Fish & Chip Specials, Afternoon Tea and Curry Express services.
Murder Mystery Evening trains.
Mother & Father's Day events.
Diesel Days.
Wizard Express trains during October.
Santa Trains during December.

▲ On 6 March 2018, BR Standard Class 7 4-6-2 70013 "OLIVER CROMWELL" hauls a mixed goods train near Oakworth on the Keighley & Worth Valley Railway. **Liam Barnes**

Keighley & Worth Valley Railway

Introduction and History

The steeply graded branch line from Keighley to Oxenhope, which follows the course of the River Worth, opened in 1867. Passenger services ceased in 1961 and freight ended in 1962. Shortly after this, a group of local people and rail enthusiasts formed a preservation society and purchased the line from British Railways, with the cost being paid in instalments over a 25 year period. The line reopened to passengers in 1968, making it one of the pioneers of railway preservation. The 1970 film 'The Railway Children' was filmed on the railway, with Oakworth station being used as a film set. This greatly raised the profile and popularity of the line, which at the time was one of a very small number of operational heritage railways. The K&WVR remains connected to the national network at Keighley, where the station has two main line and two K&WVR platforms. Occasional main line charter trains travel through to Oxenhope, such as when the railway celebrated its 50th anniversary in 2018.

Contact Details

Website: www.kwvr.co.uk
Tel: 01535 645214
Email: admin@kwvr.co.uk
Address: Keighley & Worth Valley Railway, The Railway Station, Haworth, West Yorkshire, BD22 8NJ.

Transport Links

By Rail: Main line connection at Keighley; just walk over the footbridge.
By Road: Parking is available at all stations except Damems, which it is not recommended to drive to, as the access road is unmade. All car parks are free, except Haworth (BD22 8NJ) which is pay and display. Keighley station car park (BD21 4HP) can be very busy Monday–Saturday as it is shared with the main line station. Ingrow West (BD21 5AX) has a large free car park.

Opening Times

Trains operate on Saturdays, Sundays and selected weekdays throughout the year and daily from June to August and during school holidays.

Line Mileage and Journey Time

0.00	Keighley
1.25	Ingrow West
2.00	Damems
2.25	Oakworth
3.50	Haworth
4.75	Oxenhope

A return journey takes about 1 hour 15 minutes.

Stock List

Type	Number	Builder	Details
Steam	7069	Robert Stephenson & Hawthorns	0-4-0CT
Steam	TINY (2258)	Andrew Barclay	0-4-0ST
Steam	LORD MAYOR	Hudswell Clarke	0-4-0ST
Steam	51218	Lancashire & Yorkshire	0-4-0ST
Steam	957	Beyer Peacock	0-6-0
Steam	43924	Midland Railway	0-6-0
Steam	5775	GWR	0-6-0PT
Steam	118	Hudswell Clarke	0-6-0ST
Steam	1704	Hudswell Clarke	0-6-0ST
Steam	31	Hudswell Clarke	0-6-0T
Steam	47279	Vulcan Foundry	0-6-0T
Steam	1054	LNWR	0-6-2T
Steam	85	Neilson Reid	0-6-2T
Steam	78022	British Railways	2-6-0
Steam	41241	British Railways	2-6-2T
Steam	80002	British Railways	2-6-4T
Steam	48431	GWR	2-8-0
Steam	5820	Lima Locomotive Co.	2-8-0

Steam	90733	Vulcan Foundry	2-8-0
Steam	75078	British Railways	4-6-0
Steam	45596	North British	4-6-0
Diesel	431763	Ruston & Hornsby	0-4-0
Diesel	23 MERLIN	Hudswell Clarke	0-6-0
Diesel	D2511	Hudswell Clarke	0-6-0
Diesel	32 HUSKISSON	Hunslet	0-6-0
Diesel	08266	British Railways	Class 08
Diesel	08993	British Railways	Class 08
Diesel	20031	English Electric	Class 20
Diesel	25059	British Railways	Class 25
Diesel	37075	English Electric	Class 37
Diesel	D0226 VULCAN	English Electric	Experimental 0-6-0
DMU	51189 & 51803	Metropolitan Cammell	Class 101
DMU	50928 & 51565	British Railways	Class 108
DMU	144011 (55811 & 55834)	Alexander/BREL	Class 144
DMU	79962 & 79964	Waggon und Maschinenbau	Railbus

Attractions

The K&WVR has some of the best preserved Victorian station buildings on a British heritage railway. Items of interest along the route include the Museum of Rail Travel and the Loco Maintenance & Restoration Centre at Ingrow, a well-stocked railway bookshop and the Locomotive Shed at Haworth and the Railway Exhibition Shed at Oxenhope. There is a connecting bus from Haworth station to the old village and Bronte Parsonage. Other nearby attractions include Saltaire, Bingley Five Rise Locks, the city of Bradford and the Embsay & Bolton Abbey Steam Railway.

Special Events

25–29 October 2021: Jurassic Specials.
Spring 2022: Alice in Wonderland Spring Event.

Additional events that usually take place on the railway include:

Steam and Diesel Galas.
Pullman Dining Experience trains.
The Elf Express and Mince Pie Specials during December.

▲ The Lakeside & Haverthwaite Railway's Class 4MT 2-6-4T 42073 departs from Newby Bridge on 3 November 2019. **Jamie Squibbs**

Lakeside & Haverthwaite Railway

Introduction and History

The eight-mile branch from Ulverston to Lakeside on the banks of Lake Windermere opened in 1869. Initially it predominantly carried freight, including iron ore, sulphur and coal to power the steam vessels that worked on the lake. Freight traffic declined through the 20th century and instead, the line was increasingly used by holidaymakers travelling to the Lake District. During the 1930s and 1940s passenger services were suspended for a number of long periods. The railway closed to passengers in 1965 and the final freight and enthusiast specials ran in 1967. In the same year, a group of enthusiasts formed The Lakeside Railway Society and began negotiations with British Rail to acquire the line. The trackbed was purchased in 1970; however, improvements to the A590 meant that the southern section could not be saved and its track was lifted in 1971. The line reopened as heritage railway in 1973 and trains continue to connect with cruises on Lake Windermere, as they first did in 1869.

Contact Details

Website: www.lakesiderailway.co.uk
Tel: 01539 531594
Email: Written enquiries can be made from the website.
Address: Haverthwaite Railway Station, Near Ulverston, Cumbria, LA12 8AL.

Transport Links

By Rail: Ulverston and Cark railway stations are both six miles from Haverthwaite.
By Road: Car parking is available at Haverthwaite station (LA12 8AL).
By Boat: Windermere Lake Cruises operate on most days and some services connect with L&HR trains. Please check the timetable before travelling.

Opening Times

Trains usually operate daily from April to October inclusive and on selected weekends during December. Departures are between 10.00 and 17.00 on most days, although timetables vary.

Line Mileage and Journey Time

0.00   Haverthwaite
2.00   Newby Bridge
3.00   Lakeside

A return journey takes at least half an hour.

Stock List

Type	Number	Builder	Details
Steam	2333 DAVID	Andrew Barclay	0-4-0ST
Steam	2682	Bagnall	0-6-0ST
Steam	2996 VICTOR	Bagnall	0-6-0ST
Steam	3698 REPULSE	Hunslet	0-6-0ST
Steam	No. 14 (1245)	Andrew Barclay	0-6-0T
Steam	46441	British Railways	2-6-0
Steam	42073	British Railways	2-6-4T
Steam	42085	British Railways	2-6-4T
Diesel	7120	LMS	0-6-0
Diesel	D2072	British Railways	Class 03
Diesel	D2117	British Railways	Class 03
Diesel	20214	English Electric	Class 20
DMU	52071 & 52077	BRCW	Class 110

Attractions

Visitors can look around the engine shed in Haverthwaite and see a selection of steam and diesel locomotives. The station has a picnic area, woodland adventure playground, gift shop and tea room. The Lakeland Motor Museum is a short walk from Haverthwaite station. At Lakeside, the station is adjacent to the Lakes Aquarium and the pier on Lake Windermere, where cruises to Bowness and Ambleside leave. On the opposite shore of Lake Windermere is Fell Foot National Trust Park, with views of Windermere and the fells. The railway is within the Lake District National Park, which has many other attractions and spectacular scenery.

Special Events

Events that usually take place on the railway include

Easter Egg Weekend.
Local Pensioner Days on selected dates.
Witches & Wizards Week during October.
Santa Specials during December.

Locomotion, Shildon

Introduction and History

The railway from Stockton and Darlington arrived at Shildon in 1825, when the line opened to carry coal from the area's collieries. When "Locomotion" No. 1 made its inaugural run on the route in September 1825, it was the world's first steam-hauled passenger train. After this opening day event, the railway carried passengers in horse-drawn coaches, until the horses had been replaced with locomotives by 1833. Locomotion is a railway museum with a short demonstration railway, which operates on part of the original Stockton and Darlington Railway. The museum opened in 2004 as a satellite site of the National Railway Museum in York and is adjacent to Shildon station, which is served by trains on the branch line between Darlington and Bishop Auckland.

Contact Details

Website: www.locomotion.org.uk
Tel: 0800 0478124
Email: info@locomotion.org.uk
Address: Locomotion, Dale Road Industrial Estate, Dale Road, Shildon, DL4 2RE.

Transport Links

By Rail: The nearest station is Shildon, which is a three-minute walk from the museum.
By Road: There is plenty of free parking at the site (DL4 2RE).

Opening Times

The Museum opens 11.00–16.00 each Wednesday to Sunday and these hours may be extended during 2021. Train rides operate on selected dates through the year.

Line Mileage and Journey Time

The railway at Locomotion runs for just over half a mile and trains currently operate on half of its length. Once work on the coal drops has been completed, the running length will be increased, although this may not be during 2021. The journey time is relatively short.

Stock List

Type	Number	Builder	Details
Steam	Hetton Lyon	George Stephenson	0-4-0
Steam	SANS PAREIL (Replica)	BREL	0-4-0
Steam	LOCOMOTION (Replica)	Locomotion Enterprises	0-4-0
Steam	SANS PAREIL	Timothy Hackworth	0-4-0
Steam	IMPERIAL No.1	Andrew Barclay	0-4-0F
Steam	JUNO (3850)	Hunslet	0-6-0ST
Steam	44 CONWAY	Kitson	0-6-0ST
Steam	77 (7412)	Robert Stephenson & Hawthorns	0-6-0ST
Steam	49395	LNWR	0-8-0
Steam	790	LNWR	2-4-0
Steam	30587	LSWR	2-4-0WT
Steam	4771	LNER	2-6-2
Steam	1621	NER	4-4-0
Steam	5000	LMS	4-6-0
Steam	34051	Southern Railway	4-6-2
Steam	390	Sharp Stewart	4-8-0
Gas Turbine	PC1, PC2, TC1 & TC2	BREL	APT-E
Diesel	D2090	British Railways	Class 03

Diesel	08064	British Railways	Class 08
Diesel	08911	British Railways	Class 08
Diesel	41001	BREL	Class 43 Prototype
Diesel	DELTIC	English Electric	Co-Co
Electric	755	Siemens	Bo
Electric	1 (26500)	Brush Traction	Bo-Bo
Electric	E5001	British Railways	Class 71
EMU	10656 & 12123	Southern Railway	2 Bil
EMU	11179	Southern Railway	4 Cor
EMU	65617	BRCW	Class 306
EMU	65217 & 65417	Metropolitan Cammell	Class 306
EMU	61275 & 75395	British Railways	Class 414

Attractions

The museum houses a number of unique exhibits from the National Collection, including the prototype gas turbine Advanced Passenger Train, the sole surviving prototype High Speed Train power car and the prototype DELTIC locomotive. Some exhibits periodically move to and from the National Railway Museum's main site in York and other heritage railway sites. There are guided tours of selected railway vehicles, although these were suspended during the pandemic restrictions of 2020. There is a shop with a large number of railway related books, gifts and model railway items. The Weardale Railway is only four miles from Locomotion and the Wensleydale Railway is 26 miles away. Other attractions in the area include the National Trust's Moulton Hall, the market town of Darlington and the city of Durham.

▲ Hunslet 0-6-0ST BROOKES No. 1 hauls a mixed train along the Middleton Railway during its Steampunk event on 6 July 2019.   **Ben Bucki**

Middleton Railway

Introduction and History

The Middleton Railway operates from a site to the south of Leeds city centre with a rich industrial railway history and boasts several world firsts. It was initially a horse-drawn wagonway used to carry coal on wooden tracks and in 1759 became the first railway to be authorised by an Act of Parliament. It has operated trains every year since, making it the oldest continuously operating railway in the world. It was the site where Matthew Murray's "Salamanca" became the first commercially-operated steam locomotive in 1812, and in June 1960 it became the first standard gauge preserved railway, two months before the Bluebell Railway began operating. To mark the heritage railway's 60th anniversary in 2020, Hunslet diesel 7401 repeated the landmark journey it made exactly six decades earlier, when it departed Moor Road at 16.45. Sadly, this was not open to the public due to coronavirus pandemic restrictions. The line remains connected to the national network at Leeds Midland Road, on the route between Leeds and Woodlesford. There are plans to extend the railway further south into Middleton Park, however, this was on hold while resources were channelled into the new carriage shed; the 42-metre £100 000 facility was completed in 2019.

Contact Details

Website: www.middletonrailway.org.uk
Tel: 0845 680 1758
Email: info@middletonrailway.org.uk
Address: The Middleton Railway, The Station, Moor Road, Hunslet, Leeds, LS10 2JQ.

Transport Links

By Rail: The nearest railway station is Leeds, which is under two miles away.
By Road: Free car parking is available at Moor Road station (LS10 2JQ).

Opening Times

Trains operate on Saturdays and Sundays from April to December and on some Wednesdays during school holidays, with departures between 11.00 and 16.00 on most days.

Line Mileage and Journey Time

0.00   Moor Road
1.00   Middleton Park

A return journey takes about 25 minutes.

Stock List

Type	Number	Builder	Details
Steam	68153	Sentinel	4wT
Steam	6	Hawthorn Leslie	0-4-0ST
Steam	HENRY DE LACY II	Hudswell Clarke	0-4-0ST
Steam	Mirvale	Hudswell Clarke	0-4-0ST
Steam	SLOUGH ESTATES No. 3	Hudswell Clarke	0-4-0ST
Steam	No. 11	Hunslet	0-4-0ST
Steam	2103	Peckett	0-4-0ST
Steam	1684	Hunslet	0-4-0T
Steam	1310	NER	0-4-0T
Steam	385	Hartmann	0-4-0WT
Steam	BROOKES No. 1	Hunslet	0-6-0ST
Steam	MATTHEW MURRAY	Manning Wardle	0-6-0ST
Steam	SIR BERKELEY	Manning Wardle	0-6-0ST
Steam	M.S.C No. 67	Hudswell Clarke	0-6-0T
Steam	1540	Hunslet	2-6-2T
Diesel	D2999	Beyer Peacock	0-4-0
Diesel	3900002	Fowler	0-4-0
Diesel	HARRY	Fowler	0-4-0
Diesel	CARROLL	Hudswell Clarke	0-4-0
Diesel	MARY	Hudswell Clarke	0-4-0
Diesel	1786	Hunslet	0-4-0
Diesel	6981	Hunslet	0-4-0

Diesel	AUSTINS No. 1	Peckett	0-4-0
Diesel	MD&HB 45	Hudswell Clarke	0-6-0
Diesel	7051	Hunslet	0-6-0
DMU	RDB998901	Drewry	Railcar

Attractions

The Engine House and museum have many historical and hands-on exhibits from the railway's long history and there is a shop, small café and conference facility at the Moor Road site. Middleton Park is accessible from its namesake railway station, with an ancient woodland, grassland, boating lake and visitor centre to explore. Nearby attractions in Leeds include the Royal Armouries, the Tetley and Leeds City Museum.

Special Events

Events that usually take place on the railway include:

Easter Event.
Father's Day Weekend Footplate Experience.
Mixed Traffic Weekend.
Model Railway and Bus Rally events.
Heritage Open Days and Diesel Days.
Anything Goes Event.
Santa Specials during December.

National Railway Museum, York

Introduction and History

The National Railway Museum is adjacent to York railway station and the East Coast Main Line. It opened in 1975 on the site of the former York North depot and incorporates a turntable from this. The NRM was the amalgamation of two previous railway museums, both of which closed in 1973; British Railways' Transport Museum in Clapham and York Railway Museum which was established by the London & North Eastern Railway in 1928. The Museum holds the National Collection of historically important locomotives and rolling stock and a vast number of railway artefacts. Many of the artefacts and rolling stock are on display, although at any one time some are in storage and others are at the museum's sister site at Shildon (see above), or on loan to other museums or heritage railways.

Contact Details

Website: www.railwaymuseum.org.uk
Tel: 0800 047 8124
Email: info@railwaymuseum.org.uk
Address: National Railway Museum, Leeman Road, York, YO26 4XJ.

Transport Links

By Rail: The museum is less than half a mile from York railway station.
By Road: The museum car park costs £10 per day.

Opening Times

During 2020, opening hours were reduced to 10.00–17.00 on Wednesdays to Sundays. Longer opening hours and daily opening (except 24–26 December) may be reinstated in 2021. Steam train rides are available on selected dates.

Line Mileage and Journey Time

Passenger rides are provided on the demonstration line, using a section of approximately one tenth of a mile, ending at the Network Rail boundary (the running length has been reduced recently). A return journey takes about 10 minutes.

Stock List

Type	Number	Builder	Details
Steam	ROCKET	Robert Stephenson & Co.	0-2-2
Steam	ROCKET (replica)	Locomotion Enterprises	0-2-2
Steam	ROCKET (replica)	Robert Stephenson & Co	0-2-2
Steam	BAUXITE No. 2	Black Hawthorn	0-4-0

Steam	3 "Coppernob"	Bury Curtis & Kennedy	0-4-0
Steam	Agenoria	Foster Rastrick	0-4-0
Steam	214 GLADSTONE	LBSCR	0-4-2
Steam	245	LSWR	0-4-4T
Steam	1275	Dübs & Company	0-6-0
Steam	C1 (33001)	Southern Railway	0-6-0
Steam	1247	Sharp Stewart	0-6-0ST
Steam	82 BOXHILL	LBSCR	0-6-0T
Steam	92220	British Railways	2-10-0
Steam	66	Kitson	2-2-4T
Steam	1008	Lancashire & Yorkshire	2-4-2T
Steam	13000	LMS	2-6-0
Steam	2500	LMS	2-6-4T
Steam	1	GNR	4-2-2
Steam	673	Midland Railway	4-2-2
Steam	737	SECR	4-4-0
Steam	990	GNR	4-4-2
Steam	4003	GWR	4-6-0
Steam	6229	LMS	4-6-2
Steam	4468	LNER	4-6-2
Steam	60007	LNER	4-6-2
Steam	60103	LNER	4-6-2
Steam	35029	Southern Railway	4-6-2
Steam	KF7	Vulcan Foundry	4-8-4
Diesel	7050	English Electric	0-4-0
Diesel	D2860	Yorkshire Engine Co.	Class 02
Diesel	09017	British Railways	Class 09
Diesel	D8000	English Electric	Class 20
Diesel	31018	Brush Traction	Class 31
Diesel	D6700	English Electric	Class 37
Diesel	D200	English Electric	Class 40
Diesel	43002	British Railways	Class 43
Diesel	47798	British Railways	Class 47
Diesel	D1023	British Railways	Class 52
Diesel	D9002	English Electric	Class 55
DMU	51562 & 51922	British Railways	Class 108
DMU	142001 (55542 & 55592)	BREL/Leyland	Class 142
DMU	4	Park Royal	Railcar
EMU	8143	Southern Railway	3 Sub
EMU	3308	GEC-Alsthom	Class 373
EMU	28249	Metropolitan Cammell	LNWR
EMU	22-141	Hitachi	O Series
Electric	26020	British Railways	Class 76
Electric	87001	BREL	Class 87
Battery	1	North Staffordshire Railway	2-A

Attractions

The large site has a varied collection of exhibits including "Mallard", the world's fastest steam locomotive, Queen Victoria's royal train carriages, examples of the Japanese Bullet Train, Eurostar and historically important diesel locomotives, including the recently preserved first-built High Speed Train power car. Many locomotive nameplates are mounted on the wall of the Great Hall. Hands-on activities and regular talks include signalling demonstrations, how a steam engine works and turntable demonstrations. The site has a miniature railway, standard gauge demonstration line and a viewing balcony adjacent to the East Coast Main Line. York city centre is within walking distance, where York Minster, The Shambles, City Walls and many other attractions can be found. The Derwent Valley Light Railway is four miles away.

Special Events

The Museum often has themed exhibitions; please check the NRM website for the latest information.

North Yorkshire Moors Railway

Introduction and History

The railway from Whitby to Grosmont opened in 1835 and was extended south to Pickering in 1836. It was extended further south from Pickering to Rillington in 1845, where it joined the present day York to Scarborough line. The route between Grosmont and Levisham was realigned in 1865, when the present station at Goathland opened. Passenger services between Whitby and Malton via Pickering ceased in 1965 and freight services ended in 1966. The NYMR began in 1967, when a group of local people formed the North Yorkshire Moors Railway Preservation Society, with the aim of reopening the line. After several open days, the line between Grosmont and Pickering reopened in 1973. Since 2007 the NYMR has operated trains on Network Rail's Esk Valley route to Whitby, with less frequent services continuing to Battersby too. This required the NYMR to become a registered Train Operating Company and gives it more than 40 miles of railway over which it can operate trains. A substantial programme of improvement works began recently, after a £4.4m National Lottery Heritage grant was awarded to the NYMR in 2019 – the largest sum the funding body has awarded to a heritage railway. The works include a new four-road carriage shed at Pickering, bridge renewals, an interpretation coach with exhibits at Goathland, accessibility improvements and an expanded apprenticeship scheme.

Contact Details

Website: www.nymr.co.uk
Tel: 01751 472508
Email: info@nymr.co.uk
Address: North Yorkshire Moors Railway, 12 Park Street, Pickering, North Yorkshire, YO18 7AJ.

Transport Links

By Rail: The NYMR connects with main line services at Grosmont and Whitby.
By Road: There are car parks at Pickering (YO18 7AJ), Levisham (YO18 7NN), Goathland (YO22 5NF), Grosmont (YO22 5QE) and Whitby (YO21 1YN). Charges apply at each of these.

Opening Times

Trains usually operate every day from late March to early November, between approximately 09.30 and 18.30 or 19.30, depending on which timetable is in use.

Line Mileage and Journey Time

0.00	Whitby	0.00	Grosmont
6.25	Grosmont	3.25	Glaisdale
9.75	Goathland	17.75	Battersby (Grosmont to Battersby during special events only)
15.00	Newtondale Halt		
18.25	Levisham		
24.25	Pickering		

A return journey from Whitby to Pickering (or vice versa) takes about four hours, or two hours 40 minutes between Grosmont and Pickering.

Stock List

Type	Number	Builder	Details
Steam	2702	Bagnall	0-4-0ST
Steam	"Lucie" (1625)	Cockerill	0-4-0VBT
Steam	65894	LNER	0-6-0
Steam	3180	Hunslet	0-6-0ST
Steam	29 (4263)	Robert Stephenson & Hawthorns	0-6-2T
Steam	5 (3377)	Robert Stephenson & Hawthorns	0-6-2T
Steam	63395	NER	0-8-0
Steam	92134	British Railways	2-10-0
Steam	3672	North British	2-10-0
Steam	76079	British Railways	2-6-0
Steam	62005	North British	2-6-0
Steam	80135	British Railways	2-6-4T
Steam	80136	British Railways	2-6-4T
Steam	926	Southern Railway	4-4-0
Steam	45428	Armstrong Whitworth	4-6-0

Steam	75029	British Railways	4-6-0
Steam	44806	LMS	4-6-0
Steam	61264	North British	4-6-0
Steam	825	Southern Railway	4-6-0
Steam	30830	Southern Railway	4-6-0
Steam	34101	British Railways	4-6-2
Diesel	12139	English Electric	0-6-0
Diesel	D2207	Vulcan Foundry	Class 04
Diesel	08495	British Railways	Class 08
Diesel	08556	British Railways	Class 08
Diesel	08850	British Railways	Class 08
Diesel	D5032	British Railways	Class 24
Diesel	D5061	British Railways	Class 24
Diesel	D7628	Beyer Peacock	Class 25
Diesel	37264	English Electric	Class 37
DMU	50160, 50164, 50204, 51511 & 59539	Metropolitan Cammell	Class 101

Attractions

The railway offers digital photography workshops, steam and diesel footplate experiences and engine shed tours which last two hours. These events are available on selected dates and should be booked in advance, although they had to be suspended during 2020. There are several tea rooms along the route, a railway bookshop at Pickering and a 1950s railway memorabilia shop at Grosmont. Between Whitby, Pickering and the North Yorkshire Moors National Park through which the line travels, there are many attractions, natural features and scenery to explore.

Special Events

Events that usually take place on the railway include:

1960s Festival.
Steam and Diesel Galas.
Railway in Wartime event during October (cancelled for 2021).
Halloween Trains.
Santa Specials during December.

▲ Visiting main line locomotives can be a big draw for heritage railways. On 23 March 2019, Colas Rail's 56090 made a guest appearance at the Ribble Steam Railway and is seen crossing the swing bridge at the entrance to Preston Marina, which carries both the railway and a road. **Andy Chard**

Ribble Steam Railway

Introduction and History
The steeply graded branch line, which leaves the West Coast Main Line immediately south of Preston station, was opened as far as Victoria Quay in 1846. The first one third of a mile of this involves a 1 in 29 descent, a cutting and a tunnel, before it levels off beside the River Ribble. The railway was extended to Preston Docks in 1882, where a network of lines developed and this had more than 25 miles of track at its peak. As larger container-based ports grew during the 1970s and 1980s, traffic levels to the docks declined. The Preston Docks branch remains in commercial use today, with regular oil trains travelling to the site of the Ribble Steam Railway, where the tanks are shunted into the nearby bitumen works. When Southport Railway Museum closed in 1999, many of its exhibits were transferred to the Preston site. Since 2005, the Ribble Steam Railway has been operating heritage passenger trains on a 1.5-mile section of the branch, which it continues to share with main line freight services. The site, which is adjacent to the River Ribble and Preston Marina, is in the process of being further developed, with the installation of a turntable and the café and gift shop are being renovated.

Contact Details
Website: www.ribblesteam.org.uk
Tel: 01772 728800
Email: enquiries@ribblesteam.co.uk
Address: Ribble Steam Railway, Chain Caul Road, Preston, Lancashire, PR2 2PD.

Transport Links
By Rail: The nearest railway station is Preston, which is two and a half miles away.
By Road: Free car parking is available (PR2 2PD).

Opening Times
The railway operates each Saturday and Sunday from April to September, with hourly departures from its station. Trains are usually steam-hauled, except on diesel gala days.

Line Mileage and Journey Time
0.00   Museum station
1.50   Line end / Network Rail boundary

A return journey takes about 20 minutes.

Stock List

Type	Number	Builder	Details
Steam	8024	Sentinel	4wVBT
Steam	9373	Sentinel	4wVBT
Steam	20	Sharp Stewart	0-4-0
Steam	Glenfield 1	Andrew Barclay	0-4-0CT
Steam	Heysham No. 2 (1950)	Andrew Barclay	0-4-0F
Steam	1865	Andrew Barclay	0-4-0ST
Steam	BRITISH GYPSUM No. 4	Andrew Barclay	0-4-0ST
Steam	EFFICIENT	Andrew Barclay	0-4-0ST
Steam	JN DERBYSHIRE	Andrew Barclay	0-4-0ST
Steam	JOHN HOWE	Andrew Barclay	0-4-0ST
Steam	272	Grant Richie	0-4-0ST
Steam	19	Lancashire & Yorkshire	0-4-0ST
Steam	1439	LNWR	0-4-0ST
Steam	1935 HORNET	Peckett	0-4-0ST
Steam	737 DAPHNE	Peckett	0-4-0ST
Steam	1999	Peckett	0-4-0ST
Steam	1925 CALIBAN	Peckett	0-4-0ST
Steam	2003 JOHN BLENKINSON	Peckett	0-4-0ST
Steam	7485 AGECROFT No. 2	Robert Stephenson & Hawthorns	0-4-0ST
Steam	17	Sharp Stewart	0-4-0ST
Steam	THE KING (48)	Borrows	0-4-0WT
Steam	WINDLE (53)	Borrows	0-4-0WT
Steam	NIDDRIE 7	Andrew Barclay	0-6-0ST

Steam	1568	Avonside	0-6-0ST
Steam	1883	Avonside	0-6-0ST
Steam	MDHB 26	Avonside	0-6-0ST
Steam	COURAGEOUS	Bagnall	0-6-0ST
Steam	13 (3732)	Hawthorn Leslie	0-4-0ST
Steam	21 (3931)	Hawthorn Leslie	0-6-0ST
Steam	1450	Hudswell Clarke	0-6-0ST
Steam	3155 WALKDEN	Hunslet	0-6-0ST
Steam	3696 RESPITE	Hunslet	0-6-0ST
Steam	3793 SHROPSHIRE	Hunslet	0-6-0ST
Steam	WD194 (3794)	Hunslet	0-6-0ST
Steam	GLASSHOUGHTON No. 4	Hunslet	0-6-0ST
Steam	1954	Hunslet	0-6-0ST
Steam	1636 FONMON	Peckett	0-6-0ST
Steam	30072	Vulcan Iron Works	0-6-0T
Steam	4979	GWR	4-6-0
Petrol	965 HOTTO	Howard	Petrol Loco
Diesel	21999 FLUFF	Fowler	0-4-0
Diesel	4160001 PERCIL	Fowler	0-4-0
Diesel	1031	Hudswell Clarke	0-4-0
Diesel	D628 MIGHTY ATON	Hudswell Clarke	0-4-0
Diesel	D629 SPARKY	Hudswell Clarke	0-4-0
Diesel	27653 BICC	North British	0-4-0
Diesel	10226 ENERGY	Sentinel	0-4-0
Diesel	10282 ENTERPRISE	Sentinel	0-4-0
Diesel	10283 PROGRESS	Sentinel	0-4-0
Diesel	STANLOW No. 4	Thomas Hill	0-4-0
Diesel	D2870	Yorkshire Engine Co.	0-4-0
Diesel	663	English Electric	0-6-0
Diesel	671	English Electric	0-6-0
Diesel	03189	British Railways	Class 03
Diesel	D2148	British Railways	Class 03
Diesel	D2595	Hunslet	Class 05
Diesel	D9539	British Railways	Class 14
DMU	79960	Waggon und Maschinenbau	Railbus
Battery	EE788	English Electric	Battery Loco
Battery	2000	Greenwood & Batley	Battery Loco

Attractions

The railway has the largest collection of industrial locomotives in the country. Admission includes unlimited travel for the day and access to exhibits in the museum and workshop. The line follows an interesting route, passing Preston Marina and crossing a swing bridge which it shares with a road. There is also a café, miniature railway and children's playground at the site. Preston town centre is nearby, as are the Ribble Estuary National Nature Reserve, Fylde coast and Lytham St Annes.

Special Events

Events that usually take place on the railway include:

Mother's Day Cream Tea.
Steam and Diesel Galas.
Children and family oriented events.
Spooky Trains during October.
Santa Specials during December.

Stainmore Railway

Introduction and History

The railway between Barnard Castle and Tebay via Kirkby Stephen East opened in 1861, with the northern spur to Clifton and Penrith via Appleby opening in 1862 (see the Eden Valley Railway). Passenger services were withdrawn on the Kirkby Stephen East to Tebay route in 1952, although summer Saturday holiday trains continued to use it until 1961. The line to Clifton closed to passengers in 1962 and to freight in 1974 when traffic to Hartley Quarry ceased. The first preservation group formed in 1997 and subsequently acquired the Kirkby Stephen East site. Since then, Kirkby Stephen East station building has been restored and just over one quarter of a mile of railway track has been re-laid. Heritage trains began operating in 2011 and there are long-term plans to extend the line north towards the Eden Valley Railway.

Contact Details

Website: www.kirkbystepheneast.co.uk
Tel: 07584 429481 or 01768 371700
Email: suelizjones@hotmail.com
Address: Stainmore Railway Company, Kirkby Stephen East Station, South Road, Kirkby Stephen, Cumbria, CA17 4LA.

Transport Links

By Rail: Kirkby Stephen railway station is just under one mile away.
By Road: Free car parking is available at Kirkby Stephen East (CA17 4LA).

Opening Times

Kirkby Stephen East station opens on Sundays from April until October and on selected weekdays during July and August. Steam or diesel-hauled trains are usually in operation. Please check the website or contact the railway for the latest information.

Line Mileage and Journey Time

The railway is just over a quarter of a mile long and the journey takes about 10 minutes.

Stock List

Type	Number	Builder	Details
Steam	LYTHAM ST. ANNES (2111)	Peckett	0-4-0ST
Steam	2084 FC TINGEY	Peckett	0-4-0ST
Steam	65033	NER	0-6-0
Steam	68009	Hunslet	0-6-0ST
Steam	910	NER	2-4-0
Diesel	ELIZABETH	Hibberd	0-4-0
Diesel	STANTON No. 50	Yorkshire Engine Co.	0-6-0

Attractions

Kirkby Stephen East station includes a number of restored rooms with original features, including the Booking Hall, Booking Office, Foreman's Office, Station Master's Office and Waiting Room which houses a small museum. There is a shop, children's play area and a wide range of rolling stock, including 1875-built 2-4-0 number 910 which belongs to the National Collection. The 2019-built carriage shed houses several historically important coaches, including the sole remaining 1902-built NER Stores Van 5523. Driving experiences are available, with a choice of steam or diesel locomotive. The Pennine market town of Kirkby Stephen is nearby and the Temperance Hall Museum of Costume is less than a mile away from the site. Brough Castle is five miles away and there are plenty of walking and cycling routes in the area, some of which are along the trackbed of the former Stainmore Line. In addition, the Eden Valley Railway at Appleby is only eight miles away, making a combined visit possible on a day when both sites are open.

Special Events

Events that usually take place on the railway include:

Model Railway Show at Kirkby Stephen East station.
Heritage Open Days.
Santa Event during December.

Stephenson Steam Railway

Introduction and History
The railway and museum are located on the site of former rail wagonways in an area rich in industrial and railway history. After the coal trains ceased, during the 1970s the site of the museum and current railway were used as a testing centre by the Tyne and Wear Metro before its services began in 1980. In the early 1980s North Tyneside Council then acquired the test sheds and a partnership was made with Tyne & Wear Archives & Museums to create a facility with a steam-hauled passenger railway. A single track line was relaid from the museum to Percy Main, being completed in 1989 and the first passenger trains ran on this in 1991. The museum showcases the railway pioneers George Stephenson and his son Robert.

Contact Details
Website: www.stephensonsteamrailway.org.uk
Tel: 0191 277 7135
Email: info@stephensonsteamrailway.org.uk
Address: Stephenson Steam Railway, Middle Engine Lane, North Shields, Tyne & Wear, NE29 8DX.

Transport Links
By Rail: The museum is two miles from Percy Main on the Tyne and Wear Metro, Yellow Route.
By Road: There is free parking at the museum (NE29 8DX).

Opening Times
The museum usually opens on Saturdays, Sundays and Bank Holiday from April until early November, plus on selected weekdays during school holidays. Trains operate on Sundays and Bank Holidays and they may also run on other dates during school holidays. The museum can be telephoned on the day to confirm and can provide details of which locomotive is working.

Line Mileage and Journey Time
0.00   Middle Engine Lane
1.75   Percy Main

A return journey takes around half an hour.

Stock List

Type	Number	Builder	Details
Steam	Billy	George Stephenson	0-4-0
Steam	401 SIR THOMAS BURT	Bagnall	0-6-0ST
Steam	3785	Hunslet	0-6-0ST
Steam	5 JACKIE MILBURN	Peckett	0-6-0ST
Steam	5	Kitson	0-6-0T
Steam	1 TED GARRET JP MP	Robert Stephenson & Hawthorns	0-6-0T
Electric	E4	Siemans Harton	Electric E4
Electric	3267	Metropolitan Cammell	Motor Parcel Van
Diesel	10	Consett	0-6-0
Diesel	D2078	British Railways	Class 03
Diesel	08915	British Railways	Class 08

Attractions
The Museum has a range of exhibits including George Stephenson's 1816 locomotive "Billy", which is the world's third oldest surviving steam locomotive and a forerunner to the famous "Rocket". New display panels tell the story of railway pioneers George and Robert Stephenson and the worldwide impact of their inventions. Steam or diesel locomotives carry passengers in vintage carriages on the railway line. Heritage railways within the area include the Bowes Railway (ten miles away), Tanfield Railway (12 miles) and Beamish museum (17 miles). The city of Newcastle upon Tyne, Whitley Bay and the coast are all near to the location of the museum.

Special Events
Events that usually take place on the railway include:

Drive a Diesel Locomotive may be available again from 2021.
Santa Specials during December.

Tanfield Railway

Introduction and History

The Tanfield Railway is known as the oldest railway in the world, as the first line was built to carry coal from Causey to Dunston Staithes on the River Tyne in 1725. During the 1830s it was converted from a horse-drawn wagonway to a railway. East Tanfield was the final colliery to use the line and after this closed in 1964, the railway closed and the track was lifted. Nearby Marley Hill engine shed, however, continued to be used by the National Coal Board until 1970. A group formed during the 1960s aiming to preserve the steam railway heritage of the North-East. After Marley Hill engine shed closed in 1970, it was initially used by the nearby Beamish Museum as a storage site and Beamish gave the group access, so they could restore steam locomotives and railway items belonging to both organisations. Beamish moved its rolling stock to its new railway when this opened in 1976. A connecting curve was then built from Marley Hill to the Tanfield branch. The first preserved passenger trains ran for half a mile from Marley Hill in 1977 and the railway was extended north to Sunniside in 1982. It was further extended south along the former trackbed and reached Causey in 1992 and the site of East Tanfield Colliery in 1993. There are long term aspirations to extend the railway west from Marley Hill to Byermoor, although these are not currently being pursued.

Contact Details

Website: www.tanfield-railway.co.uk
Tel: 07508 092365
Email: info@tanfield-railway.co.uk
Address: Tanfield Railway, Old Marley Hill, Gateshead, Tyne and Wear, NE16 5ET.

Transport Links

By Rail: The nearest station is Dunston (four miles), Newcastle is six miles away.
By Road: There is free parking at Marley Hill (NE16 5ET) and East Tanfield (DH9 9UY).
By Bike: The Tanfield Railway Path runs from Gateshead to Sunniside and Marley Hill. The Bowes Railway Path arrives at Marley Hill from the east.

Opening Times

Trains operate on Sundays all year round and on selected weekdays, Saturdays and Bank Holidays. The weekends before Christmas feature North Pole Express trains and these need to be booked in advance.

Line Mileage and Journey Time

0.00	Sunniside
0.75	Andrews House
1.75	Causey Arch
2.50	East Tanfield

A return journey takes about one hour.

Stock List

Type	Number	Builder	Details
Steam	4 (9559)	Sentinel	4wVBT
Steam	7007	Robert Stephenson & Hawthorns	0-4-0CT
Steam	WELLINGTON	Black Hawthorn	0-4-0ST
Steam	2711	Hawthorn Leslie	0-4-0ST
Steam	2 (2859)	Hawthorn Leslie	0-4-0ST
Steam	L&HC14	Hawthorn Leslie	0-4-0ST
Steam	1672 IRWELL	Hudswell Clarke	0-4-0ST
Steam	3 (2009)	R & W Hawthorn	0-4-0ST
Steam	21 (7796)	Robert Stephenson & Hawthorns	0-4-0ST
Steam	7409 Sir CECIL. A. COCHRANE	Robert Stephenson & Hawthorns	0-4-0ST
Steam	6	Andrew Barclay	0-4-2ST
Steam	3746	Hawthorn Leslie	0-6-0F
Steam	1015	Andrew Barclay	0-6-0ST
Steam	20 (2779)	Bagnall	0-6-0ST
Steam	STAGSHAW	Hawthorn Leslie	0-6-0ST
Steam	3575	Hawthorn Leslie	0-6-0ST

Steam	RENISHAW IRONWORKS No.6	Hudswell Clarke	0-6-0ST
Steam	16 (7944)	Robert Stephenson & Hawthorns	0-6-0ST
Steam	38 (7763)	Robert Stephenson & Hawthorns	0-6-0ST
Steam	44 (7760)	Robert Stephenson & Hawthorns	0-6-0ST
Steam	47 (7800)	Robert Stephenson & Hawthorns	0-6-0ST
Steam	49 (7098)	Robert Stephenson & Hawthorns	0-6-0ST
Steam	62 (7035)	Robert Stephenson & Hawthorns	0-6-0ST
Steam	38 (1823)	Hudswell Clarke	0-6-0T
Steam	3 TWIZELL	Robert Stephenson & Co	0-6-0T
Electric	E10 (862)	Siemens	4w
Electric	E9 (1565)	AEG, Berlin	Bo-Bo
Electric	7078	Robert Stephenson & Hawthorns	Bo-Bo
Diesel	3565	Baguley	2w-2
Diesel	758206	Hunslet	4wDM
Diesel	54781	Lister Blackstone	4wDM
Diesel	14 (D21)	Armstrong Whitworth	0-4-0DE
Diesel	2 (D22)	Armstrong Whitworth	0-4-0DE
Diesel	3716	Hibberd	0-4-0
Diesel	6980	Robert Stephenson & Hawthorns	0-4-0
Diesel	7697	Robert Stephenson & Hawthorns	0-4-0
Diesel	7901	Robert Stephenson & Hawthorns	0-4-0
Diesel	1 HUSKY	Robert Stephenson & Hawthorns	0-4-0
Diesel	35	Ruston & Hornsby	0-4-0
Diesel	4240010	Fowler	0-6-0
Diesel	501	Hunslet	0-6-0
Diesel	7746	Robert Stephenson & Hawthorns	0-6-0
Battery	3872 DEREK SHEPHERD	Hawthorn Leslie	Bo-Bo

Attractions

The railway has a particularly large collection of industrial locomotives, including steam, diese
and electric examples. The Marley Hill site, with its 1854-built engine shed, houses many o
these, along with several restored vintage carriages. Engine shed tours and afternoon tea
"Director Class" travel are usually available on Sundays between April and September. Causey
Arch, which was built in 1727 and is a Grade 1 Listed structure, is the world's oldest railway
bridge and is adjacent to Causey Arch station. There are several walking paths in the area
including the Tanfield Railway Path, which continues north on the trackbed from Sunniside
and the Bowes Railway Path, which runs east from Marley Hill. Other attractions in the area
include the North-East Land, Sea & Air Museum, Newcastle, Sunderland and the East coast
Nearby heritage railways include Beamish (three miles away), Bowes Railway (six miles), North
Tyneside Steam Railway (12 miles) and Weardale Railway (20 miles).

Special Events

Events that usually take place on the railway include:

Mothering Sunday event.
Easter Eggstravaganza trains.
Heritage Open Days.
1940s Weekend.
Tanfield Ghost Train.
North Pole Express and Mince Pie Specials during December.
"Kids for a Quid" on selected bank holidays and during school summer holidays.

Weardale Railway

Introduction and History

The railway first reached Bishop Auckland in 1843 when the line from Shildon to Crook was built. The Wear Valley line from Bishop Auckland to Stanhope opened in 1862 and was extended to Wearhead in 1895. Bishop Auckland became a major junction and at its height, seven routes converged at the station. Passenger services on the Weardale route were withdrawn in 1953, after which the line was cut back from Wearhead to the cement works at Eastgate. The heritage and tourist value of the railway was recognised as early as 1983 when intermittent charter trains ran to Stanhope and these became timetabled summer weekend services between 1988 and 1992. In 1993 rail traffic to the cement works ended and British Rail announced its intention to close the line. A preservation group formed in 1993 and trains from Wolsingham to Stanhope returned in 2004. The main line connection at Bishop Auckland was reinstated in 2009 and from 2010 the railway extended to a new station at Bishop Auckland. From 2008, the railway was owned by the American railway company Iowa Pacific Holdings (IPH), using the subsidiary British American Railway Services (BARS). IPH entered insolvency in 2019 and in 2020 the Weardale Railway was purchased by a local charity, The Auckland Project. The new owner hopes to return services to Darlington, through partnering with a train operating company and there have been long-held aims to extend the railway east by two and a half miles to Eastgate.

Contact Details

Website: www.weardale-railway.org.uk
Email: info@weardale-railway.org.uk
Address: Weardale Railway, Stanhope Station, Station Road, Stanhope, DL13 2YS.

Transport Links

By Rail: Bishop Auckland West station is a 5–10 minute walk from Bishop Auckland main line station.
By Road: Free parking is available at Stanhope (DL13 2YS). There is also limited parking at Frosterley (DL13 2SL) and Wolsingham (DL13 3BL).

Opening Times

Trains usually operate on Saturdays, Sundays and selected weekdays from late March to late October.

Line Mileage and Journey Time

0.00	Bishop Auckland West
4.25	Witton-le-Wear
10.75	Wolsingham
14.00	Frosterley
16.00	Stanhope

A return journey takes over two hours.

Stock List

Type	Number	Builder	Details
Steam	40	Robert Stephenson & Hawthorns	0-6-0T
Diesel	10232	Sentinel	4wDH
Diesel	H050	English Electric	0-6-0DE
Diesel	3994	English Electric	0-6-0DH
Diesel	6294	Hunslet	0-6-0DH
Diesel	7541	Hunslet	0-6-0DH
Diesel	10187	Sentinel	0-6-0DH
Diesel	31285	Brush Traction	Class 31
Diesel	31465	Brush Traction	Class 31
DMU	50980 & 52054	British Railways	Class 108
DMU	55012	GRCW	Class 122
DMU	144010 (55810 & 55833)	Alexander/BREL	Class 144

Attractions

The railway travels through Weardale in the North Pennines, which is an Area of Outstanding Natural Beauty. Many footpaths and bridleways are within reach from the railway's stations. Stanhope station is home to a souvenir shop and the No. 40 Café, which serves light refreshments. Other attractions in the area include High Force waterfall, Killhope Lead Mining

Museum, Raby Castle and Hamsterley Forest. Nearby heritage railways include Locomotion, Shildon (four miles away), Beamish (19 miles) and the Tanfield Railway (20 miles).

Special Events

Events that usually take place on the railway:

Easter event.
A variety of food and drink related trains including Afternoon Tea & Cream Tea Trains, Beer & Gin Specials, Cheese & Wine Specials and Fish & Chips specials.
Diesel Galas.
The Train to Christmas Town Specials during December.

Wensleydale Railway

Introduction and History

This east to west trans-Pennine line was constructed in stages across harsh terrain, with Northallerton to Leeming Bar opening in 1848, extending to Leyburn in 1856 and reaching Garsdale in 1878. It was used to carry passengers, farm produce, quarried stone and coal. Passenger services were withdrawn in 1954, after which the line remained open between Northallerton and Redmire for freight. The track between Garsdale and Redmire was lifted in the 1960s. In 1992 British Steel decided it was no longer economic to transport limestone by rail and British Rail then announced its intention to close and sell the line. The sale was delayed when the Ministry of Defence then used the line to occasionally transport military vehicles to and from Redmire. The Wensleydale Railway Association formed in 1990, obtaining a 100-year lease on the line between Northallerton (Castle Hills) and Redmire. The first preserved trains ran between Leeming Bar and Leyburn in 2003, extending to Redmire in 2004 and to Northallerton West station in 2015, although trains have been terminating at Leeming Bar recently. The railway aims to extend towards Garsdale, the next steps being the Redmire to Bolton Castle and Aysgarth sections.

Contact Details

Website: www.wensleydale-railway.co.uk
Tel: 01677 425805
Email: Written enquiries can be made from the website.
Address: Leeming Bar Station, Leases Road, Leeming Bar, Northallerton DL7 9AR.

Transport Links

By Rail: Northallerton is the nearest railway station and is five and a half miles from Leeming Bar.
By Road: Car parking is available at Leeming Bar (DL7 9AR), Leyburn (DL8 5ET) and Redmire (DL8 4ES).

Opening Times

The railway usually operates at weekends for the majority of the year and on Tuesdays, Fridays and selected other weekdays from April to September.

Line Mileage and Journey Time

0.00	Northallerton West
6.00	Leeming Bar
7.75	Bedale
13.50	Finghall Lane
17.75	Leyburn
22.00	Redmire

A return journey takes about two and a half hours.

Stock List

Type	Number	Builder	Details
Steam	266 WELLINGTON	Black Hawthorn	0-4-0ST
Diesel	01526	Thomas Hill	4wDH
Diesel	01529	Thomas Hill	4wDH
Diesel	03144	British Railways	Class 03
Diesel	D9523	British Railways	Class 14

Diesel	20166	English Electric	Class 20
Diesel	31459	Brush Traction	Class 31
Diesel	33035	BRCW	Class 33
Diesel	37250	English Electric	Class 37
Diesel	47785	Brush Traction	Class 47
DMU	50256, 50746, 51210 & 56343	Metropolitan Cammell	Class 101
DMU	51572 & 56274	British Railways	Class 108
DMU	51353, 51400, 59500 & 59509	Pressed Steel	Class 117
DMU	142018 (55559 & 55609)	BREL/Leyland	Class 142
DMU	142028 (55569 & 55619)	BREL/Leyland	Class 142
DMU	142035 (55576 & 55626)	BREL/Leyland	Class 142
DMU	142041 (55582 & 55632)	BREL/Leyland	Class 142
DMU	142060 (55710 & 55756)	BREL/Leyland	Class 142
DMU	142078 (55728 & 55774)	BREL/Leyland	Class 142
DMU	142087 (55737 & 55783)	BREL/Leyland	Class 142
DMU	142090 (55740 & 55786)	BREL/Leyland	Class 142
DMU	142094 (55744 & 55790)	BREL/Leyland	Class 142
DMU	144020 (55820, 55856 & 55843)	Alexander/BREL	Class 144
DMU	975874	BREL/Leyland	Railbus
EMU	69335	BREL	Class 422

Attractions

After the railway was awarded a £368 000 National Lottery Heritage Fund grant, work has recently begun on restoring the interior and exterior of the Victorian station building at Leeming Bar. The lengthy line runs through a scenic landscape that is very popular with walkers and the area can be explored from the railway's stations. Bolton Castle or Jervaulx Abbey for example be accessed on foot and Aysgarth Falls is four miles from Redmire station. The Yorkshire Dales National Park is also nearby.

Special Events

Events that usually take place on the railway include:

Wensley Ale.
Regular afternoon tea services.
Polar Express trains during December.

Yorkshire Wolds Railway

Introduction and History

The railway between Malton and Driffield opened in 1853, linking the two routes running south from Scarborough, both of which remain in use today. Passenger services between Malton and Driffield ended as early as 1950, although the route continued to carry chalk from local quarries until it was closed in 1958. The Yorkshire Wolds Railway formed in 2008 with the aim of restoring at least part of the route as a heritage railway. Access to the site at Fimber, roughly midway along the railway trackbed, was granted in 2012. The first locomotive arrived in 2013 and the railway opened to the public in 2015, using a short demonstration line. After planning permission was granted, work began in 2019 to extend the line southwards by one mile towards Wetwang. The railway is one of the youngest heritage railways to be featured in this book and is a good example of the small and enthusiastic beginnings from which heritage railways start.

Contact Details

Website: www.yorkshirewoldsrailway.org.uk
Tel: 01377 338053
Email: info@yorkshirewoldsrailway.org.uk
Address: Yorkshire Wolds Railway, Fimber Halt, Beverley Road, Fimber, YO25 3HG.

Transport Links

By Rail: The nearest railway stations are Driffield (ten miles) and Malton (11 miles).
By Road: Free car parking is available (YO25 3HG).

Opening Times

The site opens every Sunday from April to September inclusive.

Line Mileage and Journey Time

The demonstration line is currently approximately 600 feet long and the journey time is relatively short.

Stock List

Type	Number	Builder	Details
Diesel	5576	English Electric	0-4-0

Attractions

The diesel locomotive is used to provide cab rides and 'Driver for a Fiver' experiences, which must be booked in advance. There is a visitor centre inside a restored Mark I coach, displaying artefacts and photographs of the line during operation, and a shop selling railway related gifts and refreshments. Nearby attractions include Fimber picnic site, Sledmere House, the Driffield Navigation and the deserted medieval village at Wharram Percy. Pickering, the southern terminus of the North Yorkshire Moors Railway is 20 miles from the Fimber site.

▲ On 23 June 2018, GWR 6959 Class 4-6-0 6990 "WITHERSLACK HALL" approaches Burrs on the East Lancashire Railway, when it was visiting from the Great Central Railway.   **Liam Barnes**

▲ On 11 June 2017, BRCW Type 2 26038 passes through the North Yorkshire Moors Railway's Goathland Station after having dropped off two brake vans in a nearby siding. The locomotive is currently at the Bo'ness & Kinneil Railway in Scotland. **Ken Davies**

▼ Since the previous edition of this book, Hunslet 0-6-0T 1873 JESSIE has moved from the Llangollen Railway to the Pontypool & Blaenavon Railway, where is it was captured hauling a Blaenavon High Level–Furnace Sidings coal train on the 1 in 24 climb near the Rhymney Brewery on 13 September 2019. **Alistair Grieve**

WALES

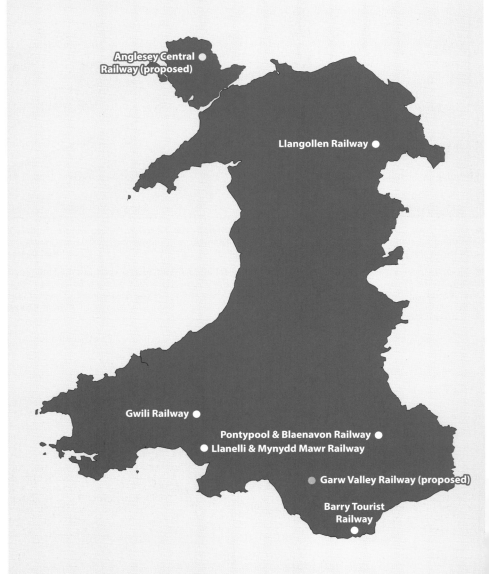

Anglesey Central Railway (proposed)

Llangollen Railway

Gwili Railway

Pontypool & Blaenavon Railway

Llanelli & Mynydd Mawr Railway

Garw Valley Railway (proposed)

Barry Tourist Railway

Region 3 – Wales

Barry Tourist Railway

Introduction and History

In 1889 Barry Docks and the railway that served them were built as an alternative to the nearby congested Cardiff Docks. Their primary purpose was the export of minerals, although passengers were also carried on the line to the docks, particularly after Barry Island Pleasure Park opened in 1897. The railway was cut back to Barry Island when Barry Pier station closed in 1976 and main line trains continue to terminate at Platform 1 of Barry Island station today. The Vale of Glamorgan Railway formed in 1994 and the first preserved trains operated from the Barry Island site in 1998. The railway was extended in stages, with heritage trains first crossing the causeway alongside the Barry Island–Barry Docks single line in 2002. They now continue to two destinations, Gladstone Bridge and a new station, Waterfront, adjacent to the site of the former Woodham's scrapyard. Since 2009 trains have been operated by Cambrian Transport and the railway shares the site with Barry Rail Centre.

Contact Details

Website: www.barrytouristrailway.co.uk
Tel: 01446 748816
Email: enquiries@barrytouristrailway.co.uk
Address: The Station Buildings, Station Approach, Barry Island, Vale of Glamorgan, CF62 5TH.

Transport Links

By Rail: Main line trains connect with the Barry Tourist Railway at Barry Island.
By Road: Parking is available outside Barry Island station (CF62 5TH) and there is free parking nearby.

Opening Times

From 2021 the railway is due to open on Saturdays and Sundays from Easter until October. Trains depart from Barry Island at 11.35, 13.10, 14.10, and 15.10.

Line Mileage and Journey Time

0.00	Barry Island		0.00	Barry Island
1.00	Waterfront		1.25	Gladstone Bridge

A return journey takes about 45 minutes.

Stock List

Type	Number	Builder	Details
Steam	SUSAN	Sentinel	4wVBGT
Steam	6686	Armstrong Whitworth	0-6-2T
Steam	92245	British Railways	2-10-0
Steam	5539	GWR	2-6-2T
Diesel	08503	British Railways	Class 08
Electro-Diesel	73118	English Electric	Class 73
DMU	50222, 50338 & 56356	Metropolitan Cammell	Class 101
EMU	61280	British Railways	Class 489

Attractions

The goods shed at the Waterfront destination has recently been redeveloped to include retail and entertainment outlets and a children's playground. The railway can operate private charter trains for a full or a half day and offers driver experiences. The station at Barry Island is also home to Barry War Museum, which opens 14.00–16.00 on Wednesdays and 11.00–16.00 on the second Sunday of the month; admission is free. Other nearby attractions include Barry Island Pleasure Park, Porthkerry Country Park, the beach and coast at Whitmore Bay. The city of Cardiff can be reached by train from Barry Island in 30 minutes.

Special Events

Events that usually take place on the railway include:

Easter Bunny Weekend.
Bonfire Night Trains during November.
Santa Specials during December.

Gwili Railway

Introduction and History

The Gwili Railway lies on part of the former line between Carmarthen and Aberystwyth in West Wales. It was originally a broad gauge line, opening in 1860 to carry both passengers and local goods. Passenger services ceased in 1964 and the line continued to carry produce such as milk until its closure in 1973. The track was lifted in 1975, the same year in which the Gwili Railway Company was formed. The company acquired an eight-mile section of trackbed between Abergwili Junction and Llanpumsaint and the first preserved trains ran from Bronwydd Arms to Cwmdwyfran in 1978. The railway has since been extended three times, across the River Gwili to Llwyfan Cerrig in 1987, to Danycoed in 2001 and to the former Abergwili Junction in 2017. There are plans to further extend after the site of Abergwili Junction has been redeveloped and a new carriage shed completed.

Contact Details

Website: www.gwili-railway.co.uk
Tel: 01267 238213
Email: info@gwili-railway.co.uk
Address: Gwili Railway, Bronwydd Arms Station, Bronwydd Arms, Carmarthenshire, SA33 6HT.

Transport Links

All trains depart from and return to Bronwydd Arms Station. There is no public access at Abergwili Junction, Llwyfan Cerrig or Danycoed Halt.
By Rail: Carmarthen station is three miles from Brownwydd Arms.
By Road: Car parking is available at Bronwydd Arms (SA33 6HT).

Opening Times

The railway usually operates at weekends, on selected weekdays between Easter and October and every day during July and August. All services begin at Bronwydd Arms.

▲ Class 47 D1566 follows the course of the River Dee as it leaves Berwyn with the 10.00 Llangollen–Carrog on 05 May 2019. The Llangollen Railway's western extension to Corwen is due to open during 2021. **Tony Christie**

Line Mileage and Journey Time

0.00	Abergwili Junction
.50	Bronwydd Arms
3.25	Llwyfan Cerrig
3.75	Danycoed Halt

A return journey takes about 1 hour 45 minutes.

Stock List

Type	Number	Builder	Details
Steam	1345	Peckett	0-4-0ST
Steam	7058	Robert Stephenson & Hawthorns	0-4-0ST
Steam	L92 (5786)	GWR	0-6-0PT
Steam	3829	Hunslet	0-6-0ST
Steam	7849	Robert Stephenson & Hawthorns	0-6-0ST
Steam	HAULWEN	Vulcan Foundry	0-6-0ST
Steam	28	Hunslet	0-6-2T
Diesel	312433	Ruston & Hornsby	4wDM
Diesel	5014	Peckett	0-6-0DM
Diesel	D2178	British Railways	Class 03
DMU	51347, 51401 & 59508	Pressed Steel	Class 117

Attractions

The railway follows a scenic route along the course of the River Gwili. There is a working signal box and gift shop at Bronwydd Arms, a miniature railway at Llwyfan Cerrig and driver footplate experiences can be arranged. The two foot gauge Teifi Valley Railway is about half an hour's drive away. Nearby attractions include Carmarthen with its 800-year-old market, the National Botanic Gardens of Wales and the Brecon Beacons National Park.

Special Events

Events that usually take place on the railway include:

Easter Special.
Teddy Bears Picnic during May.
Driver Experience Days are available between May and October.
Car Show on 18 July 2021.
Halloween Ghost Express during October.
Santa's Magical Steam Trains during December.
There are also dining trains with 'Sunday Dining', 'Cream Tea' and 'Murder Mystery Dining' services.

Llanelli & Mynydd Mawr Railway

Introduction and History

The first section of the four foot gauge horse-drawn tramway carrying ironstone to Llanelly Docks (as it was spelled at that time) opened in 1803. This was later extended to Cynheidre and Cross Hands; however, it fell into disuse as early as 1844. It was officially re-opened in 1883, although trains had been operating before 1883 and it continued to carry minerals and coal until 1989 when Cynheidre Colliery closed. The railway never had a regular passenger service, although it saw regular workmen's services and occasional charter trains. After closure, an initial preservation group was not able to raise sufficient funds to buy the line and it was sold to the local authorities and converted into the Swiss Valley Cycle Route. This is now part of Route 47 of the National Cycle Network. The Llanelli and Mynydd Mawr Railway Company formed in 1999 with the aim of opening a heritage railway. The site of the former Cynheidre Colliery and approximately one mile of trackbed have been purchased. It first opened to the public in late 2017, making it one of Britain's youngest heritage railways. Trains initially operated on a quarter-mile section of track and this has recently been increased to almost half a mile. Works to further extend the railway northwards are due to continue during 2021 and the long-term aim is to extend the line as far as possible north and south, alongside the existing cycle path. There are also plans to create a visitor centre at Cynheidre.

Contact Details

Website: www.llanellirailway.co.uk
Email: llanellirailway@gmail.com
Address: Llanelli & Mynydd Mawr Railway, Former Cynheidre Colliery, Llanelli, Carmarthenshire SA15 5YF.

Transport Links

By Rail: The nearest railway station is Llanelli, which is six miles away.
By Road: Free parking is available at Cynheidre (SA15 5YF, note this postcode is for the nearby village, turn right before Cynheidre Village sign if travelling from Llanelli).
By Bike: Route 47 of the National Cycle Network passes the Cynheidre site.

Opening Times

The usual operating dates are the last Saturday or the month between March and October, and during December for Santa Specials.

Line Mileage and Journey Time

Trains currently operate for 0.45 miles and the journey time is relatively short.

Stock List

Type	Number	Builder	Details
Diesel	394014	Ruston & Hornsby	0-4-0
Diesel	10222	Sentinel	0-4-0
Diesel	690	English Electric	0-6-0
DMU	55019	GRCW	Class 122
DMU	142006 (55547 & 55597)	BREL/Leyland	Class 142

Attractions

There is a small heritage centre and a static buffet coach selling refreshments at Cynheidre. Guided tours of the site and stock shed are available by advance arrangement, for which donations are suggested. Nature trails are organised in conjunction with a local wildlife group to explore the area's plant and animal wildlife. Nearby attractions include Gwili Railway, Llyn Llech Owain Country Park, Llanelli WWT National Wetland Centre and the National Botanic Gardens of Wales.

▲ Class 31 D5637 (the former 31465) "Steve Organ G.M." awaits departure from the Pontypool & Blaenavon Railway's Blaenavon High Level station, with the 16.00 to Furnace Sidings on 26 August 2019. **Alistair Grieve**

Special Events
Events that usually take place on the railway include:

Easter Event.
Family events during school holidays.
Santa Specials during December.

Llangollen Railway

Introduction and History
Llangollen is at the eastern end of the railway which ran across central Wales from Ruabon to Barmouth, opening in full in 1865 and closing to passengers a century later in 1965. It survived for freight use until 1968, soon after which the track was lifted and many of the stations were demolished. The first preservation group formed in 1972 and by 1975 Llangollen station had reopened. The preserved railway was extended to Berwyn in 1985, Deeside in 1990, Glyndyfrdwy in 1992 and to Carrog in 1996. It was further extended to a temporary terminus at Corwen East in 2014 and this was formally opened in 2015. At the end of the 2018 running season, the operational section was cut back to Carrog and Corwen East was dismantled, while the new Corwen Central station was completed. This is a quarter of mile to the east of the original Corwen station, which closed in 1965 and is now privately owned. The extension to Corwen Central was completed in 2020 and is due to see regular services from 2021. The new terminus has an island platform and was built within a cutting which had to be widened to accommodate the station. The 1924-built signal box from Weston Rhyn (between Chirk and Gobowen) has recently been moved to the Corwen site.

Contact Details
Website: www.llangollen-railway.co.uk
Tel: 01978 860979
Email: info@llangollen-railway.co.uk
Address: Llangollen Railway, The Station, Abbey Road, Llangollen, LL20 8SN.

Transport Links
By Rail: Ruabon is the nearest railway station and is six miles from Llangollen.
By Road: Corwen (LL21 0DN) is the best place to arrive by car as there is ample parking. There is only limited parking at Carrog (LL21 9BD), no parking at Berwyn or Glyndyfrdwy stations and limited disabled parking only at Llangollen (LL20 8SN).

Opening Times
Trains usually operate for the majority of the year, with daily services between April and October. A variety of timetables operate through the running season. Please check the railway's website for the latest information, as it came to light in March 2021 that the railway has serious financial difficulties which are expected to affect its operation.

Line Mileage and Journey Time
0.00	Llangollen
1.50	Berwyn
3.25	Deeside Halt
5.25	Glyndyfrdwy
7.25	Carrog
9.75	Corwen Central

A return journey takes at least 1 hour 40 minutes, depending on the starting point.

Stock List

Type	Number	Builder	Details
Steam	6430	GWR	0-6-0PT
Steam	7754	GWR	0-6-0PT
Steam	68030	Hunslet	0-6-0ST
Steam	1	Kitson	0-6-0ST
Steam	17 (1338)	Andrew Barclay	0-6-0T
Steam	5532	GWR	2-6-2T

Steam	80072	British Railways	2-6-4T
Steam	3802	GWR	2-8-0
Steam	4709	New build	2-8-0
Steam	61673	B17 SLT	4-6-0
Steam	5952	GWR	4-6-0
Steam	5551	LMS-Patriot Project	4-6-0
Diesel	2782	Yorkshire Engine Co.	0-4-0
Diesel	1901	English Electric	0-6-0
Diesel	03162	British Railways	Class 03
Diesel	08195	British Railways	Class 08
Diesel	D5310	BRCW	Class 26
Diesel	31271	Brush Traction	Class 31
Diesel	1566	British Railways	Class 47
DMU	50447, 50454 & 50528	BRCW	Class 104
DMU	56456	Cravens	Class 105
DMU	51933, 56223 & 56504	British Railways	Class 108
DMU	50416 & 56171	Wickham	Class 109
DMU	51618	British Railways	Class 127

Attractions

The railway has a large steam and diesel locomotive fleet and offers driver experiences using some of these. There is a railway workshop at Llangollen, where construction of new-build steam locomotive 6880 "Betton Grange" is in progress. The railway runs through part of a UNESCO World Heritage Site and an Area of Outstanding Natural Beauty, following the River Dee which is home to migratory salmon, otters and lampreys. It is also close to the Llangollen Canal and the Berwyn Mountains. Corwen Museum and the adjacent Corwen Manor and candle factory are near the town's new station. The market town of Llangollen has been popular with tourists for centuries and there are many walks, picturesque views and rural areas to explore from the railway's stations. Cambrian Heritage Railways and the Tanat Valley Railway are nearby, on the other side of the English border.

Special Events

Events that usually take place on the railway include:

Mother's and Father's Day Events.
1940s and 1960s themed events.
Steam and Diesel Galas.
Halloween Trains during October.
Santa Specials and Mince Pie Specials during December.

Pontypool & Blaenavon Railway

Introduction and History

The railway from Brynmawr to Blaenavon opened in 1869; passenger services commenced in 1870 and it was subsequently extended south to Pontypool. Passenger traffic ended in 1941 and the last of the coal trains ran from Blaenavon to Pontypool in 1980 when Big Pit closed. Heritage train services began in 1983, when the line between Furnace Sidings and Whistle Inn Halt opened. The railway was extended south to Blaenavon High Level station in 2010 and along the spur to Big Pit in 2011. There are long-term plans to further extend north to Waunavon and Brynmawr and also to the south, sharing the route with the present cycle path.

Contact Details

Website: www.bhrailway.co.uk
Tel: 01495 792263
Email: info@pbrly.co.uk
Address: Pontypool & Blaenavon Railway, The Railway Station, Furnace Sidings, Garn Yr Erw, Blaenavon, NP4 9SF.

Transport Links

By Rail: The nearest railway stations are Abergavenny and Ebbw Vale Town (both seven miles) however there are good bus connections from Cwmbran (details on P&BR website).
By Road: There is ample free parking at the Furnace Sidings base (NP4 9AX).
By Bike: On route 492 of the National Cycling Network.

Opening Times

Trains usually operate at weekends from Easter until early September, plus on selected Wednesdays during school holidays and on some days during October and December.

Line Mileage and Journey Time

0.00	Coed Avon		
0.25	Blaenavon High Level	0.00	Furnace Sidings
1.50	Furnace Sidings	0.50	Big Pit Halt
2.00	Whistle Inn Halt		

A round trip takes just over one hour.

Stock List

Type	Number	Builder	Details
Steam	1823	Andrew Barclay	0-4-0ST
Steam	2015	Andrew Barclay	0-4-0ST
Steam	2201	Andrew Barclay	0-4-0ST
Steam	FORESTER	Andrew Barclay	0-4-0ST
Steam	ROSYTH No.1	Andrew Barclay	0-4-0ST
Steam	9629	GWR	0-6-0PT
Steam	1 (2074)	Andrew Barclay	0-6-0ST
Steam	2 (1421)	Avonside	0-6-0ST
Steam	SIR JOHN (1680)	Avonside	0-6-0ST
Steam	EMPRESS	Bagnell	0-6-0ST
Steam	1873 JESSIE	Hunslet	0-6-0ST
Steam	71515	Robert Stephenson & Hawthorns	0-6-0ST
Steam	9622	Sentinel	4wVBGT
Diesel	Blaenavon No. 14	Hudswell Clarke	0-4-0
Diesel	D1387	Hudswell Clarke	0-4-0DH
Diesel	22497	Fowler	0-6-0DM
Diesel	John Roden (5511)	Hunslet	0-6-0DH
Diesel	170 (7063)	Hunslet	0-8-0DH
Diesel	03141	British Railways	Class 03
Diesel	D5627	Brush Traction	Class 31
Diesel	37023	English Electric	Class 37
Diesel	D6916	English Electric	Class 37
DMU	51351 & 51397	Pressed Steel	Class 117

Attractions

The railway, which is on the edge of the Brecon Beacons National Park, has one of the steepest gradients found on a British standard gauge heritage line. The rolling stock includes a varied collection of steam and diesel locomotives, multiple units and restored vintage saloons which are used on selected dates. 'Heritage Railway Experiences' are available, assisting the driver and train guard with their duties. The Pontypool & Blaenavon Model Railway Club is based at the Furnace Sidings site and has railways of several different gauges. The National Coal Mining Museum and Rhymney Brewery are near to Big Pit station. Blaenavon Heritage Centre and the Ironworks are a ten and 15 minute walk from Blaenavon High Level respectively. Route 492 of the National Cycle Network follows the present railway and much of the trackbed between Blaenavon and Pontypool.

Special Events

Events that usually take place on the railway include:

Steam and diesel galas.
Ghost Trains during October.
Santa Specials during December.

WEST MIDLANDS

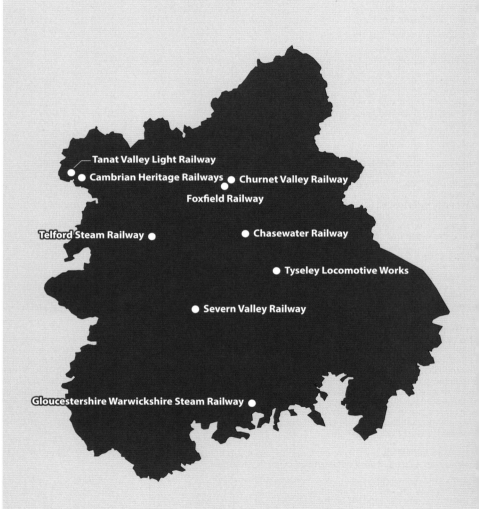

Tanat Valley Light Railway

Cambrian Heritage Railways

Churnet Valley Railway

Foxfield Railway

Telford Steam Railway

Chasewater Railway

Tyseley Locomotive Works

Severn Valley Railway

Gloucestershire Warwickshire Steam Railway

Region 4 – West Midlands

Cambrian Heritage Railways

Introduction and History

The branch line from Gobowen to Oswestry opened in 1848. A separate railway and station opened in Oswestry in 1860, heading south and this included the branch from Llynclys Junction to the quarry at Porthywaen. After the 1923 Grouping, improvements were made to what had become the Cambrian Railways station at Oswestry, enabling the former GWR station to close in 1924. Passenger services between Gobowen and Oswestry ended in 1966; stone trains from Gobowen to Blodwell continued until 1988 and the final weed killing train ran in 1993. A group of enthusiasts formed the Cambrian Railways Society (CRS) in 1972 and leased Oswestry goods yard from British Rail. The society opened a railway museum and from 1997 trains carried passengers on a short stretch of track. In 1998 the separate Cambrian Railways Trust (CRT) formed, aiming to return trains from Gobowen to Blodwell and began negotiations with Railtrack (subsequently Network Rail) to purchase the trackbed. A further group leased the trackbed between Llynclys and Pant after it was purchased by Oswestry Council. They relaid a ¾ mile length of track and started operating trains from 2005. Also in 2005, the local council bought Oswestry station and funding was obtained to restore the building and site. The CRS and CRT merged in 2009 forming Cambrian Heritage Railways, which now operates trains from both the Oswestry and Llynclys sites. Work on extending the railway south from Oswestry to a new terminus at Weston Wharf, 1.75 miles to the south, progressed during 2019 and 2020, although this was slowed by the coronavirus pandemic. The long-term aim is for heritage trains to operate for more than eight miles from Gobowen to Blodwell Quarry via Oswestry, although this will require some major engineering projects.

Contact Details

Website: www.cambrianrailways.com
Tel: 01691 728131
Email: enquiries@cambrianrailways.com
Address: Cambrian Heritage Railways, Old Station Building, Oswald Road, Oswestry, Shropshire, SY11 1RE.

Transport Links

By Rail: Gobowen railway station is two and a half miles from the Oswestry site and eight miles from Llynclys.
By Road: Chargeable car parking is available at Oswestry (SY11 1RE) and there is free parking at Llynclys (SY10 8BX).

Opening Times

Trains usually operate from Oswestry on weekends and Bank Holidays from April until mid-September. Cambrian Railway Museum at Oswestry opens 11.00–15.00 Tuesdays to Fridays from Easter to September. Regular trains are not expected to run from Llynclys during 2021 and this site will instead offer driving experiences using a Class 101 DMU and have occasional open days.

Line Mileage and Journey Time

Trains currently operate for three quarters of a mile from Llynclys and for just over half a mile from Oswestry, although this distance is expected to increase as the line is extended south. The journey time is currently relatively short.

Stock List

Type	Number	Builder	Details
Steam	2261	Andrew Barclay	0-4-0ST
Steam	2131 OLIVER VELTOM	Peckett	0-4-0ST
Steam	1430	Peckett	0-4-0ST
Steam	885	Andrew Barclay	0-6-0ST
Steam	3770 NORMA	Hunslet	0-6-0ST
Diesel	TELEMON	Drewry	0-4-0
Diesel	ALPHA	Hibberd	0-4-0
Diesel	CYRIL	Hibberd	0-4-0

Diesel	D893	Hudswell Clarke	0-4-0
Diesel	11517	Ruston & Hornsby	0-4-0
Diesel	SCOTTIE	Ruston & Hornsby	0-4-0
Diesel	D1230	English Electric	0-6-0
Diesel	H037	English Electric	0-6-0
Diesel	D3019	British Railways	Class 08
DMU	51512, 51187, 51205 & 56055	Metropolitan Cammell	Class 101
DMU	144006 (55806 & 55829)	Alexander/BREL	Class 144
DMU	144007 (55807 & 55830)	Alexander/BREL	Class 144

Attractions

There are two sites to visit, although both are not expected to operate passenger trains simultaneously during 2021. The Oswestry site is home to the original ornate Cambrian Railways station building and the Cambrian Railway Museum, which has free admission and is located within the 150-year old goods shed. Nearby attractions include Oswestry Town Museum, Pontcysyllte Aqueduct, Chirk Castle, the Tanat Valley Light Railway and the Llangollen Railway.

Chasewater Railway

Introduction and History

The industrial railways around Cannock Chase opened in the 1860s and were used to transport coal from the area's collieries. This continued until the 1960s when the coal mines and railway network were closed. The first preservation group (Railway Preservation Society, West Midlands District) formed in 1959, creating one of Britain's earliest heritage railway beginnings. The group acquired two derelict coaches and a rail-connected base at Hednesford in 1960 and the first locomotive arrived in 1961. In 1964 a 25-year lease was signed for a new site, on a section of trackbed on the former Aldridge to Brownhills branch. The first heritage trains ran on this in 1968 when Hawthorne Leslie 0-4-0ST "ASBESTOS" provided brake van rides. By 1970 all the rolling stock had been transferred from Hednesford to the Brownhills site, where regular operating days were taking place. The railway had to close between 1982 and 1985, as the funds needed to repair the line across the causeway were not available. Once this had been overcome and the repairs completed, the railway reopened and it was extended to Norton Lakeside in 1994, Chasewater Heaths in 1995 and Chasetown in 2004.

Contact Details

Website: www.chasewaterrailway.co.uk
Tel: 01543 452623
Email: admin@chasewaterrailway.co.uk
Address: Chasewater Country Park, Brownhills West Station, Pool Lane, Burntwood, Staffordshire, WS8 7NL.

Transport Links

By Rail: The nearest railway station is Landywood, which is five miles away.
By Road: There is a car park at Brownhills West, although visitors may temporarily need to park at Chasewater Country Park (both sites use the postcode WS8 7NL).

Opening Times

Trains usually operate between 11.00 and 16.00 on Saturdays, Sundays and Bank Holidays from March to October. Departure times may differ during special events.

Line Mileage and Journey Time

0.00	Brownhills West
1.00	Norton Lakeside Halt
1.50	Chasewater Heaths
1.75	Chasetown

A return journey takes about one hour.

▲ Cambrian Heritage Railways' Andrew Barclay 0-4-0ST 2261 was hauling a sole passenger coach and a brake van when it was captured at Oswestry on 5 May 2019. **Tony Christie**

▼ The Chasewater Railway's Bagnall 0-4-0ST DUNLOP No. 6 has just left Brownhills West with the 16.30 departure for Chasetown on 26 May 2019. **Alistair Grieve**

Stock List

Type	Number	Builder	Details
Steam	2 (2842)	Bagnall	0-4-0ST
Steam	DUNLOP No.6 (2648)	Bagnall	0-4-0ST
Steam	ASBESTOS (2780)	Hawthorn Leslie	0-4-0ST
Steam	750	Hudswell Clarke	0-4-0ST
Steam	2937	Neilson & Co	0-4-0ST
Steam	6 (917)	Peckett	0-4-0ST
Steam	TEDDY (2012)	Peckett	0-4-0ST
Steam	431	Hudswell Clarke	0-6-0ST
Steam	HOLLY BANK No.3	Hunslet	0-6-0ST
Steam	S100 (1822)	Hudswell Clarke	0-6-0T
Steam	5 (9632)	Sentinel	4wVBT
Diesel	3097	Bagnall	0-4-0
Diesel	3208	Bagnall	4wDH
Diesel	3027	Baguley	0-4-0
Diesel	3410	Baguley	0-4-0
Diesel	3590	Baguley	0-4-0
Diesel	4100013	Fowler	0-4-0
Diesel	21 (1612)	Hibberd	4wDM
Diesel	DERBYSHIRE STONE No.2 (1891)	Hibberd	4wDM
Diesel	6678	Hunslet	0-4-0
Diesel	D2911 (27876)	North British	0-4-0
Diesel	530003 MYFANWY	Robert Stephenson & Hawthorns	0-4-0
Diesel	111C	Thomas Hill	4wDH
Diesel	305306	Ruston & Hornsby	4wDM
Diesel	AD9118	Baguley Drewry	4wDM
Diesel	15097	Simplex	0-4-0
Diesel	15099	Simplex	0-4-0
Diesel	RRM106 (27656)	North British	0-4-0DH
Diesel	01568 HELEN	Thomas Hill	4wDH
Diesel	200V	Thomas Hill	4wDH
Diesel	5425	GEC Traction Ltd	6wDE
Diesel	5430	GEC Traction Ltd	6wDE
Diesel	3119	Bagnall	0-6-0
Diesel	10220 HARRY POTTER	Sentinel	0-6-0DH
Diesel	D615	Hudswell Clarke	0-6-0DM
Diesel	08939	British Railways	Class 08
DMU	59444	British Railways	Class 116
DMU	59603	British Railways	Class 127
DMU	142027 (55518 & 55568)	BREL/Leyland	Class 142
DMU	142029 (55520 & 55570)	BREL/Leyland	Class 142
DMU	142030 (55521 & 55571)	BREL/Leyland	Class 142
DMU	143603 (55658 & 55669)	Alexander/Barclay	Class 143

Attractions

Steam locomotive driving experiences are available and these need to be arranged in advance. At Brownhills West, there is a railway museum which has a large collection of exhibits and is free to enter, a gift and a model shop. The railway takes its name from the canal reservoir which it travels around and across, providing an interesting route. The area has a variety of walks, trails and cycling paths. Norton Lakeside is a Site of Special Scientific Interest and there is a nearby wildfowl reserve, which can also be explored on foot or bicycle (trains can carry bicycles). Nearby attractions include Chasewater Country Park, Wakelake, Beacon Park and the city of Lichfield.

Special Events

10–11 July 2021: Diesel Gala.

Other events that usually take place on the railway include:

Halloween Experience during October.
Santa Specials during December.

Churnet Valley Railway

Introduction and History

The lines that comprise today's Churnet Valley Railway are the remnants of several railways that were built at different times. The route from Macclesfield to Uttoxeter via Leek opened in 1849 and became known as the Churnet Valley Line, taking the name from the river it follows. This carried minerals from local quarries and connected with a number of industrial narrow gauge railways in the area. The line from Stoke-on-Trent to Milton Junction opened in 1864, as part of the Stoke to Congleton route. Milton Junction to Leekbrook Junction near Cheddleton opened in 1867 and Leekbrook Junction to Waterhouses opened in 1905, the line connecting with a narrow gauge line to Hulme End. Passenger services on the Waterhouses branch ended in 1935 and the line was cut back to Cauldon Lowe quarry in 1943. Passenger trains ceased on the Leek–Stoke route in 1956 and on the Macclesfield–Uttoxeter Churnet Valley Line in 1960. The first preservation group formed in the 1970s and Cheddleton became its base from 1977, while freight from Stoke-on-Trent continued to the quarries at Oakamore and Cauldon Lowe until 1988 and 1989 respectively. Preserved trains between Cheddleton and Leek Brook began in 1996 and these were extended south to Consall in 1998 and to Kingsley & Froghall in 2001. The steeply graded line from Leek Brook to Cauldon Lowe reopened in 2010, although this was cut back to today's terminating point at Ipstones in 2014. The railway has the unique and ambitious aim of extending in four different directions; track laying for the northern extension to Leek began in 2019 and completion is expected in 2021. In addition, there are longer term plans to extend west towards Stoke, south to Oakamore and to reinstate the eastern section between Ipstones and Cauldon Lowe.

Contact Details

Website: www.churnetvalleyrailway.co.uk
Tel: 01538 360522
Email: enquiries@churnetvalleyrailway.co.uk
Address: Churnet Valley Railway, Kingsley and Froghall Station, Froghall, Staffordshire, ST10 2HA.

Transport Links

By Rail: Stoke-on-Trent station is nine miles from Cheddleton and Blythe Bridge is seven miles from Kingsley & Froghall.
By Road: There is free parking at both Cheddleton (ST13 7EE) and Kingsley & Froghall (ST10 2HA) stations.

Opening Times

The railway operates on most weekends through the year and on selected weekdays, with more regular services during school holidays.

Line Mileage and Journey Time

0.00	Ipstones
4.50	Leek Brook
5.50	Cheddleton
7.75	Consall
9.75	Kingsley & Froghall

A return Kingsley & Froghall–Cheddleton journey takes about 1 hour 10 minutes, plus a further 1 hour 10 minutes for a return to Ipstones.

Stock List

Type	Number	Builder	Details
Steam	KATIE	Andrew Barclay	0-4-0ST
Steam	44422	LMS	0-6-0
Steam	2871	Fablok	0-6-0T
Steam	2944	Fablok	0-6-0T
Steam	3278	American Locomotive Co.	2-8-0
Steam	6046	Baldwin Locomotive Works	2-8-0
Steam	5197	Lima Locomotive Co.	2-8-0
Steam	48173	LMS	2-8-0
Diesel	BRIGHTSIDE	Yorkshire Engine Co.	0-4-0
Diesel	6 ROGER H BENNETT	Yorkshire Engine Co.	0-6-0

Diesel	D3800	British Railways	Class 08
Diesel	D8057	English Electric	Class 20
Diesel	25322	British Railways	Class 25
Diesel	33021	BRCW	Class 33
Diesel	33102	BRCW	Class 33

Attractions

There is a small museum at Cheddleton station, housed within the original 1849 station building and the site has a locomotive shed and goods yard. The railway offers steam footplate rides and driver experience courses. Cheddleton Flint Mill is a short walk away from the station. The region is home to Peak Wildlife Park and the market town of Leek, which is on the edge of the Peak District. The Manifold Way is a cycle and footpath along the trackbed of the former Leek & Manifold Light Railway. Nearby heritage railways include Peak Rail, the Foxfield Railway and the Ecclesbourne Valley Railway.

Special Events

The railway has a large and varied events programme which includes:

Valentine's Express Trains.
Mother's Day Lunch Trains.
A variety of food and drink themed services.
Diesel Galas.
Santa & Steam during December.

▲ The Churnet Valley Railway's line between Cheddleton and Ipstones only sees limited use. On 4 May 2019, visiting locomotive 31271 passes Fourfields Crossing on this section, while hauling the 09.15 Kingsley & Froghall–Ipstones service. **Brad Joyce**

Foxfield Railway

Introduction and History

The branch line from Blythe Bridge to Foxfield Colliery in Dilhorne, Staffordshire was built in 1893, taking a circuitous route over steep gradients to keep the railway as far away as possible from Dilhorne Hall. The colliery closed in 1965 and the site was taken over by a mineral processing firm which wanted to retain the railway for carrying minerals. At the time, the Foxfield Light Railway Society formed to operate trains over the line, with the agreement of the owning company. No further commercial freight trains operated; however, in 1967 the first heritage trains worked, carrying passengers in converted wagons. Carriages and further locomotives were subsequently acquired and a new station was built at Caverswall Road. The main line connection near Blythe Bridge has been removed and the half-mile section from Caverswall Road to the main line is currently disused. Passenger trains travel as far as Dilhorne Park, where the line continues for another three quarters of a mile to Foxfield Colliery, although at present this is not regularly used.

Contact Details

Website: www.foxfieldrailway.co.uk
Tel: 01782 396210
Email: flrenquiries@foxfieldrailway.co.uk
Address: Foxfield Railway Station, Caverswall Road, Blythe Bridge, Stoke-on-Trent, ST11 9BG.

Transport Links

By Rail: The nearest station is Blythe Bridge, which is half a mile away.
By Road: Free parking is available at Caverswall Road (ST11 9BG).

Opening Times

The railway usually operates on Sundays, Bank Holidays and on selected other dates from April to October.

Line Mileage and Journey Time

0.00   Caverswall Road
2.00   Dilhorne Park

A return journey takes about 45 minutes.

Stock List

Type	Number	Builder	Details
Steam	4101	Dübs & Company	0-4-0CT
Steam	1563	Avonside	0-4-0ST
Steam	HAWARDEN (2623)	Bagnall	0-4-0ST
Steam	1827	Beyer Peacock	0-4-0ST
Steam	3581	Hawthorn Leslie	0-4-0ST
Steam	4388	Kerr Stuart	0-4-0ST
Steam	MOSS BAY	Kerr Stuart	0-4-0ST
Steam	1803	Peckett	0-4-0ST
Steam	11 (2081)	Peckett	0-4-0ST
Steam	HENRY CORT	Peckett	0-4-0ST
Steam	6	Robert Heath	0-4-0ST
Steam	FLORENCE No.2 (3059)	Bagnall	0-6-0ST
Steam	LEWISHAM	Bagnall	0-6-0ST
Steam	WHISTON	Hunslet	0-6-0ST
Steam	WIMBLEBURY	Hunslet	0-6-0ST
Steam	1207	Manning Wardle	0-6-0ST
Steam	ACKTON HALL No.3 (1567)	Peckett	0-6-0ST
Steam	BELLEROPHON	Haydock	0-6-0WT
Steam	2	North Staffordshire Railway	0-6-2T
Steam	9535	Sentinel	4wVBGT
Electric	1130	English Electric	0-4-0
Diesel	3207	Bagnall	0-4-0
Diesel	WD820	English Electric	0-4-0
Diesel	4421	Kerr Stuart	0-4-0

Diesel	275886	Robert Stephenson & Hawthorns	4wDM
Diesel	242915	Ruston & Hornsby	4wDM
Diesel	408496	Ruston & Hornsby	4wDM
Diesel	424841	Ruston & Hornsby	0-4-0
Diesel	2262	Simplex	4wDM
Diesel	CLIVE (486)	Andrew Barclay	0-6-0
Diesel	3150	Bagnall	0-6-0
Diesel	LUDSTONE (2868)	Yorkshire Engine Co.	0-6-0
DMU	142055 (55705 & 55751)	BREL/Leyland	Class 142

Attractions

The restored Foxfield Colliery is open to visitors on selected dates only and can be reached on foot from Dilhorne Park or by shuttle bus from Caverswall Road. The railway showcases its industrial history with a large collection of industrial locomotives and wagons. Driving experiences are available, using either steam or diesel locomotives. There is a miniature railway which has steep gradients and a variety of steam, petrol and battery locomotives. This is approximately one quarter of a mile long and operates on selected Sundays. The museum at Caverswall Road has a large collection of railway exhibits and opens on Sundays, Bank Holidays and Wednesdays during school holidays from April to October. Caverswall Road has a souvenir & model railway shop, a real ale bar and station buffet. Nearby attractions include the Churnet Valley Railway, World of Wedgewood and Potteries Museum & Art Gallery in Stoke-on-Trent.

Special Events

Events that usually take place on the railway include:

Easter Weekend event.
Cream Tea Trains.
Vintage and Vehicle Rallies.
Halloween Ghost Trains.
Santa Specials.

▲ Andrew Barclay 0-6-0T No. 14 "CARRON" is based at the Lakeside & Haverthwaite Railway, where it has been restored in recent years. It visited the Foxfield Railway in 2019 to participate in its Summer Steam Gala, where it is seen on 20 July 2019. **Martyn Tattam**

Gloucestershire Warwickshire Steam Railway

Introduction and History

The railway from Stratford-upon-Avon to Cheltenham via Honeybourne opened in 1906. Passenger services were withdrawn in 1960, although freight and occasional trains to the Cheltenham races continued until 1976 when the line closed. The Cheltenham & Stratford Railway Association was created in 1977, with the aim of preserving the line. Initially, the group leased the trackbed and were given access to it from 1981. In 1984 the first preserved trains operated on a 0.4 mile section of track that was laid from Toddington. Also in 1984, the 15-miles of trackbed between Cheltenham and Broadway, along with the remaining buildings along this, were purchased from British Rail. The operational section was extended in stages, reaching Winchcombe in 1987, Gotherington in 1997, Cheltenham Race Course in 2003 and Broadway in the opposite direction in 2018. There are long-term aspirations to extend the railway four miles further north to Honeybourne, where it would connect with the national rail network and also to extend a further three quarters of a mile south to the outskirts of Cheltenham.

Contact Details

Website: www.gwsr.com
Tel: 01242 621405
Email: info@gwsr.com
Address: GWSR, Churchward House, Winchcombe Railway Station, Cheltenham, GL54 5LD.

Transport Links

By Rail: The nearest main line railway station is Cheltenham Spa. Stagecoach services D and E operate regularly between Cheltenham Spa and Cheltenham Race Course stations on Mondays to Saturdays.

By Road: There are car parks at Cheltenham Race Course (GL50 4SH) and Toddington (GL54 5DT), pay & display parking at Broadway (WR12 7DH) and limited or no parking at the other stations.

Opening Times

Trains operate at weekends for the majority of the year and on a large number of weekdays during the warmer months.

Line Mileage and Journey Time

0.00	Broadway
4.75	Toddington
5.75	Hayles Abbey Halt
7.25	Winchcombe
10.50	Gotherington
14.00	Cheltenham Race Course

A return journey takes up to three hours.

Stock List

Type	Number	Builder	Details
Steam	1976	Peckett	0-4-0ST
Steam	76077	British Railways	2-6-0
Steam	2807	GWR	2-8-0
Steam	2874	GWR	2-8-0
Steam	3850	GWR	2-8-0
Steam	4270	GWR	2-8-0T
Steam	7820	British Railways	4-6-0
Steam	7903	British Railways	4-6-0
Steam	35006	Southern Railway	4-6-2
Diesel	4210130	Fowler	0-4-0DM
Diesel	11230	Drewry	0-6-0
Diesel	372	Yorkshire Engine Co.	0-6-0
Diesel	D2182	British Railways	Class 03
Diesel	D2280	Robert Stephenson & Hawthorns	Class 04
Diesel	D8137	English Electric	Class 20
Diesel	20228	English Electric	Class 20
Diesel	5081	British Railways	Class 24

Diesel	D5343	BRCW	Class 26
Diesel	37215	English Electric	Class 37
Diesel	D6948	English Electric	Class 37
Diesel	45149	British Railways	Class 45
Diesel	47105	Brush Traction	Class 47
Diesel	47376	Brush Traction	Class 47
Electro-Diesel	E6036	English Electric	Class 73
DMU	52029	British Railways	Class 107
DMU	51360, 51363, 51372,		
	51405, 59505 & 59510	Pressed Steel	Class 117
DMU	55003	GRCW	Class 122

Attractions

There is a viewing area for the yard and locomotive depot at Toddington. The two foot gauge Toddington Narrow Gauge Railway has steam and diesel locomotives and begins from Toddington station car park, travelling for approximately half a mile. A railway carriage houses model railway displays at Winchcombe station; this opens most weekends and during special events. English Heritage Hailes Abbey is near to Hayles Abbey Halt (request stop). Cheltenham Racecourse is adjacent to its namesake station. Other nearby attractions include Berkeley Castle, Blenheim Palace, Sudeley Castle, the Cotswolds and several market towns.

Special Events

23 May & 27 June 2021: Diesel Enthusiast Days.

Other events that usually take place on the railway include:

Easter Eggspress.
Wartime in the Cotswolds.
Classic Vehicle and Bus Rallies.
Steam and Diesel Galas.
Evening Dining and Afternoon Tea Trains.
Food and drink themed events, including Real Ale Weekend.
Santa Experience Specials and Evening Carols by Steam Train during December.

▲ 7820 "DINMORE MANOR" has just brought the 14.20 Cheltenham Race Course–Broadway out of Greet Tunnel and approaches Winchcombe on the Gloucestershire Warwickshire Steam Railway on 12 September 2020. **Paul Biggs**

Severn Valley Railway

Introduction and History

The railway from Kidderminster to Bridgnorth and Shrewsbury opened in 1862. It closed as a through route in 1963, although freight traffic continued from Kidderminster to Alveley, near Highley, until 1969. The section from Kidderminster to Bewdley survived until early 1970, after which it was cut back to Foley Park, to where freight trains from Kidderminster worked until 1982. The Severn Valley Railway Society formed in 1965, with the initial aim of acquiring five and a half miles of the railway from Bridgnorth to Alveley. This was successful and the first heritage trains operated between Bridgnorth and Hampton Loade in 1970. In the early 1970s the railway sold shares to raise funds to purchase the section from Highley to Foley Park from British Rail. This was also successful and the line was extended to Bewdley in 1974. After freight services to Foley Park ceased, the final 1.5-mile section from Foley Park to Kidderminster was acquired and the new Kidderminster Town station built, allowing through trains from Bridgnorth to return to Kidderminster from 1984. The main line connection at Kidderminster has been reinstated, over which through trains occasionally pass.

Contact Details

Website: www.svr.co.uk
Tel: 01562 757900
Email: contact@svrlive.com
Address: Severn Valley Railway, Number One, Comberton Place, Kidderminster, DY10 1QR.

Transport Links

By Rail: Kidderminster main line station is adjacent to Kidderminster Town (SVR) station.
By Road: There is pay & display parking at Kidderminster (DY10 1QX), Bewdley (DY12 1BG) and Bridgnorth (WV16 5DT). Parking at Arley, Highley & Hampton Loade is very limited and not recommended.

Opening Times

The railway operates at weekends and Bank Holidays for the majority of the year and on most days from early April to late September.

Line Mileage and Journey Time

0.00	Kidderminster Town
3.50	Bewdley
5.00	Northwood Halt
7.00	Arley
9.25	Highley
10.25	Country Park Halt
11.50	Hampton Loade
16.00	Bridgnorth

A return journey takes about three hours.

Stock List

Type	Number	Builder	Details
Steam	1450	GWR	0-4-2T
Steam	4085 DUNROBIN	Sharp Stewart	0-4-4T
Steam	1501	British Railways	0-6-0PT
Steam	5764	GWR	0-6-0PT
Steam	7714	GWR	0-6-0PT
Steam	813	Hudswell Clarke	0-6-0ST
Steam	2047	Manning Wardle	0-6-0ST
Steam	71516	Robert Stephenson & Hawthorns	0-6-0ST
Steam	686	Hunslet	0-6-0T
Steam	47383	Vulcan Foundry	0-6-0T
Steam	Catch Me Who Can	Trevithick 200	2-2-0
Steam	43106	British Railways	2-6-0
Steam	46443	British Railways	2-6-0
Steam	7325	GWR	2-6-0
Steam	42968	LMS	2-6-0

Steam	82045	82045 Steam Locomotive Trust	2-6-2T
Steam	4150	GWR	2-6-2T
Steam	4566	GWR	2-6-2T
Steam	5164	GWR	2-6-2T
Steam	80079	British Railways	2-6-4T
Steam	2857	GWR	2-8-0
Steam	48773	North British	2-8-0
Steam	600	North British	2-10-0
Steam	75069	British Railways	4-6-0
Steam	4930	GWR	4-6-0
Steam	6960	GWR	4-6-0
Steam	7802	GWR	4-6-0
Steam	7812	GWR	4-6-0
Steam	7819	GWR	4-6-0
Steam	45110	Vulcan Foundry	4-6-0
Steam	34027	Southern Railway	4-6-2
Diesel	319290	Ruston & Hornsby	0-4-0
Diesel	D2960	Ruston & Hornsby	0-4-0
Diesel	D2961	Ruston & Hornsby	0-4-0
Diesel	08635	British Railways	Class 08
Diesel	08896	British Railways	Class 08
Diesel	D3022	British Railways	Class 08
Diesel	13201	British Railways	Class 08
Diesel	D3586	British Railways	Class 08
Diesel	09107	British Railways	Class 09
Diesel	D4100	British Railways	Class 09
Diesel	12099	British Railways	Class 11
Diesel	D9551	British Railways	Class 14
Diesel	33108	BRCW	Class 33
Diesel	D7029	Beyer Peacock	Class 35
Diesel	37308	English Electric	Class 37
Diesel	40106	English Electric	Class 40
Diesel	D821	British Railways	Class 42
Diesel	50031	English Electric	Class 50
Diesel	50033	English Electric	Class 50
Diesel	50035	English Electric	Class 50
Diesel	50044	English Electric	Class 50
Diesel	D1013	British Railways	Class 52
Diesel	D1015	British Railways	Class 52
Diesel	D1062	British Railways	Class 52
DMU	50933, 51941, 52064, 56208 & 59250	British Railways	Class 108

Attractions

The SVR is one of Britain's longest heritage railways and has a very large collection of locomotives, which is often embellished for its steam and diesel galas. There are plenty of exhibits at the Engine House Visitor & Education Centre at Highley and the locomotive works at Bridgnorth can be viewed from the station footbridge. Route 45 of the National Cycle Network travels through Bewdley and along the route of the former Wyre Forest railway line and continues north from Bridgnorth on the former railway to Coalport. Nearby attractions include Severn Valley Country Park, West Midland Safari Park, The Museum of Carpet, Wyre Forest and Hartlebury Castle & Museum.

Special Events planned for 2021

13–16 May: Spring Diesel Gala.
26–27 June & 3–4 July: Step Back to the 1940s.
16–19 September: Autumn Steam Gala.
30 September–3 October: Autumn Diesel Gala.
October (dates TBC): Scream Trains.
5–7 November: Season Finale Gala.
26 November–24 December: Steam in Lights.
27 November–24 December: Santa Trains.

In addition, Footplate Experiences and Photo Charters are available on selected dates.

▲ BR Class 25 D7535 (25185) passes Foley Park with the 11.18 Bridgnorth–Kidderminster during the Severn Valley Railway's annual Spring Diesel Festival on 16 May 2019. **Steve Donald**

▼ 08757 "EAGLE" sits at the buffer stops of the Telford Steam Railway's Spring Village base on 9 June 2019. **Tony Christie**

Tanat Valley Light Railway

Introduction and History

The railway from Shrewsbury to the quarries at Nantmawr and Criggion opened in 1866 and following poor revenues and inadequate maintenance, it closed in 1880. The route then became part of Cambrian Railways and reopened in 1896. The original Tanat Valley Light Railway (TVLR) from Llanyblodwell to Llangynog in central Wales opened in 1904 for carrying slate; it connected with the quarry branch to Nantmawr. Passenger services on the TVLR ended in 1951 and the line closed in 1964; however, stone traffic from Gobowen to Blodwell Quarry at the beginning of the route continued until 1988. In 2004, the newly formed TVLR Company acquired the route from Blodwell Junction to Nantmawr and ran its first trains in preservation during 2009. There is a rail connection to Cambrian Heritage Railways at Llanddu and there are long term plans for the two railways to work together and operate through trains. The TVLR suffered a major blow in 2019, when flooding caused significant damage to the trackwork and the 2020 coronavirus pandemic then compounded the difficulties. It is expected to take until at least 2022 before the necessary trackwork repairs can be completed and sadly, the railway will remain closed until then.

Contact Details

Website: www.nantmawrvisitorcentre.co.uk/tanat-valley-light-railway
Tel: 01691 780042
Email: admin@tvlr.co.uk
Address: Tanat Valley Light Railway, Tan Llwyn, Llangedwyn, Near Oswestry, SY10 9LD.

Transport Links

By Rail: Gobowen is the nearest railway station and is eight miles away.
By Road: Free car parking is available at Nantmawr (SY10 9HW).

Opening Times

As a result of the 2019 flood damage, the railway is not expected to reopen until 2022.

Line Mileage and Journey Time

0.00   Nantmawr
1.25   Llanddu Junction

Trains travel for about a third of a mile from Nantmawr and a return journey takes 10–15 minutes.

Stock List

Type	Number	Builder	Details
Diesel	HE2145	Hunslet	0-4-0
Diesel	338416	Ruston & Hornsby	0-4-0
DMU	51993, 52005, 52012, 52031 & 59791	British Railways	Class 107
EMU	61937, 75642 & 75981	British Railways	Class 309

Attractions

The railway is home to the Richard Morris Collection, which is an eclectic mix including narrow gauge items, the rail taxi, an Isetta Bubble Car converted to a rail vehicle, a steam monorail and the largest collection of industrial monorail in the country. There is a museum coach and the Clacton café is situated in a Class 309 rescued from the closed Coventry Electric Railway Museum. A number of woodland walks and nature trails are within reach from this rural setting in the Welsh-English borders. Cambrian Heritage Railways and the Llangollen Railway are four and 17 miles from Nantmawr respectively.

Telford Steam Railway

Introduction and History

The region is rich in industrial history, with the railways having played an important role in transporting raw materials and locally manufactured goods. The first wooden wagonways in the area were replaced by a cast iron plateway as early as 1769, connecting the mines and sites supplying raw materials to the iron works. The railway between Wellington and Horsehay opened in 1859 and was subsequently extended south-west to Craven Arms in 1867. The Horsehay Company Ltd was established in 1886 and occupied the site of today's steam railway. It fabricated, assembled and disassembled bridges, and had an extensive industrial railway network to aid this, before the bridges were transported to destinations throughout the British Empire. The line through Horsehay & Dawley closed to passenger services in 1962 and freight from Lightmoor Junction continued to use it until 1979. The first preservation group, the Telford Horsehay Steam Trust, formed in 1976, restoring its first steam locomotive in 1981. The heritage railway opened to the public in 1984 and was extended north to Lawley Village in 2015. Work has recently begun on a 1.5-mile southern extension from Horsehay & Dawley, which will connect to the disused Ironbridge branch at the former Lightmoor Junction. The preserved railway could then continue along the branch to Coalbrookdale and Buildwas. As the Ironbridge branch remains connected to the Wolverhampton to Telford line at Madeley Junction, this would provide the railway with a main line connection.

Contact Details

Website: www.telfordsteamrailway.co.uk
Tel: 01952 503880
Email: Written enquiries can be made from the railway's website.
Address: Telford Steam Railway, The Old Loco Shed, Bridge Road, Horsehay, Telford, TF4 3UH.

Transport Links

By Rail: The nearest railway station is Telford Central, which is three and a half miles away.
By Road: Free parking is available outside the old loco shed or in the main yard (use postcode TF4 2NF).

Opening Times

The railway opens on Sundays and Bank Holidays from Easter until late September, plus on selected Saturdays and during December for Christmas Specials.

Line Mileage and Journey Time

0.00	Lawley Village		0.00	Lawley Village
1.25	Spring Village		1.00	Horsehay & Dawley

A return journey on both spurs of the railway starting from Spring Village takes 50 minutes.

Stock List

Type	Number	Builder	Details
Steam	1944	Andrew Barclay	0-4-0F
Steam	3240 BEATTY	Hawthorn Leslie	0-4-0ST
Steam	1990	Peckett	0-4-0ST
Steam	MERLIN (1967)	Peckett	0-4-0ST
Steam	ROCKET	Peckett	0-4-0ST
Diesel	27414 TOM	North British	0-4-0
Diesel	183062	Ruston & Hornsby	0-4-0
Diesel	313394	Ruston & Hornsby	0-4-0
Diesel	382824	Ruston & Hornsby	0-4-0
Diesel	525947	Ruston & Hornsby	0-4-0
Diesel	08757	British Railways	Class 08
Diesel	D3429	British Railways	Class 08
Diesel	37263	English Electric	Class 37
DMU	50531	BRCW	Class 104
DMU	51950 & 52062	British Railways	Class 108
DMU	142004 (55545 & 55595)	BREL/Leyland	Class 142
DMU	144013 (55813 & 55836)	Alexander/BREL	Class 144

Attractions

Steam trains run on most operating days and diesel services on the other dates. The railway has a two foot gauge steam tram, a model railway, miniature railway, gift shop and tea room A variety of hands-on railway experiences are available, including a guard experience and locomotive driving experiences. The Phoenix Model Engineering Society operate a miniature railway alongside Telford Steam Railway and this opens on the last Sunday of each month and Bank Holiday Mondays. Nearby attractions include Wonderland Telford, Cosford RAF Museum, Blists Hill Victorian Town and Ironbridge Gorge museums.

Special Events

1–3 May 2021: Teddy Bears Picnic.
29–31 May 2021: Family Fun Weekend.
28–29 August 2021: 1940s Weekend.
11–12 September 2021: Anything Goes Diesel Gala.

Other events that usually take place on the railway include:

Easter Eggtravaganza Fun Day.
1940s Weekend.
Ghost Trains.
Polar Express Train Ride.

Tyseley Locomotive Works

Introduction and History

The steam locomotive depot at Tyseley opened in 1908 and has remained in continuous use as a traction maintenance depot since. When former GWR locomotive 7029 'Clun Castle' was purchased by a rail enthusiast in 1966, it was moved to Tyseley, which became its new home. The final British Railways steam locomotives allocated to Tyseley left the depot in 1967 and as preservationists acquired further steam locomotives, these were brought to Tyseley. The heritage operation grew and became known as Birmingham Railway Museum, while continuing to share the site, as it does with Tyseley DMU depot today. The first main line steam train ran in 1999 and the organisation subsequently split into two, with Tyseley Locomotive Works storing and maintaining steam locomotives and Vintage Trains promoting main line trains; Vintage Trains became a train operating company in its own right in 2018. Tyseley Locomotive Works usually opens to the public on one or two weekends each year, during which trains provide rides along a short stretch of track.

Contact Details

Website: www.vintagetrains.co.uk
Tel: 0121 708 4960
Email: tickets@vintagetrains.co.uk
Address: Tyseley Locomotive Works, 670 Warwick Road, Birmingham, B11 2HL.

Transport Links

By Rail: Tyseley railway station is adjacent to the works, a short walk away.
By Road: No on-site parking is available and visitors are encouraged to travel by public transport

Opening Times

An open weekend is planned for Saturday 23 and Sunday 24 October 2021.

Line Mileage and Journey Time

Trains carry passengers for approximately one quarter of a mile and the journey time is relatively short.

Stock List

Type	Number	Builder	Details
Steam	3 (3597)	Hawthorn Leslie	0-4-0ST
Steam	No 1 (2004)	Peckett	0-4-0ST
Steam	No.1 Cadbury	Avonside	0-4-0T
Steam	9600	GWR	0-6-0PT
Steam	7760	North British	0-6-0PT

Steam	L94 (7752)	North British	0-6-0PT
Steam	Fred (7289)	Robert Stephenson & Hawthorns	0-6-0ST
Steam	4121	GWR	2-6-2T
Steam	4588	GWR	2-6-2T
Steam	2885	GWR	2-8-0
Steam	6880	Betton Grange Society	4-6-0
Steam	7029	British Railways	4-6-0
Steam	4965	GWR	4-6-0
Steam	5043	GWR	4-6-0
Steam	5080	GWR	4-6-0
Steam	5593	North British	4-6-0
Steam	34070	Southern Railway	4-6-2
Steam	71000	British Railways	4-6-2
Diesel	299099	Ruston & Hornsby	0-4-0
Diesel	347747	Robert Stephenson & Hawthorns	0-6-0DM
Diesel	08616	British Railways	Class 08
Diesel	13029	British Railways	Class 08
Diesel	40118	English Electric	Class 40
Diesel	47773	Brush Traction	Class 47
DMU	144014 (55814, 55850 & 55837)	Alexander/BREL	Class 144
DMU	144019 (55819, 55855 & 55842)	Alexander/BREL	Class 144
DMU	144023 (55823, 55859 & 55846)	Alexander/BREL	Class 144

Attractions

Tyseley Locomotive Works has an operational turntable and is home to a large collection of locomotives, including new-build projects. Nearby attractions include Blakesley Hall and the city of Birmingham. The Severn Valley Railway is 20 miles away.

▲ The architecture and period features at many of Britain's heritage railways provide as much charm as the trains do. On 27 September 2019, D1015 "WESTERN CHAMPION" arrives at the 1862-built Bewdley station with the 11.20 Kidderminster–Bridgnorth. **Tony Christie**

EAST MIDLANDS

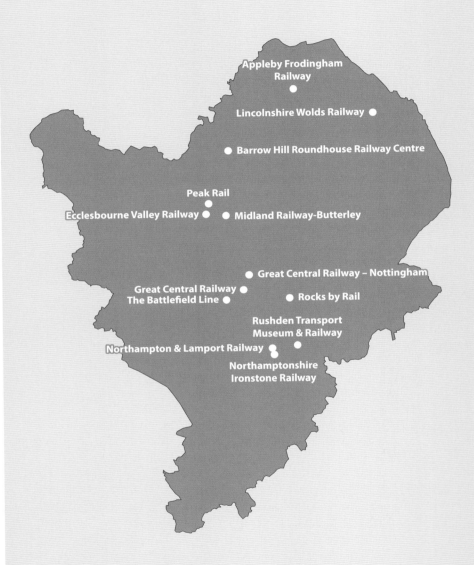

Appleby Frodingham Railway

Lincolnshire Wolds Railway

Barrow Hill Roundhouse Railway Centre

Peak Rail

Ecclesbourne Valley Railway

Midland Railway-Butterley

Great Central Railway – Nottingham

Great Central Railway
The Battlefield Line

Rocks by Rail

Rushden Transport
Museum & Railway

Northampton & Lamport Railway

Northamptonshire
Ironstone Railway

Region 5 – East Midlands

Appleby Frodingham Railway

Introduction and History

The steelworks at Scunthorpe and the extensive railway complex within them were established in the mid-19th Century. The site remains an operational steelworks today and contains more than 100 miles of working track, over which Railtours run on selected dates. Since 1990, these have been operated by the Appleby Frodingham Railway Preservation Society (AFRPS), using either a diesel multiple unit or a steam or diesel locomotive and brake van combination, giving a very different experience to that of other heritage railways. A Class 144 Pacer was acquired in 2020 and the site is now one of the few that provides second generation DMU driving experiences.

Contact Details

Website: www.afrps.co.uk
Tel: Tours are booked through Brigg Tourist Information, tel 01652 657053.
Email: bookings@afrps.co.uk or brigg.tic@northlincs.gov.uk
Address: AFRPS, Brigg Tourist Information Centre, The Buttercross, Market Place, Brigg, DN20 8ER.

Transport Links

By Rail: The nearest railway station is Scunthorpe, which is one mile from the site.
By Road: Car parking is available at the steelworks, which is accessed from Brigg Road, Scunthorpe (DN16 1XA).

Opening Times

Railtours of the steelworks operate on selected Saturdays. A donation is requested to cover the costs.

Line Mileage and Journey Time

The railway is not linear and consists of an extensive track layout around the steelworks. Railtours travel for varying distances, usually covering about 15 miles and taking up to four hours.

Stock List

Type	Number	Builder	Details
Steam	8 (2369)	Andrew Barclay	0-4-0ST
Steam	1 (1438)	Peckett	0-4-0ST
Steam	3 (1919)	Avonside	0-6-0ST
Steam	22 (3846)	Hunslet	0-6-0ST
Steam	3138	Fablok	0-6-0T
Diesel	1 (2661)	Yorkshire Engine Co.	0-6-0
Diesel	1 (2877)	Yorkshire Engine Co.	0-6-0
DMU	56207 & 59245	British Railways	Class 108
DMU	144017 (55817, 55853 & 55840)	Alexander/BREL	Class 144

Attractions

Tours through the steelworks do not necessarily cover the route that previous tours took. On some dates a restored buffet carriage is used to provide refreshments. Note that for safety reasons children under the age of 10 cannot travel on brake van tours and children under 5 cannot travel on any tour. Steam locomotive and Pacer driver experiences are available; these are unique in that they take place within an operational steelworks. Nearby attractions include North Lincolnshire Museum in Scunthorpe, Elsham Hall, Gardens & Country Park and Normanby Hall Country Park.

Special Events

There are occasional diesel locomotive events, please check the website for details.

Barrow Hill Roundhouse Railway Centre

Introduction and History

The railway through Chesterfield and Staveley opened in 1841, as part of the North Midland Railway's route from Derby to Rotherham and Leeds. A locomotive depot was built at Staveley in 1865, followed by the roundhouse in 1870. After 121 years of continuous use, British Rail closed the roundhouse in 1991 and the condition of the buildings and the site then deteriorated. In 1989 the Barrow Hill Engine Shed Action Group formed with the aim of saving the roundhouse from demolition. The group lobbied for the building to be given Grade II listed status and this was granted in 1991. The project received funding from several organisations and much restoration work was completed. The site first opened to the public in 1998, with diesel-hauled brake van rides being provided. It now has a museum and a large collection of locomotives, some of which reside there long-term and others travel to and from other locations. It remains connected to the main line, enabling occasional charter trains to travel directly for special events.

Contact Details

Website: www.barrowhill.org
Tel: 01246 475554
Email: enquiries@barrowhill.org
Address: Barrow Hill Limited, Campbell Drive, Barrow Hill, Chesterfield, S43 2PR.

Transport Links

By Rail: The nearest station is Chesterfield, which is four miles away. There is a free bus from Chesterfield station and town centre on some special event days.
By Road: There is ample free parking on site (S43 2PR).

Opening Times

The roundhouse and museum open 10.00–16.00 on Saturdays and Sundays from March to early December.

Line Mileage and Journey Time

Trains operate on a section of the former Springwell branch on selected dates. This runs north from the roundhouse site for approximately half a mile and the journey time is relatively short.

Stock List

Type	Number	Builder	Details
Steam	HENRY (2491)	Hawthorn Leslie	0-4-0ST
Steam	E B WILSON (1795)	Manning Wardle	0-4-0ST
Steam	8217	GER	0-6-0
Steam	68006	Hunslet	0-6-0ST
Steam	2000	Peckett	0-6-0ST
Steam	VULCAN (3272)	Vulcan Foundry	0-6-0ST
Steam	41708	Midland Railway	0-6-0T
Steam	506	Great Central Railway	4-4-0
Steam	1000	Midland Railway	4-4-0
Diesel	01515	Thomas Hill	0-4-0DH
Diesel	12589 HARRY	Robert Stephenson & Hawthorns	0-4-0DM
Diesel	D2868	Yorkshire Engine Co.	Class 02
Diesel	02003	Yorkshire Engine Co.	Class 02
Diesel	03066	British Railways	Class 03
Diesel	07012	Ruston & Hornsby	Class 07
Diesel	D4092	British Railways	Class 10
Diesel	D5910	Baby Deltic Project	Class 23
Diesel	26007	BRCW	Class 26
Diesel	27066	BRCW	Class 27
Diesel	45060	British Railways	Class 45
Diesel	45105	British Railways	Class 45
Diesel	45118	British Railways	Class 45
Diesel	55019	English Electric	Class 55
Diesel	D9009	English Electric	Class 55
Diesel	D9015	English Electric	Class 55
Electric	81002	BRCW	Class 81

Electric	82008	Beyer Peacock	Class 82
Electric	E3035	English Electric	Class 83
Electric	85006	British Railways	Class 85
EMU	62364 & 76762	BREL	Class 421
EMU	62321	BREL	Class 423

Harry Needle Railroad Company is based at Barrow Hill. Members of its locomotive fleet will be present, but are omitted from the stocklist as this is a commercial operator whose locomotives regularly move to and from the site.

Attractions

The roundhouse, which is now over 150 years old, has a 24-road turntable and is the only surviving operational roundhouse in Great Britain. The shear legs (lifting gear) can be seen, along with a large display of locomotives, an operational signal box, display rooms and various railway exhibits. The Deltic Preservation Society's maintenance depot and museum is adjacent to the roundhouse and are usually open on Saturdays and during some special events. Peak Rail, the Midland Railway-Butterley and the Ecclesbourne Valley Railway are all under 20 miles away. Other attractions in the area include Cliffe Park, Abbeydale Industrial Hamlet, Chesterfield and Sheffield.

Special Events

The site hosts large events such as live music productions. In addition, seasonal themed events take place throughout the year, including at Easter, Halloween and Christmas. A Real Ale Festival is planned for 9–11 September 2021.

▲ While it was visiting from the Buckinghamshire Railway Centre, GWR 6959 Class 4-6-0 6989 "WIGHTWICK HALL" passes the Battlefield Line's Shackerstone Signal Box on 11 January 2020.

Martyn Tattam

The Battlefield Line

Introduction and History

The Battlefield Line was part of the Ashby & Nuneaton Joint Railway which opened in 1873, linking Nuneaton to the Leicestershire coalfields. Before the 1923 Grouping, it was jointly operated by the London & North Western and the Midland Railways. British Rail ran the final passenger train over the line in 1965, after which it closed. The preservation era began in 1969 when the Shackerstone Railway Society formed, shortly before the track was lifted in 1970. The first heritage train worked from Shackerstone to Market Bosworth in 1973 and in 1992 the line was extended to Shenton. The railway takes its name from Bosworth Battlefield near Shenton, where the final battle of the War of the Roses took place in 1485.

Contact Details

Website: www.battlefieldline.co.uk
Tel: 07594 219979
Email: enquiries@battlefieldline.co.uk
Address: The Shackerstone Railway Society Ltd, Shackerstone Station, Leicestershire, CV13 6NW.

Transport Links

By Rail: Nuneaton and Hinckley railway stations are seven and six miles from Shenton respectively. Polesworth and Atherstone stations are both nine miles from Shackerstone.
By Road: There is ample parking at all three stations, which is free at Shakerstone (CV13 0BS) and Market Bosworth (CV13 0PF); charges apply at Shenton (CV13 6DJ).
By Boat: Narrowboats can moor at Ashby Canal Bridge 52 (a ten minute walk to Shackerstone station), Bridge 42 at Bosworth Marina (a five minute walk to Market Bosworth station) and Shenton Aqueduct or Bridge 35 (both a five minute walk to Shenton station).

Opening Times

Trains operate during weekends from late March to late October and on selected Wednesdays during school holidays.

Line Mileage and Journey Time

0.00	Shackerstone
2.50	Market Bosworth
4.25	Shenton

A return journey takes just under one hour.

Stock List

Type	Number	Builder	Details
Steam	1859 SIR GOMER	Peckett	0-6-0ST
Steam	7537 RICHARD III	Robert Stephenson & Hawthorns	0-6-0T
Steam	5526	GWR	2-6-2T
Diesel	263001 NANCY	Ruston & Hornsby	0-4-0
Diesel	268881	Ruston & Hornsby	0-4-0DE
Diesel	281271	Ruston & Hornsby	0-4-0DM
Diesel	422 HOT WHEELS	Andrew Barclay	0-6-0
Diesel	594 BIG MOMMA	Andrew Barclay	0-6-0
Diesel	D2867	Yorkshire Engine Co.	Class 02
Diesel	04110	Robert Stephenson & Hawthorns	Class 04
Diesel	12083	British Railways	Class 11
Diesel	2002 (20063)	English Electric	Class 20
Diesel	D8110 (20110)	English Electric	Class 20
Diesel	D7523	British Railways	Class 25
Diesel	33008	BRCW	Class 33
Diesel	33019	BRCW	Class 33
Diesel	33201	BRCW	Class 33
Diesel	33208	BRCW	Class 33
Diesel	37906	English Electric	Class 37
Diesel	45015	British Railways	Class 45
Diesel	47640	Brush Traction	Class 47

Diesel	58012	BREL	Class 58
Diesel	58048	BREL	Class 58
DMU	51131	British Railways	Class 116
DMU	51321	BRCW	Class 118
DMU	55005	GRCW	Class 122
DEMU	975386	British Railways	Class 202
EMU	65321 & 77112	British Railways	Class 416
Battery	905	English Electric	0-4-0

Attractions

Diesel locomotive 33201 recently moved to the railway and is often employed on passenger trains. Footplate rides, murder mystery evenings, dining and driver experiences are available on various dates. There is a working pottery business on the site of Shenton station and Bosworth Battlefield is one mile from Shenton. The Ashby Canal runs alongside the railway and boats can be hired and moored at the marina, which is a short walk from Market Bosworth station. Other attractions nearby include Conkers World of Adventure & Discovery, Ashby de la Zouch Castle, Tamworth Castle and Twycross Zoo.

Special Events

Events that usually take place on the railway include:

Mother's Day Champagne Teas.
Easter eggstravaganza.
Father's Day Pint & Ploughmans.
Rails & Ales.
Family Fun Weekend during the August Bank Holiday weekend.
Dining Trains include Fish & Chip Specials and a la carte Dining Services.
Santa Specials during December.

▲ The East Lancashire Railway's Lancashire & Yorkshire Railway-built 0-6-0 52322 had a spell at the Ecclesbourne Valley Railway during 2019, where it is seen leaving Shottle on 20 April.

Martyn Tattam

Ecclesbourne Valley Railway

Introduction and History

The branch from Duffield to Wirksworth opened in 1867 and passenger services were withdrawn 80 years later in 1947. The line was then used to carry freight and Wirksworth station was demolished in 1967 so the site could be developed as a stone terminal. The branch continued to carry local stone until 1989. The track remained in place and the route opened as a heritage railway in 2002. Initially heritage trains ran for half a mile from Wirksworth and they now make the 18-mile round trip to Duffield and up the unusually steep 1 in 27 incline of the Ravenstor extension.

Contact Details

Website: www.e-v-r.com
Tel: 01629 823076
Email: ticketoffice@e-v-r.com
Address: Ecclesbourne Valley Railway, Station Road, Coldwell Street, Wirksworth, DE4 4FB.

Transport Links

By Rail: There is a main line rail connection at Duffield; cross the footbridge to Platform 3 for the EVR. Rail tickets to Wirksworth can be purchased from any National Rail ticket office.
By Road: Car parking is available at Wirksworth (DE4 4FB) and Duffield (DE56 4EQ) where there is a smaller car park for both the EVR and national rail users.

Opening Times

Trains operate most weekends and on selected other days throughout the year.

Line Mileage and Journey Time

0.00	Ravenstor
0.50	Wirksworth
4.00	Idridgehay
5.25	Shottle
9.00	Duffield

A return journey takes about 1 hour 30 minutes.

Stock List

Type	Number	Builder	Details
Steam	2217	Andrew Barclay	0-4-0
Steam	3 (2360)	Andrew Barclay	0-4-0
Steam	68012	Bagnall	0-6-0ST
Steam	102	Hudswell Clarke	0-6-0T
Steam	9466	Robert Stephenson & Hawthorns	0-6-0PT
Diesel	402803	Ruston & Hornsby	0-4-0
Diesel	MEGAN	Thomas Hill	0-4-0
Diesel	Tom	Thomas Hill	0-4-0
Diesel	10275	Rolls Royce Sentinel	0-6-0
Diesel	08605	British Railways	Class 08
Diesel	08704	British Railways	Class 08
Diesel	D9537	British Railways	Class 14
Diesel	31206	Brush Traction	Class 31
Diesel	31601	Brush Traction	Class 31
Diesel	33103	BRCW	Class 33
Diesel	58022	BREL	Class 58
Electro-Diesel	73210	English Electric	Class 73
DMU	50170, 50253, 51505 & 59303	Metropolitan Cammell	Class 101
DMU	50599 & 51567	British Railways	Class 108
DMU	51073	GRCW	Class 119
DMU	55027 & 55031	Pressed Steel	Class 121
DMU	55006	GRCW	Class 122
DMU	79018 & 79612	British Railways	Derby Lightweight
DMU	79900	British Railways	Derby Lightweight
EMU	68500 & 68506	British Railways	Class 489

Attractions

There is a museum at Wirksworth, which opens when trains operate. There are also three smaller railways at Wirksworth; a two-foot gauge line, a 7¼ gauge railway which operates on Saturdays and selected other dates, including when standard gauge trains are running, and a model railway depicting the layout of Idridgehay in the 1940s. The railway has a large collection of heritage multiple units and offers both steam and diesel footplate experiences. The region has many attractions including the Peak District, Matlock, Matlock Bath and Carsington Water. Other nearby railway attractions include Peak Rail, Crich Tramway Village, Midland Railway-Butterley and Steeple Grange Light Railway.

Special Events

Events that usually take place on the railway include:

Diesel and railcar themed events.
Dining services include afternoon tea and ploughman's lunch trains.
Model Railway exhibition.
The Train Through Christmas Countryside.

Great Central Railway

Introduction and History

The Great Central Railway from London Marylebone to Rugby, Leicester and Nottingham opened to freight in 1898 and to passenger services in 1899, providing a new route from the North to the South East. Express trains ended in 1960 and the smaller stations, including Rothley and Quorn and Woodhouse, closed in 1963. Through services ended in 1966 when the line south of Rugby was severed and it closed fully in 1969, when Rugby–Nottingham Arkwright Street services ceased. The first preservation group, the Main Line Steam Trust, formed in the early 1970s and acquired the station and trackbed at Loughborough. The first heritage trains worked in 1973, with steam-hauled services to Quorn. In 1976 the section from Loughborough to Rothley was secured and with the assistance of the local council, the trackbed from Loughborough to Belgrave & Birstall to the south was acquired. A new station at Leicester North was built immediately south of the former Belgrave & Birstall station, with trains terminating there from 1990. The line became Britain's only double track heritage railway in 2000, with the facility for test trains to operate at 60 mph, although the maximum speed for heritage passenger trains is 25 mph. In 2015 the branch from Swithland to the former quarry site at Mountsorrel reopened and infrequent services now operate to a newly constructed halt. Plans are under way to merge with the Great Central Railway, Nottingham, creating an 18-mile railway; the bridge over the Network Rail line near Leicester was reinstated in 2017, repairs to the bridge across the Grand Union Canal have been completed and fundraising for the remaining works is ongoing. The GCR is also raising funds for a new Locomotive Shed, Visitor and Education Centre at Loughborough.

Contact Details

Website: www.gcrailway.co.uk
Tel: 01509 632323
Email: sales@gcrailway.co.uk
Address: Great Central Railway, Great Central Road, Loughborough, LE11 1RW.

Transport Links

By Rail: Loughborough (main line station) is one mile from Loughborough Central.
By Road: Parking is available at Loughborough (LE11 1RW, roadside parking), Quorn & Woodhouse (LE12 8AG), Rothley (LE7 7LD) and Leicester North (LE4 3BR).

Opening Times

Trains usually operate every weekend, on Bank Holidays and on selected weekdays. Services on the Mountsorrel branch only run on selected dates.

Line Mileage and Journey Time

0.00	Loughborough Central	0.00	Rothley
2.00	Quorn and Woodhouse	1.50	Mountsorrel Halt
4.75	Rothley		
7.75	Leicester North		

A return journey takes about 1 hour 30 minutes.

Stock List

Type	Number	Builder	Details
Steam	3809	Hunslet	0-6-0ST
Steam	4 (7684)	Robert Stephenson & Hawthorns	0-6-0T
Steam	47406	Vulcan Foundry	0-6-0T
Steam	92214	British Railways	2-10-0
Steam	46521	British Railways	2-6-0
Steam	78018	British Railways	2-6-0
Steam	78019	British Railways	2-6-0
Steam	63601	Great Central Railway	2-8-0
Steam	48305	LMS	2-8-0
Steam	48624	Southern Railway	2-8-0
Steam	246 (62712)	LNER	4-4-0
Steam	45305	Armstrong Whitworth	4-6-0
Steam	73156	British Railways	4-6-0
Steam	6990	British Railways	4-6-0
Steam	7027	British Railways	4-6-0
Steam	45491	LMS	4-6-0
Steam	777	North British	4-6-0
Steam	70013	British Railways	4-6-2
Steam	34039	Southern Railway	4-6-2
Steam	9370	Sentinel	4wVBT
Diesel	400 Bardon	Andrew Barclay	0-4-0DM
Diesel	4210079	Fowler	0-4-0DM
Diesel	D2989	Ruston & Hornsby	Class 07
Diesel	08907	British Railways	Class 08
Diesel	13101	British Railways	Class 08
Diesel	D3690	British Railways	Class 08
Diesel	10119	British Railways	Class 10
Diesel	D8098	English Electric	Class 20
Diesel	D5185	British Railways	Class 25
Diesel	D5401	BRCW	Class 27
Diesel	D6535	BRCW	Class 33
Diesel	37714	English Electric	Class 37
Diesel	D123	British Railways	Class 45
Diesel	1705	Brush Traction	Class 47
Diesel	50017	English Electric	Class 50
DMU	50193, 50203, 50266, 50321, 51427 & 56342	Metropolitan Cammell	Class 101
DMU	59575	Metropolitan Cammell	Class 111
DMU	59276	British Railways	Class 120
DMU	55009	GRCW	Class 122
EMU	70576	British Railways	Class 411

Attractions

There is a museum at Loughborough Central and a walkway from which the signal box and part of the engine shed can be seen (the shed itself is restricted). Quorn and Woodhouse has a tea room housed in an authentic recreated air raid shelter. The railway offers a large variety of dining trains, plus steam and diesel driving experiences. The Charnwood Forest Garden Railway is adjacent to Rothley station and operates at weekends and Bank Holidays. Nearby attractions include the Great Central Railway Nottingham, Stonehouse Family Farm & Motor Museum, Charnwood Museum, Bradgate Park and Gorse Hill City Farm in Leicester.

Special Events

30 September–3 October 2021: Autumn Steam Gala.

Other events that usually take place on the railway include:

Regular steam and diesel running days.
Steam and diesel galas.
1940s Wartime Event.
Murder Mystery Trains.
Vintage vehicle themed events.
Santa Steam Trains and Winter Wonderlights during December.

▲ Two liveries that are not commonly seen at heritage railways; the red of Royal Mail travelling post office vans and the original Network SouthEast blue introduced in 1986. On 8 September 2019, 50017 "Royal Oak" passes Kinchley Lane with the 14.20 Loughborough–Rothley Brook during the Great Central Railway's Diesel Gala. **Steve Donald**

▼ 37714 "Cardiff Canton" departs from the Great Central Railway's Quorn and Woodhouse station with the 14.00 Loughborough–Leicester North on 29 June 2019. The blue and yellow decals on the locomotive represent British Rail's Railfreight Metals sector and the black and silver plate on the front cab is the Cardiff Canton ram. **Brad Joyce**

Great Central Railway – Nottingham

Introduction and History

The railway from London Marylebone to Rugby and Nottingham opened in 1898 and details of the route's history and decline are given in the Great Central Railway listing above. The section from Loughborough to Ruddington survived beyond the 1969 closure as an unsignalled single line to serve the British Gypsum site at Hotchley Hill and the Ministry of Defence (MoD) depot on the spur at Ruddington. Freight traffic continued until the 1980s when the MoD depot closed and the route was never formally closed by British Rail. In the early 1990s a group of transport enthusiasts created a museum on the former MoD site and operated trains on a short section of track. Negotiations began to return trains to the route and purchase the line from British Rail. Gypsum traffic resumed; however, the railway had been severed at East Leake, separating the freight and heritage operations. This was reconnected and passenger services returned to Rushcliffe Halt in 2003. Gypsum trains to the plant at Hotchley Hill (East Leake) use the line on weekdays, accessing it from the main line connection at Loughborough, and heritage trains operate on it during weekends. Nottingham Express Transit (tram service) occupies the former railway north of Ruddington, preventing a northern extension; however, plans are under way to connect to the Great Central Railway at Loughborough (see the above listing).

Contact Details

Website: www.gcrn.co.uk
Tel: 0115 940 5705
Email: info@gcrn.co.uk
Address: Great Central Railway – Nottingham, Mere Way, Ruddington, Nottinghamshire, NG11 6JS.

Transport Links

By Rail: Nottingham railway station is six miles from Ruddington and East Midlands Parkway is six miles from Rushcliffe Halt.
By Road: Parking is available at Ruddington (NG11 6JS) and Rushcliffe Halt (LE12 6HX).

Opening Times

The railway usually operates on Sundays and Bank Holidays from April to October and on selected other dates, including Saturdays from June to August and during December.

Line Mileage and Journey Time

0.00	Ruddington Fields
4.25	Rushcliffe Halt
9.00	Loughborough (line end)

A return journey takes 1 hour 30 minutes.

Stock List

Type	Number	Builder	Details
Steam	Julia (1682)	Hudswell Clarke	0-6-0ST
Steam	1762	Manning Wardle	0-6-0ST
Steam	2009	Manning Wardle	0-6-0ST
Steam	5 (2015)	Manning Wardle	0-6-0ST
Steam	56 (7667)	Robert Stephenson & Hawthorns	0-6-0ST
Steam	63 CORBY	Robert Stephenson & Hawthorns	0-6-0ST
Steam	1631	American Locomotive Co.	2-8-0
Steam	2138	American Locomotive Co.	2-8-0
Steam	2364	Baldwin Locomotive Works	2-8-0
Steam	8274	North British	2-8-0
Diesel	D2959	Ruston & Hornsby	0-4-0
Diesel	No.2 MARBLAEGIS	Ruston & Hornsby	0-4-0
Diesel	H014	Sentinel	0-6-0DH
Diesel	03118	British Railways	Class 03
Diesel	08114	British Railways	Class 08
Diesel	08220	British Railways	Class 08
Diesel	08694	British Railways	Class 08
Diesel	13180	British Railways	Class 08
Diesel	D8154	English Electric	Class 20

Diesel	D5830	Brush Traction	Class 31
Diesel	37009	English Electric	Class 37
Diesel	46010	British Railways	Class 46
Diesel	47292	British Railways	Class 47
Diesel	56097	BREL	Class 56
DMU	50645 & 50926	British Railways	Class 108
DMU	51138 & 51151	British Railways	Class 116
DMU	59501	Pressed Steel	Class 117
DMU	144003 (55803 & 55826)	Alexander/BREL	Class 144

Attractions

There is plenty to explore at Ruddington, including a miniature railway, a large model railway, the standard gauge railway workshop, a children's play area, café and gift shop. Nottingham Area Bus Society is also based at the Ruddington site and has a large collection of vintage buses and coaches. Steam and diesel driving experiences are available along the route. The railway is home to the Inter City 125 Group which is raising funds to build a new depot at Ruddington to house its high speed trains (HST). The Great Central Railway is located near the southern end of the line. Attractions in nearby Nottingham include Green's Mill & Science Centre, Stonebridge City Farm, the National Justice Museum and City of Caves.

Special Events

Events that usually take place on the railway include:

Easter Eggspress Steam Specials.
Steam and Diesel Galas.
Heritage vehicle and transport themed events.
Santa Specials during December.

Lincolnshire Wolds Railway

Introduction and History

Trains first worked on the railway from Grimsby to Louth in 1847 and it was opened to passengers in 1848. All stations on the route except North Thoresby were closed to passengers in 1961, followed by North Thoresby and Louth, which closed in 1970 when the line was singled and reduced to a freight branch from Grimsby. This remained in use until 1980, when British Rail closed the line and then promptly demolished the stations and lifted the track. The first preservation group formed in the late 1970s, initially opposing the proposed closure, and in 1984 it established a base at Ludborough station. Since then, the LWR has purchased five miles of trackbed between Ludborough and a site on the outskirts of Louth, where a new station is planned. The first heritage trains between Ludborough and North Thoresby began in 2009. The line is currently being extended south towards the outskirts of Louth, the first stage being to Pear Tree Lane Crossing, near the site of the former Utterby Halt. The long-term aim is to extend both north and south, restoring as much of the route between Grimsby and Louth as possible.

Contact Details

Website: www.lincolnshirewoldsrailway.co.uk
Tel: 01507 363881
Email: info@lwr.co.uk
Address: Lincolnshire Wolds Railway, Ludborough Station, Station Road, Ludborough, Lincolnshire, DN36 5SQ.

Transport Links

By Rail: Grimsby Town is the nearest railway station and is nine miles from the Ludborough base.
By Road: Free parking is available at Ludborough station (use postcode DN36 5SH).

Opening Times

Trains operate on most Sundays from late March until October and on selected other dates.

Line Mileage and Journey Time

0.00	Ludborough
1.75	North Thoresby

A return journey takes 40 minutes.

Stock List

Type	Number	Builder	Details
Steam	SPITFIRE	Andrew Barclay	0-4-0ST
Steam	1749 FULSTOW	Peckett	0-4-0ST
Steam	LION	Peckett	0-4-0ST
Steam	7597	Robert Stephenson & Hawthorns	0-6-0T
Steam	1313	Motala Verkstad	4-6-0
Diesel	5308	Hunslet	4wDM
Diesel	4210131	Fowler	0-4-0
Diesel	4210145	Fowler	0-4-0
Diesel	423657	Robert Stephenson & Hawthorns	0-4-0DE
Diesel	375713	Ruston & Hornsby	0-4-0
Diesel	414303	Ruston & Hornsby	0-4-0
Diesel	421418	Ruston & Hornsby	0-4-0
Diesel	DEBBIE (3151)	Bagnall	0-6-0
Diesel	D3167	British Railways	Class 08

Attractions

There is a railway museum at Ludborough with a collection of artefacts from the route's history. Guided tours around the LWR's engine shed are available when volunteers are working (please check before visiting). Footplate rides and signal box experiences can be arranged for an additional charge. The railway is near to the market town of Louth, the coastal resort of Cleethorpes and the larger town of Grimsby.

Special Events

Events that usually take place on the railway include:

Easter Special.
Mother's Day and Father's Day Specials.
Anything Goes event using steam and diesel locomotives.
1940s Weekend.
Halloween Specials.
Santa Specials.

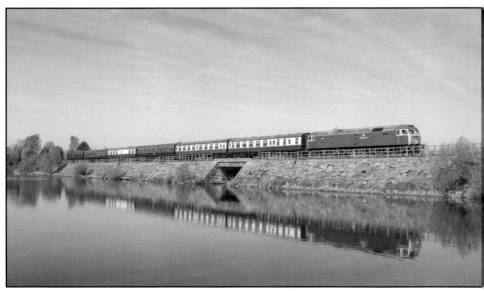

▲ On 20 April 2019, 47401 "GREAT EASTERN" passes the reservoir at Butterley with an afternoon service for Riddings Junction on the Midland Railway, Butterley. **Martyn Tattam**

Midland Railway-Butterley

Introduction and History

The railway between Pye Bridge and Ambergate opened in 1875, linking the present-day routes from Chesterfield to Nottingham and Derby to Matlock. Passenger services ended in 1947 and the line closed in 1968 after freight traffic ceased. The track was then lifted and Butterley station was demolished. In the late 1960s Derby Corporation and Derbyshire County Council planned to create a museum dedicated to the Midland Railway and three steam locomotives were purchased. A site was found on the closed Pye Bridge–Ambergate line; however, the organisations withdrew from the project due to a lack of funds. The Midland Railway Project was a volunteer group which collected and restored railway items. It revived the project in the early 1970s. Butterley became its base and Swanwick Junction was to be the site of the museum. The first open day was held in 1975. One mile of track was laid and the first preserved trains departed from the newly-constructed Butterley station in 1981. The railway has since been extended west to Hammersmith, where the A38 severs the trackbed, and east to Ironville, where the main line connection has been reinstated. New stations have been constructed and there has been considerable development of the railway's heritage attractions.

Contact Details

Website: www.midlandrailway-butterley.co.uk
Tel: 01773 570140
Email: enquiries@midlandrailway-butterley.co.uk
Address: Butterley Station, Ripley, Derbyshire, DE5 3QZ.

Transport Links

By Rail: The nearest station is Alfreton, which is four miles away.
By Road: Free parking is available at Butterley (DE5 3QZ).

Opening Times

The railway operates on Saturdays, Sundays and on selected weekdays.

Line Mileage and Journey Time

0.00	Hammersmith
0.25	Butterley
1.00	Swanwick Junction
2.75	Ironville Junction
3.00	End of Line

A return journey from Butterley takes 45–70 minutes, depending on which timetable is operating.

Stock List

Type	Number	Builder	Details
Steam	4 (454)	Naismyth Wilson	0-4-0
Steam	STANTON No.24 (1875)	Andrew Barclay	0-4-0CT
Steam	109	Markham & Co	0-4-0ST
Steam	VICTORY (1547)	Peckett	0-4-0ST
Steam	WHITEHEAD	Peckett	0-4-0ST
Steam	7214	Robert Stephenson & Hawthorns	0-4-0ST
Steam	1 (7817)	Robert Stephenson & Hawthorns	0-4-0ST
Steam	68067	Hudswell Clarke	0-6-0ST
Steam	47445	Hunslet	0-6-0T
Steam	47564	Hunslet	0-6-0T
Steam	47357	North British	0-6-0T
Steam	23 (BR No. 47327)	North British	0-6-0T
Steam	3883 LORD PHIL	Hunslet	0-6-0ST
Steam	158A	Midland Railway	2-4-0
Steam	80080	British Railways	2-6-4T
Steam	80098	British Railways	2-6-4T
Steam	92212	British Railways	2-10-0
Steam	73129	British Railways	4-6-0
Steam	6233	LMS	4-6-2
Steam	46203	LMS	4-6-2

Diesel	441	Andrew Barclay	0-4-0DH
Diesel	No. 4 (416)	Andrew Barclay	0-4-0DH
Diesel	16038	Fowler	0-4-0DM
Diesel	ALBERT	Hudswell Clarke	0-6-0DM
Diesel	MANTON	Hudswell Clarke	0-6-0DM
Diesel	RS12	Simplex	4wDM
Diesel	RS9	Simplex	4wDM
Diesel	D2858	Yorkshire Engine Co.	Class 02
Diesel	D2138	British Railways	Class 03
Diesel	08331	British Railways	Class 08
Diesel	08590	British Railways	Class 08
Diesel	12077	British Railways	Class 11
Diesel	20048	English Electric	Class 20
Diesel	D8059	English Electric	Class 20
Diesel	D8188	English Electric	Class 20
Diesel	20227	English Electric	Class 20
Diesel	D7671	British Railways	Class 25
Diesel	5580	Brush Traction	Class 31
Diesel	31108	Brush Traction	Class 31
Diesel	31418	Brush Traction	Class 31
Diesel	D5814	Brush Traction	Class 31
Diesel	40012	English Electric	Class 40
Diesel	D4	British Railways	Class 44
Diesel	45133	British Railways	Class 45
Diesel	D182	British Railways	Class 46
Diesel	47761	British Railways	Class 47
Diesel	47401	Brush Traction	Class 47
Diesel	D1516	Brush Traction	Class 47
Diesel	D1048	British Railways	Class 52
Electric	27000	British Railways	Class 77
DMU	51118 & 56097	GRCW	Class 100
DMU	51907 & 56490	British Railways	Class 108
DMU	50015, 50019, 56006 & 56015	British Railways	Class 114
DMU	59659, 51669 & 51849	British Railways	Class 115
DMU	51591, 51610, 51625 & 59609	British Railways	Class 127
DMU	141113 (55513 & 55533)	BREL/Leyland	Class 141
DMU	142011 (55552 & 55602)	BREL/Leyland	Class 142
DMU	142013 (55554 & 55604)	BREL/Leyland	Class 142
EMU	29666 & 29670	Metropolitan Cammell	MSJ&A

Attractions

There is plenty to explore at Swanick Junction; the West Shed Experience (railway museum), a second railway museum in the Matthew Kirtley Building, the demonstration signal box, the Victorian railwayman's church, the Road Transport Building and the National Fork Truck Heritage Centre. Smaller railways include the Golden Valley Light Railway and miniature railway at Swanwick, and at Butterley there is a garden railway, a model railway and carriage shed. Butterley Country Park is adjacent to the railway and other nearby attractions include Crich Tramway Village and Duffield Castle.

Special Events

Events that usually take place on the railway include:

Annual Diesel Gala.
Indietracks Music Festival.
Victorian Train Weekend.
Wizards & Spooks during October.
Fireworks Night during November.
Santa Specials during December.

Northampton & Lamport Railway

Introduction and History

The railway between Northampton and Market Harborough opened in 1859 to carry passengers and local goods. Passenger services were withdrawn in 1960; however, through traffic returned between January and May 1969 and again from 1972 to 1973. The first preservation group formed in 1981 and organised a final charter train to travel the length of the line before it closed in August 1981. The group's name was later changed to the Northampton & Lamport Railway and a base was established at Pitsford and Brampton, the first station north of Northampton. The first heritage trains ran in late 1995 and the railway formally opened in 1996. The line has recently been extended south by half a mile and a station is being built at the new terminus, Boughton. The new section is due to be formally opened during 2021. Efforts will then focus on redeveloping the Pitsford site and when that has been completed, there are plans to extend the line north to a small halt with a run round loop at Merry Tom Crossing, which will require repairs to the bridge across the River Nene.

Contact Details

Website: www.nlr.org.uk
Tel: 01604 820327
Email: enquiries@nlr.org.uk
Address: Northampton & Lamport Railway, Pitsford & Brampton Station, Pitsford Road, Chapel Brampton, NN6 8BA.

Transport Links

By Rail: The nearest station is Northampton, which is five miles away.
By Road: Free parking is available Pitsford & Brampton Station.
By Bike: Arrive on the Brampton Valley Way, a foot and cycle path which follows the railway and trackbed between Northampton and Market Harborough.

Opening Times

Trains usually operate on Sundays and Bank Holidays from March to October and on selected other dates for special events. The timetable will change when the southern extension opens. During the operating season Pitsford & Brampton station opens on some Wednesdays and Saturdays when trains aren't in service, although this is subject to volunteer availability, so checking before travelling is recommended.

Line Mileage and Journey Time

0.00   Northern limit
0.65   Pitsford & Brampton
1.50   Boughton (due to open 2021)

A round trip takes about 40 minutes.

Stock List

Type	Number	Builder	Details
Steam	776	Andrew Barclay	0-4-0ST
Steam	2323	Andrew Barclay	0-4-0ST
Steam	3718	Hawthorn Leslie	0-4-0ST
Steam	2104	Peckett	0-4-0ST
Steam	45 (5470)	Kitson	0-6-0ST
Steam	1378 WESTMINSTER	Peckett	0-6-0ST
Steam	3862	GWR	2-8-0
Steam	5967	GWR	4-6-0
Diesel	21	Fowler	0-4-0
Diesel	1	Ruston & Hornsby	4wDM
Diesel	764	Ruston & Hornsby	0-4-0
Diesel	53	Ruston & Hornsby	0-6-0
Diesel	31289	Brush Traction	Class 31
Diesel	47205	British Railways	Class 47

Attractions

At Pitsford & Brampton station, visitors can browse the gift shop and second-hand book shop. The Brampton Valley Way foot and cycle path follows the course of the present-day railway and the disused sections between Northampton and Market Harborough. Other attractions in the area include Abington Museum, Delapre Abbey and the large town of Northampton.

Special Events

Events that usually take place on the railway include:

Mothering Sunday Cream Teas.
Easter Egg Specials.
Kids for a Quid on selected dates.
Father's Day Cream Teas.
Halloween Event during October.
Santa Specials and Mince Pie Specials during December.

Northamptonshire Ironstone Railway

Introduction and History

When iron ore deposits were discovered in the area during the mid-19th Century, these were excavated and initially transported using a network of industrial narrow gauge railways. These later fell into disuse after the minerals became uneconomical to extract. The Rushden Railway Society formed in December 1971 with the intention of purchasing and restoring two Peckett industrial steam locomotives, which were previously used in the ironstone industry. At the same time, residential development was planned for the area and Northampton Development Corporation wanted to preserve the disused ironstone railway and the nearby Iron Age fort. The society gained access to the site, gradually restored it and laid the standard gauge railway. There is now approximately one and a half miles of track; however, not all of this is in operational condition.

Contact Details

Website: www.nir.org.uk
Tel: 01604 702031
Email: Written enquiries can be made from the website.
Address: Northamptonshire Ironstone Railway, Hunsbury Hill Road, Camp Hill, Northampton, NN4 9UW.

Transport Links

By Rail: Northampton is the nearest station and is three miles away.
By Road: Parking is available at the railway (NN4 9UW).

Opening Times

The railway usually operates on Sundays and Bank Holidays from April to October. The site can be viewed on days when trains are not in service.

Line Mileage and Journey Time

Passenger trains run on a quarter mile section, providing a half-mile round trip and the journey time is relatively short.

Stock List

Type	Number	Builder	Details
Steam	2130	Peckett	0-4-0ST
Steam	BELVEDERE	Sentinel	4wVBGT
Steam	MUSKETEER	Sentinel	4wVBGT
Diesel	CHARLES WAKE	Fowler	0-4-0
Diesel	0200022	Fowler	0-4-0
Diesel	3967	Hibberd	0-4-0
Diesel	D697	Hudswell Clarke	0-4-0DM
Diesel	16 (2087	Hunslet	0-4-0DM
Diesel	321734	Robert Stephenson & Hawthorns	4wDM
EMU	13004	British Railways	4DD
EMU	70284, 70510 & 70296	British Railways	Class 411
EMU	14351, 14352 & 15396	British Railways	Class 415
EMU	69304	British Railways	Class 422

Attractions

The standard gauge industrial railway has some sharp curves, steep gradients and uses a variety of different vehicles to provide passenger rides. The site also includes two garden railways of different gauges. Full and half day steam locomotive driving experiences are available and advance booking is required. The railway shares the site with the Ironstone Heritage Museum and Hunsbury Hill Country Park, which includes a children's play area and an Iron Age fort. Nearby attractions include Abington Museum, Abington Park, Delapre Abbey and the Northampton & Lamport Railway which is eight miles away.

Special Events

20–21 June 2021: Steam Rally.

Other events that usually take place on the railway include:

Easter Event.
Santa Specials during December.

Peak Rail

Introduction and History

The railway from Derby to Ambergate opened in 1840 and was extended north to Rowsley in 1849, including the section that Peak Rail now occupies. The further extension north across the more challenging terrain between Rowsley and Manchester was later completed in 1860. Local passenger services ceased in 1967 when Matlock Bath, Darley Dale, Rowsley, Bakewell and Millers Dale stations closed and the line between Matlock and Millers Dale closed in 1968, when St Pancras–Manchester express services ended. The northern section of the route has remained in continuous use with freight services to Peak Forest. The Peak Railway Preservation Society formed in 1975 and initially opened the Buxton Steam Centre with a short running track, which later closed. Peak Rail relocated to Darley Dale in the 1980s and the first heritage trains worked to Matlock Riverside in 1991. The line was extended north to a new station at Rowsley South in 1997 and south to Matlock in 2011, when the route was reconnected with the main line network. There are plans to extend further north to the original station in Rowsley and also to Bakewell. It has long been hoped that the railway could one day return to Buxton, although this would require a number of major engineering and financial obstacles to be overcome.

Contact Details

Website: www.peakrail.co.uk
Tel: 01629 580381
Email: peakrail@peakrail.co.uk
Address: Peak Rail, Matlock Station, Matlock, Derbyshire, DE4 3NA.

Transport Links

By Rail: At Matlock, cross from the main line Platform 1 to Platform 2 for Peak Rail. Through tickets are available from East Midlands Railway ticket offices.
By Road: Pay & display parking is available at Matlock (DE4 3NA) and free parking at Darley Dale (DE4 2EQ) and Rowsley South (DE4 2LF).
By Bike: The traffic-free Monsal Trail follows the railway from Matlock to Rowsley and beyond.

Opening Times

The railway operates on Saturdays, Sundays and selected weekdays from mid-February until early November. Trains run between approximately 11.00 and 17.00, depending on which timetable is in operation.

Line Mileage and Journey Time

0.00	Matlock
2.25	Darley Dale
3.25	Rowsley South

A return journey takes about one hour.

Stock List

Type	Number	Builder	Details
Steam	3138	Hawthorn Leslie	0-6-0ST
Steam	7063	Robert Stephenson & Hawthorns	0-4-0ST
Steam	150 (3892)	Robert Stephenson & Hawthorns	0-6-0ST
Steam	72	Vulcan Foundry	0-6-0ST
Steam	65	Hudswell Clarke	0-6-0T
Steam	6634	GWR	0-6-2T
Steam	5553	GWR	2-6-2T
Steam	5224	GWR	2-8-0T
Diesel	9120	Baguley	4wDM
Diesel	146C	Fowler	0-4-0
Diesel	4220015	Fowler	0-4-0
Diesel	4240015	Fowler	0-6-0
Diesel	9222	Hunslet	0-4-0
Diesel	RS8	ICI South Central Workshops	0-4-0
Diesel	27097	North British	0-4-0
Diesel	319284	Ruston & Hornsby	0-4-0
Diesel	3 (423658)	Ruston & Hornsby	0-4-0
Diesel	265V	Thomas Hill	0-4-0
Diesel	284V	Thomas Hill	0-4-0
Diesel	BIGGA (102C)	Thomas Hill	0-4-0
Diesel	WD7229	Vulcan Foundry	0-4-0
Diesel	2654	Yorkshire Engine Co.	0-4-0
Diesel	2679	Yorkshire Engine Co.	0-4-0
Diesel	2 JAMES (2675)	Yorkshire Engine Co.	0-4-0
Diesel	2480	Yorkshire Engine Co.	0-4-0DE
Diesel	319284	Ruston & Hornsby	0-4-0DM
Diesel	803	Brush Traction	0-6-0
Diesel	E1	Hudswell Clarke	0-6-0DM
Diesel	6295	Hunslet	0-6-0
Diesel	27932	North British	0-6-0
Diesel	10180	Sentinel	0-6-0
Diesel	2940	Yorkshire Engine Co.	0-6-0
Diesel	D2953	Andrew Barclay	Class 01
Diesel	D2854	Yorkshire Engine Co.	Class 02
Diesel	D2866	Yorkshire Engine Co.	Class 02
Diesel	03027	British Railways	Class 03
Diesel	03099	British Railways	Class 03
Diesel	03113	British Railways	Class 03
Diesel	03180	British Railways	Class 03
Diesel	D2139	British Railways	Class 03
Diesel	D2199	British Railways	Class 03
Diesel	D2272	Robert Stephenson & Hawthorns	Class 04
Diesel	D2284	Robert Stephenson & Hawthorns	Class 04
Diesel	D2289	Robert Stephenson & Hawthorns	Class 04
Diesel	D2337	Robert Stephenson & Hawthorns	Class 04
Diesel	D2205	Vulcan Foundry	Class 04
Diesel	D2229	Vulcan Foundry	Class 04
Diesel	D2587	Hunslet	Class 05
Diesel	06003	Andrew Barclay	Class 06
Diesel	07001	Ruston & Hornsby	Class 07
Diesel	08016	British Railways	Class 08
Diesel	08417	British Railways	Class 08
Diesel	08830	British Railways	Class 08
Diesel	09001	British Railways	Class 09
Diesel	D9500	British Railways	Class 14
Diesel	D9525	British Railways	Class 14
Diesel	D7659	Beyer Peacock	Class 25
Diesel	37152	English Electric	Class 37
Diesel	D8	British Railways	Class 44
Diesel	46035	British Railways	Class 46
Diesel	50029	English Electric	Class 50

Diesel	50030	English Electric	Class 50
Diesel	PWM650	Ruston & Hornsby	Class 97
Diesel	PWM654	Ruston & Hornsby	Class 97
Electro- Diesel	73138	English Electric	Class 73
EMU	HAZEL & CAR No. 87	Metropolitan Cammell	5 Bel
EMU	75102	British Railways	Class 307
EMU	61287 & 75407	British Railways	Class 414

The stock list includes locomotives belonging to the Heritage Shunters Trust, which has a large collection of diesel shunting locomotives and is based at Rowsey South.

Attractions

Darley Dale has a small museum displaying the history of the line. The Rowsley site has a 60-foot working turntable and several heritage railway groups are based there. These include the Heritage Shunters Trust with its extensive collection of shunting locomotives, the Renown Repulse Restoration Group which is restoring two Class 50 locomotives, 50029 & 50030 and the LMS Carriage Association. There are many attractions in Matlock Bath and the surrounding Peak District, including the Peak District Lead Mining Museum and Chatsworth House to the north. Nearby heritage railways include the Ecclesbourne Valley Railway, the Churnet Valley Railway and the Midland Railway-Butterley.

Special Events

22 August 2021: Peak Park Preserved Bus Gathering.
5 September 2021: Race The Train.
31 October 2021: Halloween Spooktacular.

Other events that usually take place on the railway include:

Various luxury dining trains.
Mother's Day & Father's Day lunch trains.
Kids Go Free on selected dates.
Shunter Hunter Enthusiast Gala.
Steam and Diesel Galas.
Car and heritage vehicle themed events.
Santa & Steam Specials during December.

▲ When it visited from the Foxfield Railway, Beyer Peacock 0-4-0ST 1827 was one of several locomotives that participated in Peak Rail's 2019 Mixed Traffic Gala. It is seen just south of Darley Dale on 10 August 2019. **Martyn Tattam**

Rocks by Rail

Introduction and History

Rocks by Rail, also known as The Living Ironstone Museum, demonstrates historic mineral extraction techniques and includes an operational railway. The site was connected to the Midland Railway branch line from Ashwell Junction to Cottesmore, which was completed in 1882 to transport quarried iron ore, and this remained in use until 1974. The three-foot gauge tramway and rope incline allowed loaded stone and minerals to be let down the steep slope and into rail wagons for onward transport to steelworks. The railway today is used to demonstrate the techniques used and carries passengers in restored brake vans.

Contact Details

Website: www.rocks-by-rail.org
Tel: 07974 171068
Email: curator@rocks-by-rail.org
Address: Rocks By Rail Living Ironstone Museum, Cottesmore, Oakham LE15 7FF.

Transport Links

By Rail: The nearest railway station is Oakham, which is five miles away.
By Road: The site has ample car parking (at LE15 7FF) and is near to the village of Cottesmore.

Opening Times

Rocks by Rail opening times are 10.00–16.00 on Tuesdays and Thursdays all year round, plus some Bank Holidays and Sundays between Easter and mid-October.

Line Mileage and Journey Time

The railway line is three quarters of a mile long and the journey time is relatively short.

Stock List

Type	Number	Builder	Details
Steam	1931	Andrew Barclay	0-4-0ST
Steam	2088 SIR THOMAS ROYDEN	Andrew Barclay	0-4-0ST
Steam	3865 SINGAPORE	Hawthorn Leslie	0-4-0ST
Steam	287	Hunslet	0-4-0ST
Steam	1759	Peckett	0-4-0ST
Steam	1257 UPPINGHAM	Peckett	0-4-0ST
Steam	2350 BELVOIR	Andrew Barclay	0-6-0ST
Steam	1972	Avonside	0-6-0ST
Steam	2668 CRANFORD No.2	Bagnall	0-6-0ST
Steam	1308	Hudswell Clarke	0-6-0ST
Steam	2521	Yorkshire Engine Co.	0-6-0ST
Diesel	178V	Thomas Hill	4wDH
Diesel	186V	Thomas Hill	4wDH
Diesel	4220007	Fowler	0-4-0
Diesel	27656	North British	0-4-0
Diesel	10201 BETTY	Rolls Royce Sentinel	0-4-0
Diesel	10204 JEAN	Rolls Royce Sentinel	0-4-0
Diesel	10207 GRAHAM	Rolls Royce Sentinel	0-4-0
Diesel	306092	Ruston & Hornsby	0-4-0
Diesel	421436	Ruston & Hornsby	0-4-0
Diesel	544997	Ruston & Hornsby	0-4-0
Diesel	1382	Yorkshire Engine Co.	0-6-0
Diesel	2872	Yorkshire Engine Co.	0-6-0
Diesel	DE5	Yorkshire Engine Co.	0-6-0

Attractions

Rocks by Rail is located within a 19-acre reclaimed quarry site which has a variety of walks, picnic spots and nature trails. The passenger brake van rides are usually steam-hauled and diesel locomotives are used on some days. Diesel locomotive "Driver for a Fiver" sessions are available on selected dates. The museum has a collection of industrial steam and diesel locomotives and wagons, plus an exhibition building and workshop where visitors can see those under restoration. There is a cab and model of the huge dragline crane "Sundew", which was the largest of its type in the world when built. Nearby attractions include Rutland Water which has an aqua park and nature reserve, and the market towns of Oakham, Melton Mowbray and Stamford.

Special Events

Events that usually take place on the railway include:

Easter Event.
Quarry Diesel Day.

Rushden Transport Museum & Railway

Introduction and History

Rushden station was the only intermediate station on the short branch from Wellingborough to Higham Ferrers, which opened in 1894 and closed to passenger services in 1959. The line remained open for freight and seasonal passenger traffic until the final train ran in 1969. This consisted of a Class 25 collecting 12 wagons from Higham station and the track was lifted not long after this. Rushden Historical Transport Society (RHTS) formed in 1976 and leased Rushden station from 1984. Rushden Transport Museum opened in 1986 and in 1996 the site was purchased by the RHTS. The first heritage train ran from Rushden in 2009, exactly 50 years after passenger services ended. In June 2017 RHTS acquired Rushden goods shed from Northamptonshire County Council and this has been restored as a community and events venue. The heritage railway has been extended to a length of half a mile and there are plans to extend it a further half-mile towards Higham Ferrers.

Contact Details

Website: www.rhts.co.uk
Tel: 0300 3023 150
Email: secretary@rhts.co.uk
Address: Rushden Transport Museum, Station Approach, Rushden, Northamptonshire, NN10 0AW.

Transport Links

By Rail: The nearest railway station is Wellingborough, which is six miles from Rushden.
By Road: There is limited car parking at Rushden station (NN10 0AW); however, free parking is available nearby on Rectory Road and at the small car park on John Clark Way.

Opening Times

Trains may not operate during 2021, as some infrastructure renewal works and updates to the safety procedures are required. Rushden Transport Museum opens 14.00–16.00 on Saturdays and Sundays from April to October and it usually opens 11.00–16.00 on special event dates.

Line Mileage and Journey Time

The railway runs for half a mile from Rushden station and the journey time is relatively short.

Stock List

Type	Number	Builder	Details
Steam	EDMUNDSONS	Andrew Barclay	0-4-0ST
Steam	2323	Andrew Barclay	0-4-0ST
Steam	2654	Bagnall	0-6-0ST
Diesel	10159	Sentinel	4wDH
Diesel	WD 70048	Andrew Barclay	0-4-0DM
Diesel	10433	Vulcan Foundry	0-4-0DM
Diesel	03179	British Railways	Class 03
DMU	55029	Pressed Steel	Class 121
DMU	142084 (55734 & 55780)	BREL/Leyland	Class 142
DMU	142091 (55741 & 55787)	BREL/Leyland	Class 142

Attractions

The Rushden site is home to the Victorian railway station, the Transport Museum, a Gresley buffet coach and a real ale bar which opens each evening and from midday at weekends. Other attractions in the area include Wellingborough Museum, Irchester Country Park, Irchester Narrow Gauge Railway Museum and the Northampton & Lamport Railway which is 20 miles away.

Special Events

8 August 2021: Classics in the Park.

Other events that usually take place on the railway include:

A variety of food and drink themed events.
Wizarding Afternoon Teas.
Christmas Craft Fair.

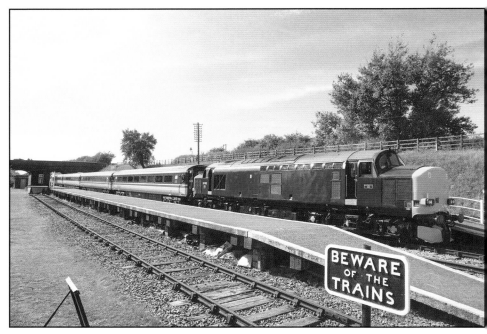

▲ Despite being older than the preserved InterCity livery coaches it is hauling, 37612 is not a preserved locomotive but a main line visitor to the Great Central Railway, Nottingham. It is about to depart from Rushcliffe Halt with the 12.02 Loughborough–Ruddington on 14 September 2019.

Andy Chard

EASTERN

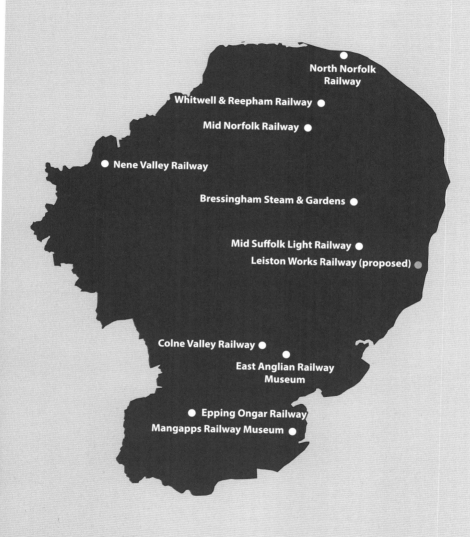

North Norfolk Railway

Whitwell & Reepham Railway

Mid Norfolk Railway

Nene Valley Railway

Bressingham Steam & Gardens

Mid Suffolk Light Railway

Leiston Works Railway (proposed)

Colne Valley Railway

East Anglian Railway Museum

Epping Ongar Railway

Mangapps Railway Museum

Region 6 – Eastern

Bressingham Steam & Gardens

Introduction and History

Bressingham was established by Alan Bloom after he purchased the 220-acre estate of Bressingham Hall in 1946. The first of several traction engines arrived in 1961 and the first narrow gauge railway was laid in 1965. The site now houses a steam museum, gardens, a garden centre and a number of different railways, all of which are open to the public. The railways consist of a standard gauge demonstration line (approximately one quarter of a mile long), the Fen Railway (2 foot gauge, one and a half miles long), the Garden Railway (10¼ inch gauge, three quarters of a mile) and the Waveney Valley Railway (15 inch gauge, one and a half miles long).

Contact Details

Website: www.bressingham.co.uk
Tel: 01379 686900
Email: info@bressingham.co.uk
Address: Bressingham Steam & Gardens, Low Road, Bressingham, Diss, Norfolk, IP22 2AA.

Transport Links

By Rail: The nearest railway station is Diss, which is three and a half miles away.
By Road: Free parking for cars and coaches is available on site (IP22 2AA).

Opening Times

The gardens and railways are open from March until October and on selected other dates. Note that the standard gauge railway does not operate on every opening day.

Line Mileage and Journey Time

The standard gauge demonstration line is approximately one quarter of a mile long and the journey time is relatively short.

▲ BR Standard Class 4 2-6-4T 80078 approaches the Mangapps Railway Museum's passenger terminus with one of the regular shuttle services during the site's 30th birthday celebrations on 25 August 2019. **Andy Chard**

Stock List

Type	Number	Builder	Details
Steam	6841 WILLIAM FRANCIS	Beyer Peacock	0-4-0+0-4-0
Steam	1472	Andrew Barclay	0-4-0F
Steam	25 (6087)	Neilson & Co	0-4-0ST
Steam	GRANVILLE (BR No. 30102)	LSWR	0-4-0T
Steam	32662	LBSCR	0-6-0T
Steam	87	GER	0-6-0T
Steam	5865	Norwegian State Railways	2-10-0
Steam	490	GER	2-4-0
Steam	377 KING HAAKON VII	Norwegian State Railways	2-6-0
Steam	80 THUNDERSLEY	LT&SR	4-4-2T
Diesel	1 (497753)	Ruston & Hornsby	0-4-0DH
Diesel	11103 (D297)	Vulcan Foundry	0-4-0DM

Attractions

Bressingham has four different railways, each with a different gauge and which together give over four miles of railway journeys. There is a collection of working and static steam and traction engines, gardens to visit and an adjacent garden centre. Visitors can ride on the 1897-built Gallopers carousel, which has been meticulously restored. Bressingham is also the home of the Dad's Army Appreciation Society and a Dad's Army Museum. Various driving experiences are available, driving trains of different gauges and traction engines. Other attractions in the region include Banham Zoo, the market town of Diss and the fens and coastlines of Norfolk.

Special Events

20 June 2021: Father's Day Ticket Deal.
26–27 June 2021: Traction Engine Gathering.
3–4 July 2021: Steampunk Weekend.
24–25 July 2021: Fire Engine Gathering.
30 July–2 August 2021: Brick Models visit Bressingham.
7–8 August 2021: Steam in Miniature Weekend.
28 November–24 December 2021: Christmas Visits at Bressingham.

▲ With Class 04 D2279 stabled on the adjacent line, Waggon & Maschinenbau railbus 79963 arrives at the East Anglian Railway Museum's platform on 15 August 2020. A lengthy restoration had recently been completed on the single-coach railbus, which was a regular visitor to Chappel & Wakes Colne between 1958 and 1961 when it worked on the branch line to Haverhill. **Alistair Grieve**

Colne Valley Railway

Introduction and History
The railway from Chappel & Wakes Colne on the present-day Sudbury branch, to Haverhill opened in stages. It reached Halstead in 1860, extending to Castle Hedingham in 1861, to Yeldham in 1862, to Haverhill in 1863 and it was connected to the Stour Valley Railway at Haverhill in 1865. Passenger services were withdrawn in 1960, followed by freight in 1965 and much of the railway infrastructure was demolished soon after. The land at the Hedingham site was bought in 1973; a heritage railway organisation was formed and the first preserved trains ran in 1976. The surviving Hedingham railway station was carefully moved from its original location one mile away and has been renamed Castle Hedingham. The railway has recently benefited from a new car park, entrance building and interactive museum.

Contact Details
Website: www.colnevalleyrailway.co.uk
Tel: 01787 461174
Email: info@colnevalleyrailway.co.uk
Address: Colne Valley Railway, Yeldham Road, Castle Hedingham, CO9 3DZ.

Transport Links
By Rail: Sudbury and Braintree are the nearest railway stations and both are nine miles away.
By Road: Ample free car parking is available at Castle Hedingham station (CO9 3DZ).

Opening Times
The Castle Hedingham site and museum open on Saturdays, Sundays and Bank Holidays from Easter until late October, plus on selected weekdays (usually Wednesdays) during Essex school holidays.

Line Mileage and Journey Time
Castle Hedingham is in the centre of the railway, which operates for slightly less than one mile and a return trip takes about half an hour.

Stock List

Type	Number	Builder	Details
Steam	1875	Avonside	0-4-0ST
Steam	1	Hawthorn Leslie	0-4-0ST
Steam	190	Hunslet	0-6-0ST
Steam	200	Hunslet	0-6-0ST
Steam	60 JUPITER	Robert Stephenson & Hawthorns	0-6-0ST
Steam	45163	Armstrong Whitworth	4-6-0
Steam	45293	Armstrong Whitworth	4-6-0
Steam	35010	Southern Railway	4-6-2
Diesel	3147	Hibberd	4wDM
Diesel	YD43	Ruston & Hornsby	4wDM
Diesel	281266	Ruston & Hornsby	0-4-0DM
Diesel	D2041	British Railways	Class 03
Diesel	D2184	British Railways	Class 03
DMU	51339 & 51382	Pressed Steel	Class 117
DMU	55033	Pressed Steel	Class 121
EMU	75023	British Railways	Class 307
EMU	75881	British Railways	Class 308
EMU	71205 & 78037	BREL	Class 312
Electric	1	Robert Stephenson & Hawthorns	Bo-Bo

Attractions
The site has four different sized railways; the standard gauge line, a 7¼ inch gauge miniature railway with steam and diesel locomotives, a garden railway and a model railway. There is a new museum which opened in 2019. Visitors can see inside the working signal box on most dates or explore the nearby woodland walk. Train driver experience courses are available on selected dates. Heritage railways within the region include the East Anglian Railway Museum, the Mid Suffolk Light Railway and the Epping Ongar Railway. Other attractions in the area include Hedingham Castle, Long Melford Country Park and Coggeshall Grange Barn.

Special Events
Events that usually take place on the railway include:

1940s themed event.
Bus & Commercial Vehicle Rally.
A variety of themed family events including Santa Specials during December.

East Anglian Railway Museum

Introduction and History
The Stour Valley Railway Preservation Society formed in 1968 to preserve the railway from Sudbury to Long Melford. This was not successful and the line now terminates at Sudbury. However, in 1969 the society instead leased the derelict goods yard, shed, signal box and station buildings at nearby Chappel & Wakes Colne from British Rail. In 1970 a Hunslet steam locomotive first carried passengers along a short stretch of relaid track and in the years that followed, the buildings were restored, as were various items of rolling stock. In 1983 the engine restoration workshop was built. In 1986 the society became the East Anglian Railway Museum focusing on the railway history of the area and in 1987 the site was purchased from British Rail. Today it is easily accessible by rail, with one platform of Chappel & Wakes Colne being the museum's home and the other platform is used by Marks Tey to Sudbury main line services.

Contact Details
Website: www.earm.co.uk
Tel: 01206 242524
Email: information@earm.co.uk
Address: East Anglian Railway Museum, Chappel & Wakes Colne Station, Colchester, Essex, CO6 2DS.

Transport Links
By Rail: Cross the footbridge at Chappel & Wakes Colne station.
By Road: Free car parking is available at the museum (CO6 2DS).

Visitors who arrive by train, bus, bike or on foot, receive a 5% "car free discount" off museum admission (except on Days Out With Thomas or Beer Festival dates).

Opening Times
The site opens on most days of the year and is closed on Christmas Day and Boxing Day. The museum and railway occasionally close during special events, such as beer festivals.

Line Mileage and Journey Time
The railway demonstration line runs for approximately one quarter of a mile and the journey time is relatively short.

Stock List

Type	Number	Builder	Details
Steam	11 (1047)	Andrew Barclay	0-4-0ST
Steam	2542 JUBILEE	Bagnall	0-4-0ST
Steam	2039	Peckett	0-4-0ST
Steam	LAMPORT No.3	Bagnall	0-6-0ST
Steam	54 (7031)	Robert Stephenson & Hawthorns	0-6-0ST
Steam	69621	GER	0-6-2T
Diesel	144 JOHN PEEL	Andrew Barclay	0-4-0
Diesel	D72229	Drewry	0-4-0
Diesel	4220039 7	Fowler	0-4-0
Diesel	2029	Simplex	0-4-0
Diesel	D2279	Robert Stephenson & Hawthorns	Class 04
DMU	51213 & 56358	Metropolitan Cammell	Class 101
DMU	79963	Waggon und Maschinenbau	Railbus

Attractions

The museum has a wealth of railway-related attractions, including the heritage centre with various interactive exhibits, the restored goods shed filled with railway memorabilia, the restoration shed where locomotives and rolling stock are restored and the active Grade I listed signal box. There is miniature railway, although this is in the process of being dismantled and rebuilt. Locomotive Driving Experiences are available. There is an escape room experience, an on-site café and pub. If arriving by train from Marks Tey, you will cross Chappel Viaduct, which is one of the largest viaducts and brick-built structures in the country. The Colne Valley Railway is 12 miles away and the Epping Ongar Railway is relatively nearby. Other nearby attractions include Clare Castle Country Park, Long Melford Country Park and Colchester Zoo.

Special Events

Events that usually take place include:

Days out with Thomas.
Beer Festival.
October Diesel Days.
Halloween Steam.

Epping Ongar Railway

Introduction and History

The railway from London reached Ongar in 1865 and was steam-hauled until 1957, when the route become part of London Underground's Central Line. Passenger numbers declined until the Underground line between Epping and Ongar closed in 1994. Fortunately, much of the infrastructure remained in place, facilitating its transition into a heritage railway and the line reopened as such in 2004. The railway doesn't currently operate into Epping (London Underground) station, but there are plans to extend there, which would provide a direct rail connection.

Contact Details

Website: www.eorailway.co.uk
Tel: 01277 365200
Email: enquiries@eorailway.co.uk
Address: Epping Ongar Railway, Ongar Station, Station Approach, Ongar, Essex, CM5 9BN.

Transport Links

By Rail: London Underground Central Line services terminate at Epping, where a connecting heritage bus service (number 339) travels to North Weald station.
By Road: There is no public parking at Ongar or North Weald stations, except limited disabled spaces which must be booked in advance. Car parking is available at Epping Underground station (CM16 4HW), from where the connecting heritage bus service starts (see above).

Opening Times

Trains usually operate on Saturdays, Sundays and Bank Holidays from April to October and on selected other weekdays.

Line Mileage and Journey Time

0.00	Ongar
1.75	Blake Hall
3.50	North Weald
5.75	Epping Ongar Boundary
6.00	Epping

A return journey takes about 1 hour 30 minutes.

Stock List

Type	Number	Builder	Details
Steam	3437	Hawthorn Leslie	0-6-0ST
Steam	3837	Hawthorn Leslie	0-6-0ST
Steam	5619	GWR	0-6-2T
Steam	4141	GWR	2-6-2T
Steam	4953	GWR	4-6-0
Diesel	RH398616	Ruston & Hornsby	0-4-0
Diesel	03119	British Railways	Class 03
Diesel	03170	British Railways	Class 03
Diesel	20001	English Electric	Class 20
Diesel	31438	Brush Traction	Class 31
Diesel	D6729	English Electric	Class 37
Diesel	45132	British Railways	Class 45
Diesel	47635	British Railways	Class 47
DMU	51342 & 51384	Pressed Steel	Class 117
DMU	56287	Pressed Steel	Class 121
DEMU	60110 & 60810	British Railways	Class 205
EMU	69013 & 70235	British Railways	Class 412

Attractions

Railway related activities include driver and signal box experiences and the "Epping Fryer" evening fish and chip specials. The Penny Salon Micro Gallery can be found at Ongar station; North Weald Airfield and Museum is a short walk from North Weald station and Epping Forest is also nearby. Other heritage railways in the area include the Colne Valley Railway and Mangapps Railway Museum.

Special Events

Events that usually take place on the railway include:

Easter Egg Hunt.
Steam and Diesel Galas.
1940s Weekend.
Family Fun Days.
Epping Ongar Light Fantastic during the winter months.
Santa Specials during December.

▲ American-built 2-8-0 5197 passes GWR 4200 Class 2-8-0T 4270, as it runs round at the Epping Ongar Railway's North Weald station on 7 June 2019. **Alisdair Anderson**

Mangapps Railway Museum

Introduction and History

The Mangapps Railway Museum is situated on a private site and, unlike most heritage railways and museums, it is not on the site of a former railway. All the station buildings, signal boxes, infrastructure and rolling stock have been brought from other locations. The site includes a museum with a large collection of railway exhibits, many of which are from East Anglia and the former Great Eastern Railway. An operational railway line has been created and this is used by a variety of locomotives, including examples of industrial steam, industrial diesel and main line diesels.

Contact Details

Website: www.mangapps.co.uk
Tel: 01621 784898
Address: Mangapps Railway Museum, Southminster Road, Burnham-on-Crouch, Essex, CM0 8QG.

Transport Links

By Rail: The nearest station is Burnham-on-Crouch, which is just over one mile away.
By Road: There is ample parking on-site (CM0 8QG).

Opening Times

The railway usually operates on Saturdays, Sundays and Bank Holidays from March to October and every day during August.

Line Mileage and Journey Time

The railway consists of two spurs and a return journey takes about 20 minutes.

0.00	Mangapps		0.00	Mangapps Yard
0.40	Old Heath		0.25	Southminster Road
0.55	Line End			

Stock List

Type	Number	Builder	Details
Steam	1619	Andrew Barclay	0-4-0ST
Steam	8 (2157)	Andrew Barclay	0-4-0ST
Steam	2613	Bagnall	0-6-0PT
Steam	MINNIE	Fox Walker	0-6-0ST
Steam	80078	British Railways	2-6-4T
Diesel	ELLAND No 1	Hudswell Clarke	0-4-0
Diesel	11104	Drewry	0-6-0
Diesel	03018	British Railways	Class 03
Diesel	03020	British Railways	Class 03
Diesel	03081	British Railways	Class 03
Diesel	03089	British Railways	Class 03
Diesel	D2158	British Railways	Class 03
Diesel	03399	British Railways	Class 03
Diesel	D2325	Robert Stephenson & Hawthorns	Class 04
Diesel	31105	Brush Traction	Class 31
Diesel	31233	Brush Traction	Class 31
Diesel	33018	BRCW	Class 33
Diesel	33110	BRCW	Class 33
DMU	51381	Pressed Steel	Class 117
EMU	75033 & 75250	British Railways	Class 302

Attractions

The Mangapps site has two stations, a sizeable collection of locomotives, wagons and a museum housing a substantial collection of railway artefacts, including many locomotive nameplates, station signs and signalling equipment. There is a demonstration signal box, where the lever frame and sub-floor workings are visible. Other attractions in the area include National Trust Danbury Commons & Blakes Wood, Northey Island and Dengie National Nature Reserve.

Mid Norfolk Railway

Introduction and History

The railway between Wymondham and Dereham opened in 1847. It was extended to King's Lynn in 1848 and to Wells-next-the-Sea in 1857. The decline began when passenger services between Dereham and Wells ended in 1964 and the line from Wymondham to Dereham was singled in 1965. Passenger services between Dereham and King's Lynn ceased in 1968, followed by Wymondham–Dereham in 1969. Freight north of Wymondham continued but was progressively cut back, running to Fakenham until 1980, to Ryburgh until 1983 and to North Elmham until 1989, when the branch north of Wymondham closed. A group that formed in 1974 had been campaigning for passenger trains to return and this resulted in at least one charter train operating on the line each year between 1978 and 1988. The group leased Hardingham station and yard in 1983, at which it initially established a museum and base. This closed in 1989 and a number of groups then merged in 1990, creating the beginning of today's Mid Norfolk Railway. The first heritage trains ran from Yaxham in 1995 and services returned to Dereham in 1997. In 1998 the Wymondham–Dereham section was purchased and through trains from the main line were reinstated. The railway was extended north to Hoe Crossing in 2013 and to Worthing Crossing in 2018. The line to North Elmham station is in-situ but does not yet see regular trains. The railway owns the trackbed north to County School and there are long term aims to further extend the line to Fakenham.

Contact Details

Website: www.mnr.org.uk
Tel: 01362 851723
Email: Written enquiries can be made from the website.
Address: Dereham Railway Station, Station Road, Dereham, Norfolk, NR19 1DF.

Transport Links

By Rail: Wymondham railway station is just under one mile from Wymondham Abbey station.
By Road: Parking is available at Dereham station (NR19 1DF) and is very limited at Wymondham Abbey.

Opening Times

The railway usually operates on Saturdays, Sundays and Bank Holidays from mid-March to mid-October, plus on selected weekdays.

Line Mileage and Journey Time

0.00	Wymondham Abbey
3.00	Kimberley Park
6.25	Thuxton
8.75	Yaxham
10.50	Dereham
12.25	Hoe Level Crossing
14.25	Worthing Hoe Road Crossing
15.00	North Elmham (regular services don't yet reach this point)

A return journey takes about 1 hour 45 minutes.

Stock List

Type	Number	Builder	Details
Steam	9596	Sentinel	4wVBGT
Steam	2 (7818)	Robert Stephenson & Hawthorns	0-4-0ST
Steam	75008 SWIFTSURE	Hunslet	0-6-0ST
Diesel	BSC1 (D1049)	English Electric	0-6-0DH
Diesel	03197	British Railways	Class 03
Diesel	D2334	Robert Stephenson & Hawthorns	Class 04
Diesel	31255	Brush Traction	Class 31
Diesel	33202	BRCW	Class 33
Diesel	47367	Brush Traction	Class 47
Diesel	47596	Brush Traction	Class 47
Diesel	50019	English Electric	Class 50
DMU	56301	GRCW	Class 100

DMU	51226, 51434, 51499, 51503, 56347 & 59117	Metropolitan Cammell	Class 101
DMU	51942 & 56270	British Railways	Class 108
DMU	51370 & 51412	Pressed Steel	Class 117
DMU	142038 (55579 & 55629)	BREL/Leyland	Class 142
DMU	142061 (55711 & 55757)	BREL/Leyland	Class 142
DMU	144018 (55818, 55854 & 55841)	Alexander/BREL	Class 144
EMU	75120	British Railways	Class 307
EMU	68004	British Railways	Class 419
EMU	69318	British Railways	Class 422

Attractions

The Mid Norfolk is one of Britain's longer heritage railways and is actively extending northwards. Steam and diesel driver experience days can be arranged. The North Norfolk Railway, the narrow gauge Bure Valley Railway and Bressingham Steam & Gardens are all nearby. Other attractions in the area include Lenwade Dinosaur Adventure and Gressenhall Farm and Workhouse. Wymondham Abbey is a short walk from the railway's southern terminus and there is plenty to explore in Wymondham and Dereham.

Special Events

17 July 2021: Summer Craft Fair.
7–8 August 2021: 1940s Railway at War Weekend.
2–18 October 2021: Flying Scotsman Visits.
November & December: The Polar Express at the Mid Norfolk Railway.

▲ 33202 "Dennis G. Robinson" operates on the Mid Norfolk Railway in top and tail format with the National Railway Museum's prototype High Speed Train power car 41001 and the InterCity 125 Group's preserved Mark 3 coaches. The unusual combination pass Garvestone with the 16.10 Wymondham Junction–Dereham on 5 April 2019. **Aubrey Evans**

Mid Suffolk Light Railway

Introduction and History
The light railway, with reduced speed and safety requirements, from Haughley near Stowmarket to Laxfield, opened to goods traffic in 1904 and to passenger services in 1908. It was intended for the railway to continue to Halesworth on the present-day Ipswich–Lowestoft line, but a lack of finances meant that it only reached Laxfield. The railway was effectively bankrupt before it opened and was never profitable, leading to its closure in 1952 and the track was lifted in 1953. In 1991 a group of railway enthusiasts formed and initially created a railway museum close to the current Brockford site. The station at Brockford was re-established, a short stretch of track was laid and the first heritage trains worked in 2002. The railway is in the process of extending to a new station which will be called Aspall Halt and this will double the length of the line. The project is expected to be completed for the 2022 running season.

Contact Details
Website: www.mslr.org.uk
Tel: 01449 766899
Email: secretary@mslr.org.uk
Address: Mid Suffolk Railway, Brockford Station, Wetheringsett, Stowmarket, Suffolk, IP14 5PW.

Transport Links
By Rail: The nearest railway station is Stowmarket, which is nine miles away.
By Road: Free car parking is available at Brockford (IP14 5PW).

Opening Times
The railway usually opens on Sundays and Bank Holidays from May until early September and on selected weekdays.

Line Mileage and Journey Time
Train currently run for a quarter of a mile from Brockford and a return journey takes about 20 minutes.

Stock List

Type	Number	Builder	Details
Steam	2565	Bagnall	0-4-0ST
Steam	1604	Hudswell Clarke	0-4-0ST
Steam	985	LNER	0-4-0T
Steam	2525	Cockerill	0-4-0WT
Diesel	294266	Ruston & Hornsby	0-4-0
Diesel	ALSTON	Ruston & Hornsby	0-4-0
Diesel	20337	Fowler	0-4-0DM

Attractions
Unlike many other heritage railways, there is no ex-British Rail coaching stock. Instead, vintage carriages are used, including the recently restored Victorian four-wheel coach and the 1865 Great Eastern Railway First Class smoking coach No. 140. Visitors can explore the Arts Council accredited museum which tells the story of the railway and see the carriage and wagon workshop which houses active renovation projects. Tours of the workshop are available, subject to staffing. There is also a café, shop and the Kitchener Arms restored real ale bar coach. Attractions in the region include Suffolk Owl Sanctuary and the Museum of East Anglian Life in Stowmarket. The East Anglian Railway Museum and Colne Valley Railway are both about 35 miles away.

Special Events
30–31 May 2021: Middy in the War Years.
4 July 2021: Land Rover Day – Series 1, 2 & 3.
25 July 2021: Norfolk & Suffolk Narrow Gauge Modellers.
8 August 2021: Steam Railway Day with visiting ALN 825 Preservation Group.
22 August 2021: Steam Railway Day and Steam Punk.
29–30 August 2021: Model Mania & Hornby Collectors Club.
4–5 September 2021: Country Railway Gala.
4–5, 11–12 & 18–19 December 2021: Santa Specials.

Nene Valley Railway

Introduction and History

The railway from Blisworth (near Northampton), on the present-day West Coast Main Line, to Peterborough opened in 1845 and was the first railway to reach Peterborough. Wansford subsequently grew in importance, becoming a junction with four lines converging after the railway to Stamford was built in 1867 and the route to Seaton in 1879. Passenger trains from Peterborough to Rugby via Seaton ceased in 1966, although freight continued until 1972. In 1969 a group that was to become the Peterborough Railway Society (PRS) formed and after the Peterborough Development Corporation purchased the railway in 1974, it was leased to the PRS. The first trains in preservation ran between Orton Mere and Wansford in 1977, using continental locomotives and rolling stock, a theme which continues with some of the railway's rolling stock today. The railway was extended from Orton Mere to Peterborough in 1986 and from Wansford to Yarwell Junction in 2007. The main line connection remains and is used for transferring visiting locomotives and by occasional railtours. There are aspirations to extend the railway towards Elton on the original route to Blisworth.

Contact Details

Website: www.nvr.org.uk
Tel: 01780 784444
Email: adminassistant@nvr.org.uk
Address: Nene Valley Railway Ltd, Wansford Station, Stibbington, Peterborough, PE8 6LR.

Transport Links

By Rail: The nearest railway station is Peterborough, which is just over one mile away.
By Road: Free parking is available at Wansford (PE8 6LR) and Orton Mere (PE2 7DA) stations. Alternatively, there is chargeable parking in Ferry Meadows Country Park (PE2 5UU) adjacent to Overton station or Pleasure Fair Meadow car park (PE2 9NR) near Peterborough NVR station.

Opening Times

Trains operate on weekends and on selected weekdays between 10.00 or 11.00 and 16.00, depending on which timetable is in operation.

Line Mileage and Journey Time

0.00	Peterborough NVR
1.50	Orton Mere
2.50	Overton for Ferry Meadows
6.25	Wansford
7.25	Yarwell Junction

A return journey takes about 1 hour 30 minutes, but slightly less when the railcar is operating.

Stock List

Type	Number	Builder	Details
Steam	1626	Cockerill	0-4-0VBT
Steam	4612	GWR	0-6-0PT
Steam	DEREK CROUCH	Hudswell Clarke	0-6-0ST
Steam	3193	Hunslet	0-6-0ST
Steam	75006	Hunslet	0-6-0ST
Steam	JACKS GREEN	Hunslet	0-6-0ST
Steam	656	Danske Statsbaner	0-6-0T
Steam	THOMAS	Hudswell Clarke	0-6-0T
Steam	5485	Fablok	0-8-0T
Steam	THE BLUE CIRCLE	Aveling & Porter	2-2-0WT
Steam	64305	DB, Germany	2-6-2T
Steam	1178	Motala Verkstad	2-6-2T
Steam	73050	British Railways	4-6-0
Steam	101	Motala Verkstad	4-6-0
Steam	34081	British Railways	4-6-2
Diesel	2895	Hibberd	Petrol Loco
Diesel	BARABEL	Sentinel	0-4-0
Diesel	D1123	English Electric	0-4-0DH

Diesel	304469	Ruston & Hornsby	0-4-0DM
Diesel	DL83	Sentinel	0-6-0
Diesel	323.674-2	Gmeinder & Co.	4wDH
Diesel	2896	Hibberd	4wDM
Diesel	77120	American Locomotive Co.	Bo-BoDE
Diesel	9529	British Railways	Class 14
Diesel	D9520	British Railways	Class 14
Diesel	45041	British Railways	Class 45
DMU	1212	Hagglund and Soner	Swedish Railcar

Attractions

A new 5 inch gauge miniature railway is being built at Wansford. It is hoped that this will open during 2021, when steam and battery locomotives will carry passengers between the children's play area and the engineering shed. The viewing platform at Wansford gives access to the restoration work in progress and shed tours are available (advance arrangement may be needed). There is a second-hand book carriage, café and gift shop. The railway offers driving and signal box experiences, for which advance booking is required. At nearby Peterborough is the city's Cathedral and Railworld, which has a variety of railway and wildlife exhibits. Ferry Meadows Country Park is close to Overton station and Thorpe Meadows, with a sculpture walk and rowing lake, is also nearby.

Special Events

Events that usually take place on the railway include:

Steam and Diesel Galas.
Various family themed events.
The Jolly Fisherman (fish & chip specials).
The Wizard's Express during October.
Santa Steam during December.

▲ Class 20 D8059, which was visiting from the Chinnor & Princes Risborough Railway, passes Ailsworth with the 13.25 Peterborough–Wansford during the Nene Valley Railway's Autumn Diesel Gala on 13 October 2018. **Aubrey Evans**

North Norfolk Railway

Introduction and History

The railway between Cromer and Melton Constable opened in 1887 as part of the Midland & Great Northern Joint Railway network. The route became known as the Poppy Line, due to the abundance of the distinct flowers in the area. Despite public protest beforehand, the line was closed in 1959. The North Norfolk Railway (NNR) was one of Britain's earlier heritage railways, forming in 1965. The first two steam locomotives were delivered in 1967 and in 1973 the Royal Train episode of Dad's Army was filmed at Weybourne station. Services between Sheringham and Holt began in 1975. A major milestone was achieved in 2010 when Sheringham East level crossing was reinstated, reconnecting the NNR with the national rail network. In 2019, an appeal was launched to raise funds to rebuild the station building and canopy at Sheringham, which BR destroyed during the 1960s. There is a long-term plan to join the NNR with the Mid Norfolk Railway, creating the Norfolk Orbital Railway, a rail circuit that would include the current routes of both railways.

Contact Details

Website: www.nnrailway.co.uk
Tel: 01263 820800
Email: enquiries@nnrailway.co.uk
Address: North Norfolk Railway, Station Approach, Sheringham, Norfolk, NR26 8RA.

Transport Links

By Rail: Main line connection at Sheringham; the two stations are adjacent, separated by a road.
By Road: Car parking is available at Sheringham (NR26 8RA, charges apply), Weybourne (NR25 7HN) and Holt (NR25 6AJ) stations. Parking space at Weybourne is limited.

Opening Times

Trains usually operate for the majority of the year, with regular weekend trains from March and daily services from April. The NNR website shows the latest timetables, which differ through the year.

Line Mileage and Journey Time

0.00	Sheringham
2.75	Weybourne
3.25	Kelling Heath Halt
5.00	Holt

A return journey takes about 50 minutes.

Stock List

Type	Number	Builder	Details
Steam	564	GER	0-6-0
Steam	1982	Hunslet	0-6-0ST
Steam	1700 WISSINGTON	Hudswell Clarke	0-6-0ST
Steam	1744	North British	0-6-2T
Steam	76084	British Railways	2-6-0
Steam	53809	Robert Stephenson & Co	2-8-0
Steam	92203	British Railways	2-10-0
Steam	90775	North British	2-10-0
Steam	8572	Beyer Peacock	4-6-0
Diesel	D2051	British Railways	Class 03
Diesel	D2063	British Railways	Class 03
Diesel	D3935	British Railways	Class 08
Diesel	D3940	British Railways	Class 08
Diesel	12131	British Railways	Class 11
Diesel	20227	English Electric	Class 20
Diesel	D5631	Brush Traction	Class 31
Diesel	D6732	English Electric	Class 37
DMU	51188, 51192, 51228, 56062 & 56352	Metropolitan Cammell	Class 101
DMU	50479 & 56182	BRCW	Class 104
EMU	68004	British Railways	Class 419

Attractions

The William Marriott Museum, which tells the story of East Anglia's railways, is located at Holt station. Reedham signal box was secured by the railway in 2019 and is to be relocated to Holt, where it will become a working museum. The NNR's locomotive yard and a model railway can be found at Weybourne. A variety of visitor experiences can be booked in advance, including Steam Driving, Diesel Driving and Signalling Experiences. The Mid Norfolk Railway and the narrow gauge Bure Valley Railway are about eight and ten miles from the NNR respectively. Sheringham town centre, the Norfolk Coastal Path, Sheringham Park and several other National Trust sites are near to the railway.

Special Events

Events that usually take place on the railway include:

A variety of dining services including Cream Tea, Gin, Fish & Chips and Prosecco & Pudding trains.
Days out with Thomas.
Steam, Diesel & Mix Traction Galas.
Vintage Transport Day.
1940s Weekend.
Halloween Event.
Santa & Mince Pie Specials.
North Norfolk Lights Express between November and January.

Whitwell & Reepham Railway

Introduction and History

The Midland & Great Northern Joint Railway (M&GNJR) from Norwich City to Melton Constable opened in 1882 and Whitwell & Reepham station was situated roughly half way along the rural route. The Great Eastern Railway had opened a more conveniently located station in Reepham in 1881, creating competition from the beginning. After declining use, passenger services to Whitwell & Reepham ceased in 1959, although freight continued until 1981, running via Themelthorpe Curve, which BR built in 1960. The final weedkilling train passed through Whitwell & Reepham in 1983 and track lifting began the following year. From 1993, much of the trackbed became part of Marriott's Way, a traffic-free cycle and footpath named after William Marriott, Chief Engineer of the M&GNJR, which runs through both former stations in Reepham. The derelict Whitwell & Reepham station site was offered for sale by Norfolk County Council in 2006 and bought by a rail enthusiast who restored it and relaid railway track in the yard behind the station; the line extends for a short distance to the south. The first heritage trains ran when the station reopened in 2009 and it now has a growing collection of rolling stock. There are plans to extend the railway north towards Themelthorpe Curve.

Contact Details

Website: www.whitwellstation.com
Tel: 01603 871694
Email: info@whitwellstation.com
Address: Whitwell & Reepham Station, Whitwell Road, Reepham, Norfolk, NR10 4GA.

Transport Links

By Rail: The nearest stations are on other heritage railways. Aylsham on the narrow gauge Bure Valley Railway is nine miles away, Dereham on the Mid Norfolk Railway (see page 119) is 11 miles away and Norwich station is 15 miles away.
By Road: Car parking is available at Whitwell & Reepham.
By Bike: Whitwell & Reepham station is situated on the Marriott's Way route. Cycle hire is available nearby.

Opening Times

The station is usually open every day and trains operate during weekends. They run on demand rather than to a set timetable and are diesel-hauled, except on the first Sunday of the month when they are steam-hauled.

Line Mileage and Journey Time

The railway runs for a quarter of a mile from Whitwell & Reepham and the journey time is relatively short.

Stock List

Type	Number	Builder	Details
Steam	2199 VICTORY	Andrew Barclay	0-4-0ST
Steam	945 ANNIE	Andrew Barclay	0-4-0ST
Steam	AGECROFT No.3 (7681)	Robert Stephenson & Hawthorns	0-4-0ST
Diesel	1 (3733)	Baguley	0-4-0
Diesel	D2700	North British	0-4-0
Diesel	466629 TIPOCKITY	Ruston & Hornsby	0-4-0
Diesel	518494 SWANWORTH	Ruston & Hornsby	0-4-0
Diesel	D1171	Hudswell Clarke	0-6-0
EMU	70527	British Railways	Class 411

Attractions

The site includes the restored station building, signal box and a museum with exhibits relating to the station and railway's history. There is a model and miniature railway club based at the site. Steam driving experiences are available at a price that compares favourably with those at other heritage railways. Whitwell & Reepham station is directly on the 26-mile-long traffic-free Marriott's Way through rural Norfolk. The region is also home to the North Norfolk Railway, the Mid Norfolk Railway, the historic city of Norwich and several coastal destinations.

Special Events

Events that usually take place on the railway include:

Easter Egg Hunt.
Mother's Day Event.
Classic Car Evenings.
Gin Trains.
1940s Weekend.

▲ The North Norfolk Railway's Weybourne station provides an idyllic rural railway setting for this view of a Class 101 DMU on 14 June 2019. **Glen Batten**

SOUTH-EAST

Region 7 – South-East

Bluebell Railway

Introduction and History

This railway was the first of two routes between Oxted and Lewes and was built by the London, Brighton & South Coast Railway, opening in 1882. Closure of the East Grinstead–Lewes route was proposed in 1954 and effected in 1958, with the Haywards Heath–Horsted Keynes route surviving until 1963. A preservation group formed in 1959 and in 1960 the Bluebell Railway became one of the first standard gauge preserved railways in the world to operate trains, initially from Sheffield Park to Bluebell Halt, with the line extending north to Horsted Keynes in 1962, Kingscote in 1994 and East Grinstead in 2013. The East Grinstead extension required vast quantities of 30-foot deep landfill rubbish to be excavated from the railway cutting, before the line could continue over the impressive Imberhorne Viaduct to re-join the national rail network. The railway owns the trackbed of the line from Horsted Keynes to Ardingly and plans to reinstate this and connect to the main line at Copyhold Junction, north of Haywards Heath. There is also a long-term aspiration to extend south from Sheffield Park to Lewes, which would make the railway unique in connecting to the main line network at three different locations.

Contact Details

Website: www.bluebell-railway.com
Tel: 01825 720800
Email: info@bluebell-railway.com
Address: The Bluebell Railway, Sheffield Park Station, East Sussex, TN22 3QL.

Transport Links

By Rail: There is a rail connection at East Grinstead; the main line and Bluebell stations are adjacent and a short walk between the two is needed.
By Road: There is plenty of parking space at Sheffield Park (TN22 3QL) and Horsted Keynes (RH17 7BB). There is pay and display parking near to East Grinstead (RH19 1EB) and there is no road access at Kingscote.

Opening Times

Trains usually operate during weekends from February and every day between April and October.

Line Mileage and Journey Time

0.00	Sheffield Park
4.50	Horsted Keynes
8.50	Kingscote
10.75	East Grinstead

A return journey takes 1 hour 40 minutes from Sheffield Park or about two hours from East Grinstead.

Stock List

Type	Number	Builder	Details
Steam	3 CAPTAIN Baxter	Fletcher Jennings	0-4-0T
Steam	96 NORMANDY	LSWR	0-4-0T
Steam	263	SECR	0-4-4T
Steam	65	SECR	0-6-0
Steam	592	SECR	0-6-0
Steam	30541	Southern Railway	0-6-0
Steam	4 (641)	Manning Wardle	0-6-0ST
Steam	55 STEPNEY	LBSCR	0-6-0T
Steam	FENCHURCH (32636)	LBSCR	0-6-0T
Steam	58850	North London Railway	0-6-0T
Steam	31027	SECR	0-6-0T
Steam	178	SECR	0-6-0T
Steam	323 BLUEBELL	SECR	0-6-0T
Steam	1959 (30064)	Vulcan Iron Works	0-6-0T
Steam	32473	LBSCR	0-6-2T

Steam	1638	Southern Railway	2-6-0
Steam	31618	Southern Railway	2-6-0
Steam	84030	Bluebell Railway SC2P	2-6-2T
Steam	80064	British Railways	2-6-4T
Steam	80100	British Railways	2-6-4T
Steam	80151	British Railways	2-6-4T
Steam	9017	GWR	4-4-0
Steam	928	Southern Railway	4-4-0
Steam	32424	Bluebell Railway Atlantic Group	4-4-2
Steam	488	LSWR	4-4-2T
Steam	73082	British Railways	4-6-0
Steam	75027	British Railways	4-6-0
Steam	847	Southern Railway	4-6-0
Steam	34059	Southern Railway	4-6-2
Steam	21C123 (BR No.34023)	Southern Railway	4-6-2
Steam	92240	British Railways	2-10-0
Diesel	957	Howard	0-4-0
Diesel	10241	Rolls Royce Sentinel	0-4-0
Diesel	D4106	British Railways	Class 09

Attractions

The Bluebell Railway has the largest collection of British steam locomotives after the National Railway Museum. This, along with the engine shed and museum at Sheffield Park and carriage & wagon works with its viewing gallery at Horsted Keynes, give plenty of railway interest. Attractions in the region include Sheffield Park Gardens and Standen House & Garden (both National Trust), Bluebell Vineyard which is two miles from Sheffield Park and Sackville College at East Grinstead. The Royal Botanic Gardens' Wakehurst site is a few miles from Horsted Keynes.

Special Events

19–20 June 2021: Road Meets Rail.
26–27 June 2021: Model Railway Weekend.
July 2021 (date TBC): Diesel Gala.
7–8 August 2021: 60 Plus 1 Celebration.
24–26 September 2021: Giants of Steam Autumn Gala.
30–31 October 2021: Halloween Ghost Train.
November 2021–January 2022: SteamLights
December 2021: Santa Specials.

▲ The Cholsey & Wallingford Railway's popular Santa Special services are being operated by two of its Class 08 shunters; 08022 "LION" is nearest the camera and 08123 is at the far end of the train. The seasonal service is seen at Wallingford on 8 December 2019. **Tony Christie**

Buckinghamshire Railway Centre

Introduction and History

The Buckinghamshire Railway Centre is based at Quainton Road station, which opened in 1868 on the line from London to Verney Junction via Aylesbury. It grew in significance after becoming part of the Great Central Railway in 1899. However, passenger services no longer stopped at the station from 1963 and the route was closed to passenger traffic in 1966. The Quainton Road Society was formed in 1969 and in 1971 it absorbed the London Railway Preservation Society with its collection of railway exhibits. Today the 25-acre site has one of the country's largest collections of locomotives, rolling stock and railway memorabilia and a short operational steam railway. The station remains connected to the national railway network and freight trains continue to pass through the site.

Contact Details

Website: www.bucksrailcentre.org
Tel: 01296 655720
Email: office@bucksrailcentre.org
Address: Buckinghamshire Railway Centre, Station Road, Quainton, Aylesbury, Bucks, HP22 4BY.

Transport Links

By Rail: Aylesbury Vale Parkway is the nearest railway station and is less than five miles away.
By Road: There is ample free parking for cars and coaches (HP22 4BY).

Opening Times

The Centre usually opens on Sundays and on selected weekdays between April and September. Trains operate on Sundays, Bank Holidays and some weekdays during school holidays.

Line Mileage and Journey Time

There are two operational lines on the site, both of which run for one third of a mile and the journey time is relatively short.

Stock List

Type	Number	Builder	Details
Steam Railcar	5208	Sentinel-Cammell	Steam Railcar
Steam	1477	Andrew Barclay	0-4-0F
Steam	2243	Andrew Barclay	0-4-0F
Steam	699	Andrew Barclay	0-4-0ST
Steam	2469	Bagnall	0-4-0ST
Steam	1742	Hudswell Clarke	0-4-0ST
Steam	3717	Hawthorn Leslie	0-4-0ST
Steam	1159	Peckett	0-4-0ST
Steam	2105	Peckett	0-4-0ST
Steam	807	Aveling & Porter	0-4-0T
Steam	9366	Sentinel	0-4-0T
Steam	1900	Peckett	0-4-0T
Steam	3567	Aveling & Porter	0-4-0WT
Steam	No. 1	Metropolitan Railway	0-4-4T
Steam	7715	GWR	0-6-0PT
Steam	3890	Hunslet	0-6-0ST
Steam	3782	Hunslet	0-6-0ST
Steam	2498	Yorkshire Engine Co.	0-6-0ST
Steam	1334	Hudswell Clarke	0-6-0T
Steam	24564	North British	0-6-0T
Steam	3020	LNWR	2-2-2
Steam	30585	LSWR	2-4-0WT
Steam	7200	GWR	2-8-2T
Steam	6984	British Railways	4-6-0
Steam	6989	British Railways	4-6-0
Steam	3405	North British	4-8-4
Diesel	20067	Fowler	0-4-0
Diesel	2102	Hibberd	0-4-0
Diesel	3271	Hibberd	0-4-0

Diesel	3765	Hibberd	0-4-0
Diesel	2067	Hunslet	0-4-0
Diesel	K4428	Hunslet	0-4-0
Diesel	425477	Ruston & Hornsby	0-4-0
Diesel	463153	Ruston & Hornsby	0-4-0
Diesel	459518	Ruston & Hornsby	0-6-0
Diesel	D2298	Robert Stephenson & Hawthorns	Class 04
DMU	51886, 51899 & 59761	British Railways	Class 115

Attractions

The museum and visitor centre have extensive exhibits including a royal dining coach from 1901 and one of the most complete sets of British Rail goods vehicles. Visitors can ride the 1 km long miniature railway and see the projects awaiting renovation in the restoration sheds. The Travelling Post Office tells the story of moving mail by rail. There is a second-hand bookshop and steam engine driver experiences are available. Nearby attractions include Quainton Windmill, Waddesden Manor, Buckinghamshire County Museum and the town of Aylesbury.

Special Events

Events that usually take place on the railway include:

1940s Event.
Halloween event during October.
Santa at the Station during December.

▲ GWR 6400 Class 0-6-0PT creates a typical branch line scene with a short engineer's train at the Chinnor & Princess Risborough Railway's Chinnor station on 19 July 2020. **Martyn Tattam**

Chatham Dockyard Railway

Introduction and History

Chatham Dockyard was a Royal Navy dockyard that was established in the mid-16th Century. A standard gauge railway within the dockyard was built in 1865 to move materials within the site and to serve the shipbuilding yards. This was connected to the main line network in 1877. A narrow gauge railway and locomotives were introduced in 1871; however, this had ceased operating by the 1930s. At its peak, it is estimated that there were approximately 17 miles of railway within the Royal Navy dockyard and when it closed in 1984, this had been reduced to two miles. The site opened the following year as Chatham Historic Dockyard, a maritime museum. The Chatham Dockyard Railway runs demonstration trains through the site. The railway is not able to carry passengers.

Contact Details

Website: www.dockyardrailway.co.uk or www.thedockyard.co.uk
Tel: 01634 823800
Email: nkils2@hotmail.co.uk or info@chdt.org.uk
Address: Chatham Historic Dockyard, Main Gate, Chatham, ME4 4TY.

Transport Links

By Rail: The nearest stations are Chatham and Gillingham (Kent); both are just over a mile away.
By Road: Parking is available at the dockyard site (ME4 4TY).

Opening Times

The dockyard opens daily from February to early November and trains operate on selected weekends.

Line Mileage and Journey Time

The dockyard has nearly two miles of track and demonstration trains use about one mile of this. The operational section has recently been increased to include Anchor Wharf. It takes about half an hour for trains to make a return journey.

Stock List

Type	Number	Builder	Details
Steam	INVICTA (2220)	Andrew Barclay	0-4-0ST
Steam	1903	Peckett	0-4-0ST
Steam	AJAX (7042)	Robert Stephenson & Hawthorns	0-4-0ST
Diesel	WD42	Andrew Barclay	0-4-0
Diesel	THALIA (2503)	Drewry	4wDM
Diesel	ROCHESTER CASTLE (FH3738)	Hibberd	4wDM

Attractions

The dockyard railway operates demonstrations using steam cranes, steam and diesel locomotives and wooden wagons, most of which pre-date the 1923 railway Grouping. Special steamings can be arranged in advance for photographers, railway enthusiasts or private functions. Trains travel through the dockyard, which is a maritime museum covering an 80-acre site, with warships, a historic RNLI lifeboat collection and the Victorian ropery. Additional attractions nearby include Fort Amherst, Chatham Snowsports Centre and Diggerland Kent.

Special Events

3 March–31 October 2021: Call the Midwife Official Location Tours.
3–4 July 2021: Medway Rapture Gaming & Creative Festival.
18–19 September 2021: Salute to the 1940s.

Chinnor & Princes Risborough Railway

Introduction and History

The branch line from Princes Risborough to Watlington opened in 1872, with intermediate stations at Chinnor and Aston Rowant. Passenger services ceased in 1957 although trains carrying goods and parcels continued until early 1961, after which the track beyond Chinnor was lifted. The station and platform at Chinnor were demolished during the 1970s; trains continued to work to Chinnor Cement Works until 1989, when Class 47 47258 hauled the final revenue-earning service. The Chinnor & Princes Risborough Railway Association took over the route in 1990 and in 1994 it purchased the freehold for the line, built a new station and ran its first trains from Chinnor. The railway was extended in 1995 and again in 1996 when it reached the former main line junction at Princes Risborough. In 2018 the line was extended into Platform 4 of Princes Risborough station, returning connecting passenger services to the branch for the first time since 1957. There are aspirations to extend the railway south-west along the former Watlington branch in the future.

Contact Details

Website: www.chinnorrailway.co.uk
Tel: 07979 055366 (between 10.00–16.00)
Email: enquiries@chinnorrailway.co.uk
Address: Chinnor & Princes Risborough Railway, Station Approach, Station Road, Chinnor, OX39 4ER.

Transport Links

By Rail: The heritage railway operates from Platform 4 of Princes Risborough station.
By Road: Parking is available opposite Chinnor station (use postcode OX39 4BZ).

Opening Times

Trains usually operate on Sundays from April to October and on selected other dates for special events.

Line Mileage and Journey Time

0.00   Princes Risborough
3.75   Chinnor

A return journey between Chinnor and Princes Risborough takes about an hour. In addition, on occasional special event days, passenger rides are available on the quarter mile spur that runs south from Princes Risborough.

Stock List

Type	Number	Builder	Details
Diesel	IRIS (459515)	Ruston & Hornsby	0-6-0
Diesel	08629	British Railways	Class 08
Diesel	08825	British Railways	Class 08
Diesel	D3018	British Railways	Class 08
Diesel	D8568	Clayton	Class 17
Diesel	97205 (31163)	Brush Traction	Class 31
Diesel	37227	English Electric	Class 37
DMU	51375 (977992)	Pressed Steel	Class 117
DMU	55023 & 55024	Pressed Steel	Class 121
EMU	61736, 61737 & 70573	British Railways	Class 411

Attractions

The railway's Chinnor base is home to the Cambrian Tea Room and a shop selling railway books, models and souvenirs. Nearby attractions include Chinnor Windmill, Chinnor Beehive Lime Kiln and Chinnor St. Andrews Church. The historic market town of Princes Risborough is less than a mile from its station and has several 17th and 18th Century buildings, including the National Trust-owned Manor House. The railway is on the edge of the Chiltern Hills, an Area of Outstanding Natural Beauty, which has many walks, hills and woodlands that can be explored.

Special Events

3–5 September 2021: Vintage Diesel Gala.

Other events that usually take place on the railway:

Mothering Sunday event (reduced price travel for Mums).
Father's Day event in June (reduced price travel for Dads).
Spooks & Ghouls event.
Santa Specials & Mince Pie Specials during December.
Several Kids for £1 days and various dining trains through the year.

Cholsey & Wallingford Railway

Introduction and History

The branch line from Cholsey to Wallingford opened 1866. It was originally planned for the railway to continue to Watlington and meet the branch from Princes Risborough, part of which forms the Chinnor & Princes Risborough Railway today, but this was not built. Passenger services ceased in 1959; freight trains to Wallingford continued until 1965, after which the station was closed and the land sold. Freight traffic continued to the malting plant to the south of Wallingford until 1981. A final railtour ran from London Paddington to Wallingford in May 1981, before British Rail closed the junction at Cholsey. The C&WR Preservation Society was then formed and heritage services began in 1985 from a temporary platform at Wallingford. The railway returned to Cholsey station in 1994, with trains working into a dedicated bay platform, although there is no main line rail connection. Wallingford station has recently benefited from improvement works, which included installing the Victorian canopy from Maidenhead station and a platform extension.

Contact Details

Website: www.cholsey-wallingford-railway.com
Tel: 01491 835067
Email: Written enquiries can be made from the website.
Address: Cholsey & Wallingford Railway, Wallingford Station, 5 Hithercroft Road, Wallingford, Oxfordshire, OX10 9GQ.

Transport Links

By Rail: Heritage trains depart from Platform 5 at Cholsey station. Through tickets to Wallingford can be purchased from GWR stations (the Wallingford Rover).
By Road: Parking is available at Wallingford (OX10 9GQ) and there is a small pay & display car park outside Cholsey station (OX10 9QD).

Opening Times

Trains operate on selected weekends and bank holidays through the year and are steam hauled on some dates.

Line Mileage and Journey Time

0.00	Cholsey
2.25	Wallingford

A return journey takes about 45 minutes.

Stock List

Type	Number	Builder	Details
Steam	6515	Sentinel	4wVBT
Steam	NORTHERN GAS BOARD No. 1	Peckett	0-4-0ST
Diesel	3270	Hibberd	0-4-0
Diesel	08123	British Railways	Class 08
Diesel	08022 LION	British Railways	Class 08
Diesel	08060 UNICORN	British Railways	Class 08

Attractions

The railway has a number of locomotives with an industrial and shunting history. Wallingford station has a museum coach, a café and shop with many railway-related items and second-hand books. In Wallingford, there is a 15th Century marketplace, a castle, views of the River Thames and a local museum. Cholsey Church is the burial place of Agatha Christie and is a short walk from Cholsey station. Didcot Railway Centre is six miles away and the Chinnor & Princes Risborough Railway is 16 miles away.

Special Events

An event to commemorate the 40th anniversary of the last through train to Wallingford is due to take place in May 2021. Other events that usually take place include:

Easter Running Days.
Cream Tea Specials.
1940s Event.
Halloween trains during October.
Santa Specials during December.

▲ Didcot Railway Centre is a former GWR depot which is now home to a large collection of GWR-built locomotives. On 1 August 2020, 6000 "King" Class 6023 "KING EDWARD II", 5600 Class 6697 and newbuild 2900 Class 2999 "LADY OF LEGEND" recreate an authentic depot scene.

Martyn Tattam

Didcot Railway Centre

Introduction and History

There has been a railway at the Didcot site since the original broad gauge line was built in 1839. Didcot station opened in 1844 and it has been an important junction, depot and stabling point since. The depot became surplus to British Rail's requirements and closed in 1965; however, in 1967 the Great Western Society gained access to the site and since then has used it to restore, exhibit and demonstrate an array of rolling stock and items of railway interest. The site is in the middle of the busy triangle of railway lines at Didcot and includes a number of short railway lines on which a variety of traction carries passengers.

Contact Details

Website: www.didcotrailwaycentre.org.uk
Tel: 01235 817200
Email: info@didcotrailwaycentre.org.uk
Address: Didcot Railway Centre, Didcot, Oxfordshire, OX11 7NJ.

Transport Links

By Rail: The subway inside Didcot Parkway railway station leads directly to the Centre.
By Road: Car parking is available at Didcot Parkway (OX11 7NJ) or the nearby larger Foxhall Road site (OX11 7NR) and both are chargeable. Note that as the Railway Centre is entirely surrounded by railway lines, the route to the Centre includes crossing a footbridge or using the station subway, both of which involve stairs.

Opening Times

The Centre usually opens on Saturdays & Sundays and regular weekdays from Spring until October. Advance booking is recommended, please refer to the website for the latest information.

Line Mileage and Journey Time

The main section of standard gauge line used to carry passengers is one third of a mile long and the journey time is relatively short.

Stock List

Type	Number	Builder	Details
Steam Railcar	93	GWR	Steam Railmotor
Steam	1340	Avonside	0-4-0ST
Steam	1338	Kitson	0-4-0ST
Steam	1 BONNIE PRINCE CHARLIE	Robert Stephenson & Hawthorns	0-4-0ST
Steam	5	George England	0-4-0WT
Steam	1466	GWR	0-4-2T
Steam	3650	GWR	0-6-0PT
Steam	3738	GWR	0-6-0PT
Steam	1363	GWR	0-6-0ST
Steam	2409	Hunslet	0-6-0ST
Steam	6697	Armstrong Whitworth	0-6-2T
Steam	FIRE FLY (replica)	Fire Fly Trust	2-2-2
Steam	5322	GWR	2-6-0
Steam	4144	GWR	2-6-2T
Steam	5572	GWR	2-6-2T
Steam	6106	GWR	2-6-2T
Steam	3822	GWR	2-8-0
Steam	5227	GWR	2-8-0T
Steam	7202	GWR	2-8-2T
Steam	IRON DUKE	Resco Railways	4-2-2
Steam	6998	British Railways	4-6-0
Steam	1014	Great Western Society	4-6-0
Steam	2999	Great Western Society	4-6-0
Steam	7808	GWR	4-6-0
Steam	4079	GWR	4-6-0
Steam	5051	GWR	4-6-0
Steam	5900	GWR	4-6-0

Steam	6023	GWR	4-6-0
Gas Turbine	18000	Brown Boveri	A1A-A1A
Diesel	DL26	Hunslet	0-6-0
Diesel	604	British Railways	Class 08
Diesel	D9516	British Railways	Class 14
DMU	22	GWR	Railcar

Attractions

The 21-acre site has a wealth of railway-related exhibits and a large collection of locomotives, which includes steam, diesel and gas turbine engines. The passenger line uses a varied selection of traction and the roster showing what is due to work on each date is shown on the website. Visitors can see the engine shed, carriage display shed, transfer shed with broad and standard gauge railways and the signalling centre with a modern panel and mechanical levers which can be pulled. The site is close to the centre of Didcot; the city of Oxford is 12 miles away and nearby heritage railways include Cholsey & Wallingford (six miles away), Chinnor & Princes Risborough (19 miles) and Swindon & Cricklade (29 miles).

Special Events

An event celebrating the 60th anniversary of the Great Western Society is due to take place during 2021. Other events include:

Hallowsteam during autumn.
Steam Into Christmas.

East Kent Railway

Introduction and History

The East Kent Light Railway, as it was originally known, was built in stages between 1911 and 1917, primarily to carry coal. It ran from Shepherdswell to Wingham and Richborough. The first passengers were carried in 1916; however, passenger services between Eastry and Sandwich Road ended as early as 1928 and the remaining passenger services ceased in 1948. The stretch between Shepherdswell and Tilmanstone Colliery continued to carry coal until 1986 and closed in 1987. The preservation era began in 1985 when the East Kent Railway Society formed and the first heritage trains ran in 1993. There are plans to extend the railway south along the trackbed towards Coldred.

Contact Details

Website: www.eastkentrailway.co.uk
Tel: 01304 832042
Email: Written enquiries can be made from the EKR website.
Address: East Kent Railway Trust, Station Road, Shepherdswell, Dover, CT15 7PD.

Transport Links

By Rail: The main line station at Shepherdswell is next to the EKR station.
By Road: There is plenty of free parking at Shepherdswell station (CT15 7PD).

Opening Times

The railway usually operates on Sundays and Bank Holidays from April to October, plus on Saturdays during July and August and at weekends during December for Santa services.

Line Mileage and Journey Time

0.00   Shepherdswell
1.50   Eythorne

A return journey takes just under one hour.

Stock List

Type	Number	Builder	Details
Steam	2087	Peckett	0-4-0ST
Steam	2004 ST DUNSTAN	Avonside	0-6-0ST
Diesel	4160002	Fowler	0-4-0
Diesel	01530	Thomas Hill	0-4-0

Diesel	01543	Thomas Hill	0-4-0
Diesel	D1197	English Electric	0-6-0
Diesel	427	Ruston & Hornsby	0-6-0
Diesel	08502	British Railways	Class 08
Diesel	08676	British Railways	Class 08
Diesel	08685	British Railways	Class 08
Diesel	08799	British Railways	Class 08
Diesel	08804	British Railways	Class 08
Diesel	NS687	English Electric	Dutch 600 Series
Electric	42 (Kearsley No.1)	Hawthorn Leslie	Bo-Bo
DMU	142017 (55558 & 55608)	BREL/Leyland	Class 142
DMU	142036 (55577 & 55627)	BREL/Leyland	Class 142
DEMU	60100 & 60800	British Railways	Class 205
DEMU	54000	BREL	Class 210
EMU	11161 & 11187	Southern Railway	4 Cor
EMU	62385	BREL	Class 421
EMU	76875	BREL	Class 423
EMU	70904, 76397 & 76398	British Railways	Class 423

Attractions

The railway has a varied selection of traction, including steam and diesel locomotives, and multiple units. Visitors can ride on the standard gauge line and the 7¼ inch gauge Woodland Miniature Railway. There is also a model railway, two signal boxes which house historical information on the EKR and a nature trail to explore. There are various other attractions in the area, with Canterbury, Sandwich and the Kent Coast all nearby.

Special Events

Events that usually take place at the railway include:

Dining Trains serving Cream Teas and Fish & Chip Suppers.
Beer Festival.
Santa by Train.

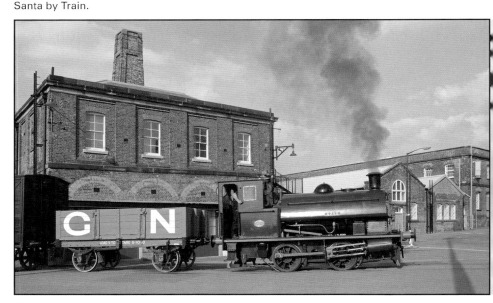

▲ Robert Stephenson & Hawthorns 0-4-0ST AJAX has spent its entire 80-year life at Chatham Dockyard. It was owned and operated by the Admiralty between 1941 and 1984 and since 1985 it has been a feature at the visitor attraction that superseded the working dockyard. It is seen working a mixed goods train on 7 July 2018.   **Alistair Grieve**

Fawley Hill

Introduction and History

Fawley Hill is the home of Lady McAlpine and was built in 1960 by the late Sir William McAlpine. In 1961, Hudswell Clarke 0-6-0ST number 31 was bought for scrap value by Sir William and became the first of many railway items that were brought to Fawley Hill. A railway with a length of approximately one mile has been built; this operates on selected dates and is also available for private hire. Some of the larger items which have been brought to the site include Somersham station from Cambridgeshire, a Midland Railway signal box and a footbridge from the Isle of Wight's Ryde–Shanklin line. There is a museum with a large collection of exhibits, which began as a home for Sir William's traction engines and car collection.

Contact Details

Website: www.fawleyhill.co.uk
Tel: 01491 574873
Email: events@fawleyhill.com
Address: Fawley Hill, Fawley, Henley-on-Thames, Bucks, RG9 6JA.

Transport Links

By Rail: The nearest station is Henley-on-Thames, which is three miles away.
By Road: There is on-site parking for visitors.

Opening Times

Fawley Hill is a private estate, which only opens to the public on a few days each year and these are advertised on its website. Entrance at other times is only by arrangement for private functions or by invitation.

Line Mileage and Journey Time

The railway is nearly one mile long and the journey time is relatively short.

Stock List

Type	Number	Builder	Details
Steam	31	Hudswell Clarke	0-6-0ST
Diesel	3817	Hibberd	4wDM
Diesel	3894 ERNIE	Hibberd	4wDM
Diesel	D2120	British Railways	Class 03

Attractions

Fawley Hill has the steepest standard gauge railway in the world, with a gradient of 1 in 13 at its steepest point. The site and museum have a large collection of railway artefacts and some of the larger exhibits include the Great Eastern Railway Chairman's private wooden saloon and two Royal Train carriages; Her Majesty's private carriage and the nursery coach for Prince Charles and Princess Anne. There are two 'O' gauge railways and Iron Henge, which is a large circle of supports from the undercroft of St Pancras station. Fawley Hill has an animal sanctuary with over 20 different animal types, which have been transferred from several zoos and animal sanctuaries. Animal feeding trips can be arranged in advance. The museum, Victorian railway station and waiting room can all be used as a venue for weddings and events.

Isle of Wight Steam Railway

Introduction and History

The railway from Ryde to Newport opened in 1875 and was one of several lines on the Isle of Wight which have generally used older rolling stock than those on the mainland. The final steam trains ran in 1966 and the railway from Ryde to Newport and Cowes then closed. In 1967 a group of enthusiasts formed the Wight Locomotive Society and purchased steam locomotive 24 "Calbourne", which remains at the railway today. In 1971 the Isle of Wight Railway Company formed with the aim of acquiring the line between Wooton and Havenstreet. This was successful and the first preserved trains ran in 1971. The railway was extended to Smallbrook Junction, where it connects with the Ryde–Shanklin line, in 1991. There are plans to reinstate the connection to the Ryde–Shanklin Island Line at Smallbrook Junction, which would allow through running to Ryde. In addition, there are aspirations to extend the railway west towards Newport.

Contact Details

Website: www.iwsteamrailway.co.uk
Tel: 01983 882204
Email: info@iwsteamrailway.co.uk
Address: The Railway Station, Havenstreet, Near Ryde, Isle of Wight, PO33 4DS.

Transport Links

By Rail: Change at Smallbrook Junction on the Ryde–Shanklin route (Island Line). Note, there is no road or footpath access at Smallbrook Junction.
By Road: Free car parking is available at Havenstreet (PO33 4DS).

Opening Times

Regular train services operate from late March until November and during the Christmas and New Year period. The railway is closed on some dates and please check the website for details of which timetable is in operation.

Line Mileage and Journey Time

0.00	Smallbrook Junction
1.75	Ashey
3.25	Havenstreet
4.75	Wooton

A return journey takes about one hour.

Stock List

Type	Number	Builder	Details
Steam	INVINCIBLE	Hawthorn Leslie	0-4-0ST
Steam	24	LSWR	0-4-4T
Steam	192	Hunslet	0-6-0ST
Steam	198	Hunslet	0-6-0ST
Steam	38 AJAX	Andrew Barclay	0-6-0T
Steam	2 YARMOUTH	LBSCR	0-6-0T
Steam	8 (BR No. 32646)	LBSCR	0-6-0T
Steam	W11 (BR No. 32640)	LBSCR	0-6-0T
Steam	41313	British Railways	2-6-2T
Steam	41298	British Railways	2-6-2T
Diesel	235	Andrew Barclay	0-4-0
Diesel	D2059	British Railways	Class 03
Diesel	D2554	Hunslet	Class 05

Attractions

There is plenty to explore at the railway's Havenstreet base, including the Train Story Centre, Haven Falconry Bird of Prey Centre, a small museum, a railway gift & model shop, the carriage & wagon workshop, a picnic & children's play area and a woodland walkway. Attractions in the area include Appley Park, Dinosaur Isle, Butterfly & Fountain World and there are hundreds of miles of walking and cycling routes on the island.

Special Events
23 May 2021: Festival of Transport.
4–6 June 2021: 50th Anniversary Gala.
26–27 June 2021: Real Ale Festival.
3–4 July 2021: The 1940s Experience.
10–11 July 2021: The Island Motor Show.
18 July 2021: Island Highland Gathering.
31 July 2021: Summer Concert.
27–30 August 2021: Island Steam Show.
5 September 2021: Morris Minor Rally.
11–12 September 2021: Cider & Cheese Festival.
25–26 September 2021: 1960s Weekend.
16 October 2021: Teddy Bear Day.
25–29 October 2021: Wizard Week.
30–31 October 2021: Fright Nights.
December 2021: Santa Specials.

Kent & East Sussex Railway

Introduction and History
The first section of the Kent & East Sussex Light Railway opened between Robertsbridge and Rolvenden in 1900. It was extended to Tenterden Town in 1903 and to Headcorn in 1905, when it met the main line from Tonbridge to Ashford. After declining use, the Tenterden to Headcorn section closed in 1954 and the track was lifted soon afterwards. The branch from Robertsbridge to Tenterden continued to see freight and occasional charter trains until 1961 when it was closed. During the 1960s, a preservation group worked towards reinstating the railway; however, the Robertsbridge to Bodiam section had to be abandoned due to the number of roads crossing the line. The heritage railway between Tenterden and Rolvenden opened in 1974 and this was extended to Wittersham Road in 1977, Northiam in 1990 and to Bodiam in 2000. Plans are under way to extend and reconnect the railway to the main line under the auspices of the Rother Valley Railway (see the Proposed Railways section).

Contact Details
Website: www.kesr.org.uk
Tel: 01580 765155
Email: enquiries@kesr.org.uk
Address: Tenterden Town Station, Station Road, Tenterden, Kent, TN30 6HE.

Transport Links
By Rail: Robertsbridge station is five miles from Bodiam and the nearest stations to Tenterden are Ham Street (eight miles) and Headcorn (nine miles).
By Road: Parking is available at Tenterden Town (TN30 6HE) and Northiam (TN31 6QT).

Opening Times
Trains usually operate on Saturdays, Sundays and on a variety of weekdays between April and October.

Line Mileage and Journey Time
0.00 Tenterden Town
1.50 Rolvenden
4.75 Wittersham Road
6.50 Northiam
10.25 Bodiam

A return journey from Tenterden takes about 1 hour 50 minutes.

Stock List

Type	Number	Builder	Details
Steam	12 (1631)	Peckett	0-4-0T
Steam	1	Dodman & Co	0-4-2WT
Steam	1638	British Railways	0-6-0PT
Steam	23 (3791)	Hunslet	0-6-0ST

Steam	25 (3797)	Hunslet	0-6-0ST
Steam	14 CHARWELTON (1955)	Manning Wardle	0-6-0ST
Steam	32670	LBSCR	0-6-0T
Steam	32678	LBSCR	0-6-0T
Steam	5753	SECR	0-6-0T
Steam	65	Vulcan Iron Works	0-6-0T
Steam	300	Vulcan Iron Works	0-6-0T
Steam	5668	GWR	0-6-2T
Steam	6619	GWR	0-6-2T
Steam	376	Norwegian State Railways	2-6-0
Steam	4253	GWR	2-8-0T
Diesel	423661	Ruston & Hornsby	0-4-0DE
Diesel	D2023	British Railways	Class 03
Diesel	D2024	British Railways	Class 03
Diesel	3174	British Railways	Class 08
Diesel	D4118	British Railways	Class 08
Diesel	D9504	British Railways	Class 14
Diesel	7594	British Railways	Class 25
Diesel	D6570	BRCW	Class 33
DMU	50971 & 51571	British Railways	Class 108
DMU	20	GWR	Railcar
Electro-Diesel	40	British Thomson-Houston	Bo-Bo

Attractions

The Colonel Stephens Railway Museum is at the railway's Tenterden base and opens on the days when trains operate. Behind the scenes tours can be arranged at Tenterden, which include a visit inside the carriage and wagon workshop. There is a viewing gallery for the locomotive engineering workshop at Rolvenden. Various walks can be taken from each of the stations along the course of the railway. Other attractions in the area include Lashenden Air Warfare Museum, Bodiam Castle, Camber Sands, Rye Castle and Rye Harbour Nature Reserve.

Special Events

Events that usually take place on the railway include:

Sunday Lunch and Evening Dining Trains.
Mother's Day Event.
1940s Weekend.
Family Event during October.
Santa Specials during December.

▲ On 26 August 2019, LSWR 0-4-4T 24 "CALBOURNE" approaches the Isle of Wight Steam Railway's western terminus, Wootton. This locomotive is now 130 years old and has been on the Isle of Wight since 1925.   **Tony Christie**

The Lavender Line

Introduction and History

The railway between Uckfield and Lewes opened in 1858, providing an alternative route between London and Brighton. Closure of the line was suggested in Dr Beeching's 1963 report; however, due to considerable opposition, it did not close until 1969 and the track was lifted in 1970. Isfield station was purchased privately in 1983 after which the owner renovated the station, signal box and rebuilt the waiting room (the original building had been moved to the Bluebell Railway's nearby Sheffield Park site). A stretch of track was laid and a steam locomotive subsequently arrived at Isfield. In 1991 ownership of the station and railway was transferred to the Lavender Line Preservation Society, the name being taken from Lavender & Sons, a local firm that was previously based at Isfield station. In recent years there has been a campaign for the Uckfield–Lewes line to reopen as a commercial railway, connecting to the main line network. The Lavender Line aims to extend; however, that would be subject to the main line project not proceeding.

Contact Details

Website: www.lavender-line.co.uk
Tel: 01825 750515
Email: Written enquiries can be made from the website.
Address: The Lavender Line, Isfield Station, Near Uckfield, East Sussex, TN22 5XB.

Transport Links

By Rail: The nearest stations are Uckfield (three miles) and Lewes to the south (six miles).
By Road: Free parking is available at Isfield (TN22 5XB).

Opening Times

The railway usually operates each Sunday and Bank Holiday (except Good Friday and between Christmas and New Year) and on selected other dates for special events. Trains depart from Isfield approximately every half hour between 11.00 and 16.30.

Line Mileage and Journey Time

The railway is just over three quarters of a mile long and a return journey takes about 20 minutes.

Stock List

Type	Number	Builder	Details
Steam	2945	Cockerill	0-4-0VBT
Diesel	354	Andrew Barclay	0-4-0
Diesel	830	Drewry	0-4-0
Diesel	15	Hibberd	4wDM
Diesel	422	Ruston & Hornsby	0-6-0
Diesel	D4113	British Railways	Class 09
DMU	56279	British Railways	Class 108
DMU	999507	Wickham	Railbus
DEMU	60117, 60122, 60151, 60820, 60828 & 60832	British Railways	Class 205
EMU	61928, 75965 & 75972	British Railways	Class 309
EMU	69333	BREL	Class 422

Attractions

Driver experiences have recently been introduced, using the railway's Class 205 "Thumper" units and these should be arranged in advance. Brake van rides are available, using the demonstration freight train. Isfield station has a restored Grade II listed signal box, a gift shop, station buffet, picnic area and children's play area. There is a five inch gauge miniature railway which operates on selected Sundays and the proceeds from this are given to charity. Children's parties can be hosted in a decorated static carriage. The Bluebell Railway's southern terminus at Sheffield Park is eight miles from Isfield. Other attractions in the area include Wilderness Wood, the market town of Lewes and the South Coast.

Special Events

A Steam and Car Rally usually takes place in October.

Mid Hants Railway

Introduction and History

The railway between Alton and Winchester via Alresford opened in 1865 and became known as the Watercress Line, due to the large volumes of the locally produced crop that it carried. The line from London to Alton was electrified in 1937, which brought an end to regular through trains and when the London–Southampton line was electrified in 1967, the line through Alresford became an isolated diesel section. The route survived the mass rural line closures of the 1960s, but only until 1973 when British Rail closed it between Alton and Winchester Junction. The Alresford–Alton section was purchased from BR in 1975 and the first heritage trains worked between Alresford and Ropley in 1977. The railway was extended to Medstead in 1983 and to Alton in 1985 where the line is now connected to the national network.

Contact Details

Website: www.watercressline.co.uk
Tel: 01962 733810
Email: Written enquiries can be made from the website.
Address: Mid Hants Railway Ltd, New Alresford, Hampshire, SO24 9JG.

Transport Links

By Rail: There is a rail connection at Alton; cross to the Mid Hants Railway platform.
By Road: Car parking is available at Alresford (SO24 9JG) and Alton (GU34 2PZ). It is chargeable at both locations and the rates are lower at Alresford.

Opening Times

Trains operate on most weekends and Bank Holidays through the year and on selected weekdays, including most weekdays between April and August.

Line Mileage and Journey Time

0.00	Alton
4.50	Medstead and Four Marks
7.25	Ropley
10.25	Alresford

A return journey takes about 2 hours 30 minutes.

Stock List

Type	Number	Builder	Details
Steam	1 (3781)	Hunslet	0-6-0T
Steam	76017	British Railways	2-6-0
Steam	41312	British Railways	2-6-2T
Steam	80150	British Railways	2-6-4T
Steam	53808	Robert Stephenson & Co	2-8-0
Steam	925	Southern Railway	4-4-0
Steam	73096	British Railways	4-6-0
Steam	75079	British Railways	4-6-0
Steam	30499	LSWR	4-6-0
Steam	30506	LSWR	4-6-0
Steam	30828	Southern Railway	4-6-0
Steam	850	Southern Railway	4-6-0
Steam	34105	British Railways	4-6-2
Steam	34007	Southern Railway	4-6-2
Steam	34058	Southern Railway	4-6-2
Diesel	08032	British Railways	Class 08
Diesel	08377	British Railways	Class 08
Diesel	D3358	British Railways	Class 08
Diesel	12049	British Railways	Class 11
Diesel	47579	Brush Traction	Class 47
Diesel	50027	English Electric	Class 50
DEMU	60124 & 60824	British Railways	Class 205

Attractions

Behind the scenes tours of the engineering hub are available on selected dates at Ropley, where there is also a miniature railway. There is a Goods Shed Exhibition and Photo Exhibition at Medstead & Four Marks and a gift shop and model railway at Alton. The railway operates various food and drink themed services, including cream tea, evening dining and real ale trains. The Curtis Museum in Alton town centre is nearby and Jane Austen's house in Chawton village is a few miles away. There are several themed walks in the area, including the Jane Austen Trail linking Alton with her home in Chawton, the one-mile Alresford Millennium Trail exploring Alresford and the Watercress Way which continues along the route of the former railway west of Alresford.

Special Events

22–23 May 2021: Traction Engine & Vintage Vehicles.
29 May–6 June 2021: Day Out with Thomas.
12–13 June 2021: War on the Line.
19 June 2021: Uire Locomotive Society Open Day.
25–27 June 2021: Diesel Gala.
7–15 August 2021: Day Out with Thomas.
28–30 August 2021: 1950s Weekend.
1–3 October 2021: Autumn Steam Gala.
29–31 October 2021: Wizard Weekend.
November & December 2021: Steam Illuminations.

▲ The National Railway Museum's "Schools Class" 4-4-0 30925 and the Mid Hants Railway's Ropley station effectively recreate a scene from the past at dusk on 8 February 2020. **Martyn Tattam**

Spa Valley Railway

Introduction and History

The railway from East Grinstead to Groombridge and Tunbridge Wells West opened in 1866 and the Groombridge to Eridge, Uckfield and Lewes section opened in 1868. After declining use and with costly upgrade work being necessary, British Rail announced its intention to close the line between Tunbridge Wells and Eridge in 1983. Objections were overridden and the line was closed in 1985. In the same year, the Tunbridge Wells and Eridge Railway Preservation Society formed with the aim of reopening the line. The Tunbridge Wells site was reduced in size after planning permission was given for a supermarket to be built on the rail yard; however, this was subject to the company covering the cost of a new station platform. In 1996 the group acquired the railway line as far as Birchden Junction near Eridge and operated its first trains from Tunbridge Wells West for about half a mile. The operational section was extended to Groombridge in 1997, Birchden Junction in 2005 and to Eridge in 2011, where the railway now connects with main line trains.

Contact Details

Website: www.spavalleyrailway.co.uk
Tel: 01892 300141
Email: Written enquiries can be made from the website.
Address: Spa Valley Railway, West Station, Nevill Terrace, Royal Tunbridge Wells, TN2 5QY.

Transport Links

By Rail: The railway shares Eridge station with main line services which arrive from Uckfield and London; discounted fares are available if travelling by rail to Eridge, when SVR tickets are purchased with a main line ticket. Alternatively, Tunbridge Wells West is less than a mile from Tunbridge Wells main line station.
By Road: Free parking is available at High Rocks (TN3 9JJ) and and there is pay & display parking near to Eridge (TN3 9LE) and Tunbridge Wells West (TN2 5QY) stations.

Opening Times

The railway operates on most weekends and Bank Holidays, and on selected weekdays between February and October and during December.

Line Mileage and Journey Time

0.00	Tunbridge Wells West
1.25	High Rocks
3.00	Groombridge
5.00	Eridge

A return journey takes about 1 hour 10 minutes.

Stock List

Type	Number	Builder	Details
Steam	3 (2315)	Andrew Barclay	0-4-0ST
Steam	6435	GWR	0-6-0PT
Steam	68077	Andrew Barclay	0-6-0ST
Steam	2193	Bagnall	0-6-0ST
Steam	1589	Hunslet	0-6-0ST
Steam	2890	Hunslet	0-6-0ST
Steam	57 (7668)	Robert Stephenson & Hawthorns	0-6-0ST
Steam	62 (7673)	Robert Stephenson & Hawthorns	0-6-0ST
Steam	32650	LBSCR	0-6-0T
Steam	47493	Vulcan Foundry	0-6-0T
Steam	34053	Southern Railway	4-6-2
Diesel	SOUTHERHAM (2591)	Drewry	0-4-0
Diesel	09026	British Railways	Class 09
Diesel	D3489	British Railways	Class 10
Diesel	15224	British Railways	Class 12
Diesel	31430	Brush Traction	Class 31
Diesel	33063	BRCW	Class 33
Diesel	33065	BRCW	Class 33

Electro-Diesel	73140	English Electric	Class 73
DMU	56408	Metropolitan Cammell	Class 101
DEMU	60142, 60616 & 60916	British Railways	Class 207
EMU	62402, 76764 & 76835	BREL	Class 421
EMU	69306	British Railways	Class 422
EMU	61277	British Railways	Class 489

Attractions

The Spa Valley line runs through High Weald, which is an Area of Outstanding Natural Beauty. At the railway's Tunbridge Wells West base, the 1886 engine shed can be seen and there is a buffet housed within a multiple unit. Steam and diesel locomotive driving experiences can be arranged. Nearby heritage railways include the Bluebell Railway (13 miles away), the Lavender Line (14 miles), the Rother Valley Railway (17 miles) and the Kent & East Sussex Railway (24 miles). Groombridge Place and Enchanted Forest are a 15–20 minute walk from Groombridge station. Other attractions in the area include Ashdown Forest, Dunorlan Park and Royal Tunbridge Wells, home of the Pantiles and the Chalybeate Spring.

Special Events

6–8 August 2021: Diesel Gala.

Other special events that usually take place on the railway include:

Steam and Real Ale Trains.
Santa Specials during December.

▲ The driver of BR Standard Class 4 2-6-4T 80078 pauses to take in the surroundings of the Spa Valley Railway's High Rocks station on 10 August 2020.
Martyn Tattam

SOUTH-WEST

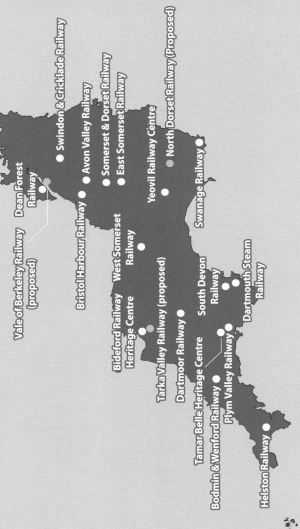

Swindon & Cricklade Railway

Avon Valley Railway

Somerset & Dorset Railway

East Somerset Railway

North Dorset Railway (Proposed)

Yeovil Railway Centre

Swanage Railway

Dean Forest Railway

Bristol Harbour Railway

West Somerset Railway

Vale of Berkeley Railway (proposed)

South Devon Railway

Dartmouth Steam Railway

Bideford Railway Heritage Centre

Tarka Valley Railway (proposed)

Dartmoor Railway

Tamar Belle Heritage Centre

Plym Valley Railway

Bodmin & Wenford Railway

Helston Railway

Alderney Railway

Pallot Steam, Motor & General Museum

Region 8 – South-West

Alderney Railway

Introduction and History
The Alderney Railway was built by the British Government to carry the stone quarried from the east of the island which was used to construct the breakwater and Victorian forts. The line opened in 1847 and the first official passengers to be carried were Queen Victoria and Prince Albert in 1854. Stone quarrying ceased for several years from 1940, when German forces occupied Alderney and replaced part of the railway with a 60 cm gauge system. After the war, the British Home Office took over the railway and the standard gauge line was reinstated. It was later converted to a passenger line and services began in 1980. Today the railway follows a coastal route from Braye Road to Mannez Quarry and Lighthouse, using a diesel shunter to haul two 1959 former London Underground coaches, providing a unique view of Alderney.

Contact Details
Website: www.alderneyrailway.com
Tel: 07911 739572
Email: alderneyrailway@suremail.gg
Address: 7 Rue de Beaumont, St Anne, Guernsey.

Transport Links
By Rail: There are no other railways on Alderney.
By Road: Car parking is available at Braye Road station.
By Air: There are direct flights to Alderney from Southampton and Guernsey.
By Sea: Ferries to Alderney sail from Guernsey and Cherbourg, France.

Opening Times
Trains operate on Sunday afternoons from May to September and also on Saturday afternoons during July and August. Two return trips are made, departing from Braye Road at 14.15 and 15.30.

Line Mileage and Journey Time
0.00   Braye Road
1.75   Mannez Quarry

A return journey takes about 45 minutes.

Stock List
Type	Number	Builder	Details
Diesel	D100	English Electric	0-4-0
Diesel	2	Ruston & Hornsby	0-4-0

Attractions
At Mannez Quarry visitors can ride the quarter mile long 7¼ inch gauge railway, which operates at times that connect with the standard gauge train services. The rail shed at Mannez Quarry, which houses the Wickham cars and diesel locomotives, can also be visited. Mannez Quarry station is close to the coast, lighthouse and forts at the north-eastern end of the island. Braye Road station is adjacent to the beach, harbour and breakwater, and is a short walk from the centre of St Anne.

Special Events
Events that usually take place on the railway include:

Easter Special on Easter Sunday.
Santa Specials on the Sunday before Christmas.
Trains can be chartered for weddings and private functions.

Avon Valley Railway

Introduction and History

The railway through Bitton was part of the Midland Railway's Mangotsfield and Bath branch line which opened in 1869 as a through route from the Midlands to the south coast and connected with the Somerset & Dorset Railway. After being earmarked for closure in Dr Beeching's Reshaping Britain's Railways report, the final trains ran in 1966. A preservation group then formed in 1972, initially leasing Bitton station and the first heritage trains operated on a short stretch of track in 1974. The line has since been extended to a length of nearly three miles and there is potential for the railway to extend further south towards Bath.

Contact Details

Website: www.avonvalleyrailway.org
Tel: 0117 932 5538
Email: info@avonvalleyrailway.org
Address: Bitton Station, Bath Road, Bristol, South Gloucestershire, BS30 6HD.

Transport Links

By Rail: Keynsham is the nearest railway station and is one and a half miles away.
By Road: There is free parking at Bitton station (BS30 6HD), which is on the A431 between Bristol and Bath.
By Bike: Bitton station has a cycle parking area and can be reached on the Bristol and Bath Railway Path (Route 4 of the National Cycling Network).

Opening Times

The station buffet at Bitton opens daily and trains operate on selected days through the year, including most weekends and school holidays, with one of three different timetables operating.

▲ During the peak holiday season in 2018, the Dartmouth Steam Railway hired GWR 4-6-0 6023 "KING EDWARD II" from the Didcot Railway Centre to operate passenger services on the line. The "King" follows the River Dart estuary and approaches Kingswear station on 29 August 2018.

Martyn Tattam

Line Mileage and Journey Time

0.00	Oldland Common
1.00	Bitton
2.50	Avon Riverside

A round trip from Bitton to Oldland Common and Avon Riverside takes about one hour.

Stock List

Type	Number	Builder	Details
Steam	7492	Sentinel	0-4-0
Steam	44123	LMS	0-6-0
Steam	1798 EDWIN HULSE	Avonside	0-6-0ST
Steam	132	Hunslet	0-6-0ST
Steam	65 (3163)	Hunslet	0-6-0ST
Steam	5	Manning Wardle	0-6-0ST
Steam	4015	Fablok	0-6-0T
Steam	7151	Robert Stephenson & Hawthorns	0-6-0T
Diesel	235519	Robert Stephenson & Hawthorns	4wDM
Diesel	RH252823	Robert Stephenson & Hawthorns	4wDM
Diesel	446	Andrew Barclay	0-4-0
Diesel	70043 Grumpy	Ministry of Defence	0-4-0
Diesel	429	Ruston & Hornsby	0-6-0
Diesel	610	Sentinel	0-8-0
Diesel	D2994	Ruston & Hornsby	Class 07
Diesel	08202	British Railways	Class 08
Diesel	08663	British Railways	Class 08
Diesel	09015	British Railways	Class 09
Diesel	31101	Brush Traction	Class 31
Diesel	31130	Brush Traction	Class 31
DMU	52006 & 52025	British Railways	Class 107

Attractions

The railway is based at the beautifully restored Bitton station. This is part way along the 13-mile Bristol and Bath Railway Path, which connects the two cities and runs alongside the heritage railway. There is a small museum and a buffet at Bitton which opens every day of the year except Christmas Day. Driving Experiences are available, with the choice of a steam locomotive, diesel locomotive or diesel multiple unit. The Avon Valley Adventure and Wildlife Park is very close and the nearby cities of Bath and Bristol have many attractions, including the Roman Baths and Bristol Zoo.

Special Events

5–6 June 2021: Brick Express.
26–27 June 2021: Teddy Bears' Picnic.
11–12 September 2021: Teddy Bears' Picnic.
18–19 September 2021: 1940s Weekend.
Santa & Mince Pie Specials usually run during December.

In addition, themed trains, including Murder Mystery and Dining Services, usually operate on the railway.

Bideford Railway Heritage Centre

Introduction and History

The broad gauge railway from Barnstaple first reached Instow and Bideford in 1855 and was extended south to Torrington in 1872. It was converted to a standard gauge line in 1877 and lost its passenger services in 1965. Milk traffic from Torrington continued until 1978 and ball clay from Petrockstow and Meeth used the route through Torrington until 1982. A final railtour visited Torrington in November 1982 and the line then closed. The track was lifted in 1985, which was when the first preservation group formed. Devon County Council purchased the trackbed from British Rail to create a coastal walkway and assisted the group's preservation efforts. These included redeveloping both the Bideford and Instow sites and laying a short stretch of railway track on part of the former route at Bideford, along which trains have operated since 2004. A new museum, located within a former parcels van, was opened at Bideford in 2019.

Contact Details

Website: www.bidefordrailway.co.uk
Tel: 07854 590503
Email: Written enquiries can be made from the website.
Address: Bideford Railway Heritage Centre, 4 Station Hill, Bideford EX39 4BB.

Transport Links

By Rail: Instow is six miles from Barnstaple station and the Bideford site is nine miles from both Barnstaple and Chapelton stations.
By Road: There are car parks a short walk from both Bideford station (EX39 4BB) and Instow signal box (EX39 4HW).
By Bike: Both sites are conveniently located on the traffic-free Tarka Trail and bicycles can be hired from various outlets along the trail, including at Bideford.

Opening Times

Bideford Station usually opens 10.30–16.00 on Saturdays and Sundays from Easter until late October and daily during school holidays. Instow signal box opens on occasional Sunday afternoons; please telephone or check the website for the latest opening times. Both sites can be seen from the outside on dates when they are not open.

Line Mileage and Journey Time

The track at Bideford is nearly a quarter of a mile long and the journey time is relatively short.

Stock List

Type	Number	Builder	Details
Diesel	3832	Hibberd	4wDM

Attractions

Diesel-hauled brake van rides are provided on the demonstration line at Bideford station. The site includes a new museum (opened 2019), an interactive visitor centre, a model railway and a rebuilt signal box with a working lever frame. At Instow, the signal box is preserved as it was when train services ended; visitors can pull the levers and turn the level crossing gate wheel. Bideford is also home to the medieval Long Bridge, a museum, gallery and various other attractions. Bideford station and Instow signal box are on the Tarka Trail, which is one of the country's longest traffic-free walking and cycling trails and forms part of the Devon Coast to Coast cycle route. The former Torrington Station, the base of the Tarka Valley Railway, is five miles to the south on the Tarka Trail (see the Proposed Railways section).

Bodmin & Wenford Railway

Introduction and History

The broad gauge railway between Plymouth and Truro opened in 1859, with a station at Bodmin Road, which is now known as Bodmin Parkway. The standard gauge branch from Bodmin Road to Bodmin General opened in 1887, extending to Boscarne in 1888 and making a connection with the existing Bodmin & Wadebridge Railway which had opened as early as 1834. Passenger services from Padstow to Bodmin ended in 1967, with freight continuing to Wadebridge until 1978 and china clay traffic to Wenfordbridge (via Bodmin General) surviving until 1983. The branch from Bodmin Parkway then closed. Shortly after closure, in 1984, the Bodmin Railway Preservation Society formed and the trackbed from Bodmin Parkway to Boscarne Junction was subsequently purchased from British Rail. The first shunting operations were carried out at Bodmin General station in 1986 and the first heritage passenger trains ran from Bodmin General to Bodmin Parkway in 1990, with services being extended to Boscarne Junction in 1996. A second platform has recently been built at Bodmin General and this will be brought into use once the track and signalling work have been completed. The railway plans to extend to the outskirts of Wadebride in stages, sharing the route with the Camel Trail.

Contact Details

Website: www.bodminrailway.co.uk
Tel: 01208 73555
Email: enquiries@bodminrailway.co.uk
Address: Bodmin & Wenford Railway, General Station, Bodmin, Cornwall, PL31 1AQ.

Transport Links

By Rail: There is a main line rail connection at Bodmin Parkway; simply cross to Platform 3.
By Road: Free parking is only available at Bodmin General station (PL31 1AG).
By Bike or on Foot: The traffic-free Camel Trail runs from Padstow and Wadebridge, directly to Boscarne Junction station. There are several locations along the route where bikes can be hired.

Opening Times

Trains operate on selected dates from mid-February until the end of October and every day from mid-May until early October, plus for Santa Specials in December. The times vary, depending on which timetable is in operation, with trains usually operating 11.00–16.00, or longer.

Line Mileage and Journey Time

0.00	Bodmin Parkway
1.25	Colesloggett Halt
3.50	Bodmin General
6.25	Boscarne Junction

A return journey takes around two hours, depending on the starting station.

Stock List

Type	Number	Builder	Details
Steam	2962	Bagnall	0-4-0ST
Steam	2572 JUDY	Bagnall	0-4-0ST
Steam	3058 ALFRED	Bagnall	0-4-0ST
Steam	75178	Bagnall	0-6-0ST
Steam	5552	GWR	2-6-2T
Steam	4247	GWR	2-8-0T
Diesel	22928	Fowler	0-4-0
Diesel	443642	Ruston & Hornsby	0-4-0
Diesel	P403D	Sentinel	0-4-0
Diesel	08444	British Railways	Class 08
Diesel	D3452	British Railways	Class 10
Diesel	37142	English Electric	Class 37
Diesel	47306	Brush Traction	Class 47
Diesel	50042	English Electric	Class 50
DMU	51947	British Railways	Class 108
DMU	55020	Pressed Steel	Class 121

Attractions

The branch line from Bodmin travels through the scenery of rural Cornwall. Luxury dining trains and train driving experiences are available. The traffic-free Camel Trail to Wadebridge and Padstow follows the route of the current and former railway and the River Camel. There are many other attractions in the region, including Bodmin Moor and many Cornish coastal walks and beaches, which can be reached from the railway and the Camel Trail.

Special Events

Events that usually take place on the railway include:

Mother's Day Cream Tea Train.
Easter at the Railway.
Santa Specials during December.

Bristol Harbour Railway

Introduction and History

When it opened in 1872, the Bristol Harbour Railway was a commercial system operating within Bristol Harbour. A heritage railway was established in 1978 as part of Bristol Museum (now known as M Shed) and this ran on the line between the museum site and the SS Great Britain. When commercial rail traffic ceased in 1987, the museum railway expanded to include the section along the northern bank of the River Avon. Unfortunately, recent episodes of subsidence have led to the suspension of trains on this longer section and trains currently only run between M Shed and the SS Great Britain. Repair work has begun, but it is likely to be 2022 before this is completed and train journeys can be extended.

Contact Details

Website: www.bristolmuseums.org.uk/m-shed
Tel: Written enquiries can be made from the M Shed website.
Email: 0117 352 6600
Address: M Shed, Princes Wharf, Wapping Road, Bristol, BS1 4RN.

Transport Links

By Rail: Bristol Temple Meads station is just under one mile from M Shed.
By Road: Chargeable parking is available nearby at The Grove (BS1 4RB) and Wapping Wharf (BS1 4RH).
By Bike: There is a cycle path to the south of M Shed; bicycle stands are on Museum Street.
By Boat: Ferries from Temple Meads station and Hotwells run to Prince Street Bridge and these are operated by Bristol Ferry Boats.

Opening Times

M Shed is open 10.00–17.00 Tuesday to Sunday. Train services operate at selected times, subject to availability.

Line Mileage and Journey Time

The operational section between M Shed and SS Great Britain runs for 0.4 miles and a return journey takes about 15 minutes. The southern spur, which runs for 0.7 miles from the site of M Shed, in not currently in use.

Stock List

Type	Number	Builder	Details
Steam	1764	Avonside	0-6-0ST
Steam	242	Fox Walker	0-6-0ST
Steam	1940 HENBURY	Peckett	0-6-0ST
Diesel	418792	Ruston & Hornsby	0-4-0

▲ Class 37 37142 was based in the South-West for several years during the late 1970s and early 1980s, before it moved to the Bodmin & Wenford Railway in 2003. On 22 June 2019, it is ready to leave Boscarne Junction with the 12.38 departure to Bodmin General. **Andy Chard**

▼ Avonside 0-6-0ST 1764 hauls passengers through the industrial environs of the Bristol Harbour Railway on 27 May 2019. **Glen Batten**

Attractions

As well as an operational railway, M Shed has a 1950s working dockside with electric cranes, boats, train transit and quayside operations. The site also has a café and shop. M Shed is located within Bristol Harbour, a short walk from SS Great Britain and it is close to the city centre, Bristol Museum & Art Gallery and Bristol Zoo.

Special Events

5 June–31 October 2021: British Street Art Exhibition.

Dartmoor Railway

Introduction and History

The railway from Exeter to Plymouth via Okehampton opened in stages. From Exeter, it reached North Tawton in 1865, Sampford Courtenay in 1867, Okehampton in 1871, Lydford in 1874 and it opened as through route in 1876. The line west of Meldon Quarry was closed in 1968 and passenger services between Exeter and Okehampton ended in 1972. The railway between Coleford Junction and Meldon Quarry continued to carry stone traffic and was later sold to Aggregate Industries. A collaboration between the owner and local organisations enabled seasonal passenger trains from Exeter to return to Okehampton each year from 1997. The railway was acquired by British American Railway Services in 2008 (see Weardale Railway) and then leased to the Dartmoor Railway, which began operating heritage trains between Okehampton and Meldon Viaduct. Stone trains from Meldon Quarry continued to use the line until the quarry was mothballed in 2011. The owning company went into administration in 2020 and the line between Coleford Junction and Okehampton has since become the possession of Network Rail. Main line passenger services between Exeter and Okehampton are due to return in 2021, but it is not currently clear when heritage trains between Okehampton and Meldon Quarry will be reinstated.

Contact Details

Website: www.dartmoor-railway-sa.org
Email: info@dartmoor-railway-sa.org
Address: Dartmoor Railway, Okehampton Station, Station Road, Okehampton, Devon, EX20 1EJ.

Transport Links

By Rail: Regular services between Exeter and Okehampton are due to return during 2021, providing a main line connection. At other times, the nearest stations are Copplestone, Morchard Road and Lapford, all of which are 14 miles from Okehampton.
By Road: Parking is available at Okehampton (EX20 1EJ).
By Bike: Travel on the Granite Way or Devon Coast to Coast Path, arriving via Meldon Viaduct.

Opening Times

When trains are operating, services usually run on Saturdays, Sundays and Bank Holidays between April and September.

Line Mileage and Journey Time

0.00	Meldon Viaduct
2.00	Okehampton
5.75	Sampford Courtenay
16.50	Yeoford
27.00	Exeter St Davids

A return journey from Okehampton to Meldon Quarry takes about 45 minutes.

Stock List

Type	Number	Builder	Details
Diesel	D4167	British Railways	Class 08
DMU	59520	Pressed Steel	Class 117
DEMU	60146, 60150, 60673, 60677, 60827 & 60831	British Railways	Class 205
EMU	61742, 61743 & 70273	British Railways	Class 411
EMU	76747, 69310 & 69332	British Railways	Class 421
EMU	76277	British Railways	Class 491

Attractions

There is a tea room and small museum located at Okehampton station and the Castle and Museum of Dartmoor Life are both less than one mile away. Many walks can be taken from the area, such as to the summit of nearby Yes Tor. The traffic-free Granite Way runs from Meldon Quarry station, crossing Meldon Viaduct and this continues along the railway trackbed to Lydford and beyond. The route is also part of the Devon Coast to Coast Path. There are many other attractions in the region, including the narrow gauge Lynton & Barnstaple Railway, the Dartmouth Steam Railway (see below) and the South Devon Railway.

Dartmouth Steam Railway

Introduction and History

The broad gauge railway reached Torre in 1848 and this was extended to Paignton in 1859 and to Kingswear in 1864. The line was converted to a standard gauge railway in 1892. The Dart Valley Railway was a commercial venture established in 1962 to operate the line from Totnes to Buckfastleigh, after the route was closed by British Rail in 1962 (see South Devon Railway). The line from Paignton to Kingswear was first threatened with closure in 1968. In 1972 the Dart Valley Railway acquired the route and started operating trains on it from the start of 1973. In 2010 the Dart Valley Railway acquired two passenger carrying boats and its two heritage railways became separate organisations. The route from Paignton to Kingswear, with its connecting river cruises, is now known as the Dartmouth Steam Railway & River Boat Company.

Contact Details

Website: www.dartmouthrailriver.co.uk
Tel: 01803 555872
Email: Written enquiries can be made from the website.
Address: Dartmouth Steam Railway, Queens Park Station, Torbay Road, Paignton, TQ4 6AF.

Transport Links

By Rail: The railway connects with the main line network at Paignton.
By Road: Churston (TQ5 0LL) is the only station with free parking and this is very limited. There are chargeable car parks near to Paignton (TQ4 6AF), Goodrington (TQ4 6LN) and Kingswear stations (TQ6 0AA), which can be very busy during the peak season.
By Boat: River crossings from Dartmouth to Kingswear carry foot passengers. As the River Dart is tidal, the crossing times vary.

Opening Times

Trains operate on most days of the year, with no services on selected weekdays between November and March inclusive.

Line Mileage and Journey Time

0.00	Paignton
0.75	Goodrington Sands
3.00	Churston
4.00	Greenway Halt
6.75	Kingswear

A return journey takes one hour 15 minutes.

Stock List

Type	Number	Builder	Details
Steam	2253	Baldwin Locomotive Works	2-8-0
Steam	4277	GWR	2-8-0T
Steam	5239	GWR	2-8-0T
Steam	7827	British Railways	4-6-0
Steam	75014	British Railways	4-6-0
Diesel	03371	British Railways	Class 03
Diesel	D2192	British Railways	Class 03
Diesel	D3014	British Railways	Class 08
Diesel	6975	English Electric	Class 37
DMU	59719	British Railways	Class 115
DMU	59003 & 59004	British Railways	Class 116
DMU	59488, 59494, 59503, 59507, 59513 & 59517	Pressed Steel	Class 117

Attractions

The railway offers a variety of round trips, with different combinations of rail, river cruise, paddle steamer and bus tours available. Trains offer views of the English Channel and River Dart and there are various walks which can be taken from or between the railway's stations. The visitor centre situated in a railway carriage at Kingswear is free to enter. Steam locomotive footplate experiences can be arranged. Greenway House and Garden are a short walk (or shuttle bus ride) from Greenway Halt. The region, which includes the towns of Brixham, Torquay, Totnes and Dartmouth, is a popular holiday destination, with plenty of coastlines, beaches and attractions within reach from the railway.

Special Events

Events that usually take place on the railway include:

Dartmouth Regatta in August, during which additional trains operate.
Candlelit Dartmouth during November.
Santa Express and Train of Lights during December.

▲ On 10 July 2019, GWR 4-6-0 7820 "DINMORE MANOR" and a rake of "chocolate and cream" livery Mark 1 coaches cross Waterhead Creak and approach Kingswear, the southern terminus of the Dartmouth Steam Railway. **Glen Batten**

Dean Forest Railway

Introduction and History

A three foot six inch gauge horse-drawn plateway from Lydney to Parkend opened in 1810. This was used to carry minerals from the Dean Forest to the River Severn for onward transit and it became part of a larger tramway network. When the broad gauge main line from Gloucester to Chepstow opened in 1851, an interchange station was built at Lydney, allowing the minerals to be carried further by rail. The railway's owners purchased five three foot six inch gauge steam locomotives in the 1860s. However, the line was converted to Brunel's seven foot broad gauge in 1872 and then further converted to standard gauge within 20 years. Traffic on the route increased as passenger services from Lydney to Parkend and beyond commenced in 1875 and when the original Severn Bridge opened in 1879, it connected the railway with Sharpness Docks (see Vale of Berkeley Railway). Passenger services ended in 1929 and freight on the line declined through the 20th Century. Traffic across the Severn Bridge ended when it was damaged beyond repair in 1960 and by 1967 there was just one daily goods train from Lydney Junction to Parkend. A preservation group formed in 1970 and held its first event in 1971. The trackbed was purchased from British Rail in 1985 and the heritage railway has been extended in stages, reaching Norchard, then Lydney Junction in 1995 and Parkend in 2005. There are various plans to develop the railway; a new carriage shed and restoration works are planned for Lydney and a passing loop and second platform are to be built at Whitecroft. It is hoped that work can begin soon on a three-mile northern extension to a new station near Beechenhurst Lodge and there are long-term plans for the railway to be extended a further three miles north to Cinderford.

Contact Details

Website: www.deanforestrailway.co.uk
Tel: 01594 845840
Email: contact@deanforestrailway.co.uk
Address: Dean Forest Railway, Forest Road, Lydney, Gloucestershire, GL15 4ET.

Transport Links

By Rail: The nearest station is Lydney, which is a five-minute walk to Lydney Junction.
By Road: Free parking is available at Norchard (GL15 4ET). There is no parking at the other stations.

Opening Times

The railway operates on most weekends, Wednesdays and Bank Holidays and on selected other dates.

Line Mileage and Journey Time

0.00	Lydney Junction
0.75	Lydney Town
1.50	Norchard Low Level & High Level
3.00	Whitecroft Halt
4.25	Parkend

A return journey takes about one hour 45 minutes, depending where the journey starts from.

Stock List

Type	Number	Builder	Details
Steam	2221	Andrew Barclay	0-4-0ST
Steam	USKMOUTH 1 (2147)	Peckett	0-4-0ST
Steam	9681	British Railways	0-6-0PT
Steam	9682	British Railways	0-6-0PT
Steam	65 (3889)	Hunslet	0-6-0ST
Steam	2411	Hunslet	0-6-0ST
Steam	2413	Hunslet	0-6-0ST
Steam	WARRIOR (3823)	Hunslet	0-6-0ST
Steam	WILBERT (3806)	Hunslet	0-6-0ST
Steam	152	Robert Stephenson & Hawthorns	0-6-0ST
Steam	5541	GWR	2-6-2T
Diesel	3947	Hibberd	4wDM

Diesel	4210127	Fowler	0-4-0
Diesel	6688	Hunslet	0-4-0
Diesel	DON CORBETT (5622)	Hunslet	0-4-0
Diesel	D2069	British Railways	Class 03
Diesel	08238	British Railways	Class 08
Diesel	08473	British Railways	Class 08
Diesel	08769	British Railways	Class 08
Diesel	D9521	British Railways	Class 14
Diesel	D9555	British Railways	Class 14
Diesel	31210	Brush Traction	Class 31
Diesel	31235	Brush Traction	Class 31
Diesel	31466	Brush Traction	Class 31
DMU	50619, 50632, 51566, 51914, 52044, 56492 & 59387	British Railways	Class 108

Attractions

There is a railway museum at Norchard, which has a large number of exhibits. The site also has a locomotive restoration shed (guides are usually available to show visitors around), a shop and café. There are various food themed trains and footplate experiences can be arranged. Many walks can be made, with routes from each of the railway's stations, including a one mile walk from Lydney Junction along the trackbed to Lydney Harbour, where there are views of the River Severn and Sharpness. Parkend station is less than half a mile from route 42 of the National Cycle Network, some of which continues along the railway trackbed. Other attractions in the area include Clearwell Caves and the Dean Forest, with its sculpture trail.

Special Events

Events that usually take place on the railway include:

Brake Van Specials.
Diesel Gala.
Evening Steam Fish & Chip Trains.
Evening Steam & Beer Trains.
Murder Mystery on a Steam Train.
Santa Specials during December.

▲ On 4 July 2019, when Peckett 0-4-0WT 1788 "KILMERSDON" was on loan to the Helston Railway, the 1929-built locomotive is about to leave Prospidnick with the 11.30 to Truthall Halt. **Ian Beardsley**

East Somerset Railway

Introduction and History

The railway from Witham (between the extant Frome and Bruton stations) to Shepton Mallet opened in 1858 and was later extended to Wells where the railway continued to Yatton. The line carried locally quarried rock as well as passengers, originally as a broad gauge railway, until it was converted to standard gauge in 1874. Passenger traffic ended in 1963 and freight ceased the following year. In the early 1970s, when the late artist David Shepherd was looking for a home for two steam locomotives he had acquired, he purchased and then developed the Cranmore site. This became the East Somerset Heritage Railway, which first opened in 1974 and this line is still connected to the main line network via the nearby Torr Works Quarry. It is hoped that the railway will be extended, with the potential to do so in either direction, however there are no immediate plans to proceed with this.

Contact Details

Website: www.eastsomersetrailway.com
Tel: 01749 880417
Email: info@eastsomersetrailway.com
Address: Cranmore Railway Station, Cranmore, Shepton Mallet, Somerset, BA4 4QP.

Transport Links

By Rail: The nearest railway stations are Frome (nine miles) and Bruton (eight miles).
By Road: There is a large, free car park a short walk from Cranmore Station (BA4 4QP).

Opening Times

Trains usually operate on Saturdays, Sundays and selected weekdays from mid-March until late October, plus Santa Specials in December.

Line Mileage and Journey Time

0.00   Cranmore
0.50   Cranmore West
1.00   Merryfield Lane
2.00   Mendip Vale

A return journey takes about 40 minutes.

Stock List

Type	Number	Builder	Details
Steam	1719	Andrew Barclay	0-4-0ST
Steam	1 (7609)	Robert Stephson & Hawthorns	0-6-0T
Steam	46447	British Railways	2-6-0
Steam	4110	GWR	2-6-2T
Steam	4555	GWR	2-6-2T
Diesel	10165	Sentinel	0-4-0
Diesel	10175	Sentinel	0-4-0
Diesel	10199	Sentinel	0-4-0
Diesel	10218	Sentinel	0-6-0
Diesel	10221	Sentinel	0-6-0
DMU	51909 & 56271	British Railways	Class 108

Attractions

Cranmore station was refurbished in 2020 and now houses a museum. The Cranmore base is also home to the David Shepherd Discovery Centre which showcases the artist's life and the railway's history, a museum, signal box, miniature railway, children's play area and café. Visitors can also explore the engine shed and workshop, where restoration projects are underway. The railway offers footplate and driving experiences, with a choice of a steam locomotive or a multiple unit. Nearby attractions include Nunney Castle, Shepton Mallet, Glastonbury and Wells. The Strawberry Line Trail is located to the west and this mainly traffic-free route between Yatton and Cheddar follows the course of the former railway.

Special Events

Events that usually take place on the railway include:

Steam Gala.
Easter Event.
Various child and family themed events.
Santa Specials during December.

Helston Railway

Introduction and History

The branch line from Gwinear Road, between Hayle and Camborne, to Helston opened in 1887, creating the most southerly railway and station in mainland Britain. Despite much opposition to the threatened closure, the final passenger train left Helston behind Class 22, D6312 in November 1962. Freight services continued until October 1964 and the track was lifted in 1965. The first preservation group formed 40 years later in 2005; a base was established at Trevarno Halt and vegetation clearance along the disused trackbed began. One mile of track was relaid and the first trains from Truthall Halt to Prospidnick ran in 2011. Two sections of trackbed have recently been acquired and the railway plans to extend south to Nancegollan and Water-Ma-Trout on the outskirts of Helston, which would increase the length of the line to around three miles.

Contact Details

Website: www.helstonrailway.co.uk
Tel: 07901 977 597
Email: info@helstonrailway.co.uk
Address: Trevarno Farm, Prospidnick, Helston, Cornwall, TR13 0RY.

Transport Links

By Rail: The nearest railway station is Camborne, which is seven miles away.
By Road: Free car parking is available at Prospidnick Halt (TR13 0RY).

Opening Times

The railway usually operates on Sundays, Bank Holidays and Thursdays, and on selected other weekdays between mid-March and early November, with services between 10.30 and 16.00.

Line Mileage and Journey Time

0.00 Truthall Halt
1.00 Prospidnick Halt

A return journey takes about 30 minutes from Prospidnick.

Stock List

Type	Number	Builder	Details
Steam	WILLIAM MURDOCH	Peckett	0-4-0ST
Diesel	97649	Ruston & Hornsby	0-4-0
Diesel	395305	Ruston & Hornsby	0-4-0
DMU	50413 & 56169	Park Royal	Class 103
DMU	59521	Pressed Steel	Class 117
DMU	51616 & 51622	British Railways	Class 127

Attractions

Two of the three surviving Class 103 Park Royal multiple unit vehicles are based at the railway, although these are not currently operational and are used as a buffet. There is also a gift shop with railway books and souvenirs. Truthall Halt has been rebuilt as an exact replica of the original building and the quality of the rebuild was recognised with a Heritage Railway Association award in 2019. There are many other attractions in western Cornwall, including the National Seal Sanctuary, Poldark Mine, Lizard Peninsula and the South West Coastal Path.

Special Events

Events that usually take place on the railway include:

Easter Family Fun & Easter Egg Trail.
Return to the 1940s.
Heritage Weekend.
Kids for a Quid.
Santa Specials.

Pallot Steam, Motor & General Museum, Jersey

Introduction and History

The museum is one of the few sites within this book which is not located on the site of a former railway. Don Pallot (1910–1996) was an engineer and inventor, who after collecting various mechanical items including steam engines, created a museum to house these and this opened in 1990. The collection includes locomotives from mainland Britain, Belgium and Alderney. In 1996 the engine shed, railway line and station were opened and the engine shed was extended in 2002.

Contact Details

Website: www.pallotmuseum.co.uk
Tel: 01534 865307
Email: info@pallotmuseum.co.uk
Address: The Pallot Steam, Motor & General Museum, Rue de Bechet, Trinity, Jersey, Channel Islands, JE3 5BE.

Transport Links

By Rail: There is no rail service on Jersey.
By Road: There is ample free car parking at the museum (JE3 5BE).

Opening Times

The museum usually opens Monday to Saturday from the start of April until the end of October, with the exception of some bank holidays. Steam trains usually depart on the hour between 11.00 and 16.00 on Thursdays and during occasional specials events.

Line Mileage and Journey Time

Trains operate on an oval shaped circuit, which runs for just over a quarter of a mile and the journey time is relatively short.

Stock List

Type	Number	Builder	Details
Steam	J T DALY	Bagnall	0-4-0ST
Steam	2085	Peckett	0-4-0ST
Steam	2129 Kestrel	Peckett	0-4-0ST
Steam	LA MEUSE	Belgian	0-6-0T
Diesel	27734	North British	0-4-0

Attractions

The museum's exhibits include a 1912 steam roller, steam locomotives, tractors, classic and vintage motor vehicles, toys, a church pipe organ, a Compton theatre organ and details of Jersey's history. The museum is close to Jersey Zoo (two miles), St Helier (three and a half miles), the island's coast and various other attractions.

Special Events

Events that usually take place at the museum include:

Liberation Day Steam & Motor Fayre in May.
Steam Threshing & Motor Fayre in September.

Plym Valley Railway

Introduction and History

The original broad gauge railway from Devonport Junction (to the east of Plymouth) to Tavistock South and Lydford opened in 1859. This was extended to Launceston in 1865 and the line was converted to standard gauge in 1892. Passenger services ended in 1962 and it closed as a through route when freight ceased in 1964. A group formed in 1980 and began working towards creating a heritage railway. The first section of track was laid in 2001 and preserved train services began in 2008, travelling north along the original route from Marsh Mills. The line was extended to a new station at Plym Bridge in 2012, which opened exactly 50 years after the final passenger train ran in 1962. There are long-term aims to extend the railway further north towards Tavistock.

Contact Details

Website: www.plymrail.co.uk
Tel: 01752 345078
Email: plymrail@yahoo.co.uk
Address: Plym Valley Railway, Coypool Road, Plympton, Plymouth, PL7 4NW.

Transport Links

By Rail: The nearest station is Plymouth, which is four miles from Marsh Mills.
By Road: There are car parks at Coypool Park and Ride (PL7 4TB) and Plymbridge Road (PL7 4SR), which are very close to Marsh Mills and Plym Bridge stations respectively.
By Bike: Route 27 of the National Cycle Network follows the course of the present and former railway.

Opening Times

The railway usually operates on Sundays from March to November and on selected other dates.

Line Mileage and Journey Time

0.00   Marsh Mills
1.25   Plym Bridge

A return journey takes about half an hour.

▲ On 20 July 2019, Class 04 D2271 brings the 11.25 Buckfastleigh–Totnes Riverside round Caddaford Curve on the South Devon Railway. **Tony Christie**

Stock List

Type	Number	Builder	Details
Steam	3121	Bagnall	0-4-0F
Steam	705	Andrew Barclay	0-4-0ST
Steam	ALBERT (2248)	Andrew Barclay	0-4-0ST
Steam	BYFIELD (2655)	Bagnall	0-6-0ST
Steam	TKH49 (5374)	Fablok	0-6-0T
Diesel	10077	Sentinel	0-4-0
Diesel	125V	Thomas Hill	0-4-0
Diesel	D2046	British Railways	Class 03
Diesel	13002	British Railways	Class 08
Diesel	31190	Brush Traction	Class 31
Diesel	51365 & 51407	Pressed Steel	Class 117
Diesel	142023 (55564 & 55614)	BREL/Leyland	Class 142

Attractions

The 7¼ inch gauge Plym Valley Miniature Railway can be found at the railway's Marsh Mills base, along with the locomotive shed, a shop and café. The Devon Coast to Coast walking and cycle route (Route 27 of the National Cycle Network) travels alongside the railway on its journey from Plymouth to Barnstaple. Saltram House is near to Marsh Mills and Plymbridge Woods is adjacent to Plym Bridge station (both National Trust). Further nearby attractions include Plymouth Ski Centre, Crownhill Fort, the National Marine Aquarium and Merchant's House Museum.

Special Events

Events that usually take place on the railway include:

New Year Mince Pie Specials.
Easter Egg Hunt.
Summer Family Fun Day.
Halloween Event during October.
Santa Specials during December.
Evening dining and cream tea trains operate on selected dates.

▲ The Somerset & Dorset Railway has recently extended its running length. On 7 March 2020, Class 03 D2128 sits at the front of a mixed goods train at Midsomer Norton station, with Class 08 D4095 and English Electric 0-6-0 D1120 to its right.
Tony Christie

Somerset & Dorset Railway, Midsomer Norton

Introduction and History

Midsomer Norton South station opened in 1874, when the single-track extension of the Somerset & Dorset Railway (S&D) to Bath was completed. The track was doubled in 1886, but after declining use, Midsomer Norton station and the S&D route were closed in 1966. The Somerset & Dorset Railway Heritage Trust acquired the Midsomer Norton site in 1995 and has since restored the station building, signal box and goods shed. A stretch of operational track was laid, running south from the station and this was extended towards Chilcompton Tunnel in 2019, increasing the railway's length to one mile. There is potential to extend the line in both directions, although before it can be extended further south, substantial quantities of landfill waste will need to be excavated.

Contact Details

Website: www.sdjr.co.uk
Tel: 01761 411 221
Email: general@sdjr.co.uk
Address: Somerset & Dorset Railway, Midsomer Norton Station, Silver Street, Midsomer Norton, BA3 2EY.

Transport Links

By Rail: The nearest stations are Frome (11 miles), Bath (11 miles) or Trowbridge (14 miles).
By Road: There is limited disabled parking at Midsomer Norton South station (BA3 2EY). Free parking is available at Norton Hill School (BA3 4AD) at weekends and during school holidays, or nearby in the town centre.
By Bike: The Five Arches Cycle & Walkway from Radstock to Midsomer Norton is a spur off the Colliers Way, which is route 24 of the National Cycle Network.

Opening Times

Trains usually operate on selected Saturdays and Sundays. The station, shop and museum are usually open every Sunday, subject to volunteer availability.

Line Mileage and Journey Time

0.00   Midsomer Norton
1.00   Southern limit

A return journey takes about 25 minutes.

Stock List

Type	Number	Builder	Details
Steam	7109	Sentinel	4wVBT
Diesel	D1120	English Electric	0-6-0
Diesel	03901	British Railways	Class 03
Diesel	D4095	British Railways	Class 08
DMU	59664	British Railways	Class 115

Attractions

The Midsomer Norton base is home to the restored Victorian station buildings, a museum devoted to the S&D, a small pillar box war museum, a gift and second-hand bookshop. The East Somerset Railway and Avon Valley Railway are eight and 13 miles away respectively. Other nearby attractions include Radstock Museum, The Colliers Way cycle route, the city of Bath and the Mendip Hills.

Special Events

22–23 May 2021: Grand Re-opening.
29–31 May 2021: Family Weekend.
20 June 2021: Fathers' Day Cream Teas.
2 July 2021: Summer Mixed Traffic Gala.
16–17 October 2021: End of Season Gala.

South Devon Railway

Introduction and History

The broad gauge branch line from Totnes to Ashburton opened in 1872 and was converted to standard gauge over a single weekend in 1892. After usage declined, it was closed to passengers in 1958 and to freight in 1962. The Dart Valley Light Railway formed in 1962 to operate the route as a commercial tourist railway; the first locomotives arrived in 1965 and the railway was formally opened by Dr Richard Beeching in 1969. The northern Buckfastleigh to Ashburton section of the railway was lost in 1971, when the A38 was redeveloped and the line was severed. The independent railway later became uneconomical and was threatened with closure in 1989. It survived when an existing charity based at the railway took it over and this was renamed the South Devon Railway Association. The first trains to officially operate in preservation ran in 1991 and in the years since, the railway has continued to grow in popularity and success. Ashburton station building survives; plans to redevelop the site have been successfully fought off, with the hope that it might be reconnected to the South Devon Railway in future.

Contact Details

Website: www.southdevonrailway.co.uk
Tel: 01364 644370
Email: trains@southdevonrailway.org
Address: South Devon Railway, Dartbridge Road, Buckfastleigh, Devon, TQ11 0DZ.

Transport Links

By Rail: Totnes railway station is less than half a mile away and the journey to Totnes Riverside involves crossing a footbridge over the River Dart.
By Road: Ample car parking is available at Buckfastleigh (TQ11 0DZ). There are a number of car parks near Totnes Riverside station, the nearest of which is about half a mile away.

Opening Times

The railway usually operates during most weekends through the year, with regular weekday running from mid-March until early November and during December for Santa and Mince Pie Specials.

Line Mileage and Journey Time

0.00   Buckfastleigh
3.00   Staverton
6.75   Totnes Riverside

A return journey takes about 1 hour 15 minutes.

Stock List

Type	Number	Builder	Details
Steam	151 TINY	Sara & Co	0-4-0 Broad Gauge
Steam	1690	Peckett	0-4-0T
Steam	2031	Peckett	0-4-0T
Steam	1420	GWR	0-4-2T
Steam	3205	GWR	0-6-0
Steam	1369	GWR	0-6-0PT
Steam	6412	GWR	0-6-0PT
Steam	GLENDOWER	Hunslet	0-6-0ST
Steam	5474	Kitson	0-6-0ST
Steam	4160	GWR	2-6-2PT
Steam	5542	GWR	2-6-2T
Steam	2873	GWR	2-8-0
Steam	3803	GWR	2-8-0
Diesel	MFP4	Fowler	0-4-0
Diesel	2745	Yorkshire Engine Co.	0-6-0
Diesel	D2246	Robert Stephenson & Hawthorns	Class 04
Diesel	D2271	Robert Stephenson & Hawthorns	Class 04
Diesel	D3721	British Railways	Class 09
Diesel	D7535	British Railways	Class 25
Diesel	D7541	British Railways	Class 25

Diesel	D7612	British Railways	Class 25
Diesel	D6501	BRCW	Class 33
Diesel	6737	English Electric	Class 37
Diesel	D402	English Electric	Class 50
DMU	59740	British Railways	Class 115
DMU	51352, 51376 & 59493	Pressed Steel	Class 117
DMU	55000	GRCW	Class 122

Attractions

The railway travels along a secluded and scenic route that follows the River Dart. There is a museum at Buckfastleigh which tells the story of the line and houses the UK's only surviving original broad gauge locomotive. There is a large gift and model shop at Buckfastleigh and footplate driving experiences can be arranged. Nearby attractions include Totnes Rare Breeds Farm, Dartmoor Otters & Buckfast Butterflies, Buckfast Abbey and Totnes with its historic market.

Special Events

Events that usually take place on the railway include:

Days Out with Thomas.
Diesel Gala.
South Devon 1940s Festival.
The Polar Express and Mince Pie Specials during December.

▲ One of the Swanage Railway's Class 117 DMUs leaves Corfe Castle with the 13.20 Swanage–Norden service on 21 July 2018.
Glen Batten

Swanage Railway

Introduction and History

The branch line from Wareham to Swanage opened in 1885 and remained in use until it was closed by British Rail in early 1972, after which the track was promptly lifted. The Swanage Railway Society formed in 1972 and successfully thwarted several attempts to demolish Swanage station which became its base. Trains first worked on a short section of track in 1979 and the line was lengthened in several stages, reaching Norden in 1992 and reconnecting to the main line at Wareham in 2017. From 2018, main line operator South Western Railway has run summer Saturday trains from Salisbury to Corfe Castle, brining through services to the Swanage branch for the first time in many years.

Contact Details

Website: www.swanagerailway.co.uk
Tel: 01929 425800
Email: info@swanagerailway.co.uk
Address: Swanage Railway, Station House, Swanage, Dorset, BH19 1HB.

Transport Links

By Rail: There is a main line rail connection at Wareham. However, the railway only operates through trains to Wareham seasonally.
By Road: Norden station has a 350-space car and coach park just off the A351 and charges apply (BH20 5DW). There is no car parking at Corfe Castle station or Herston Halt. Harmans Cross has a small car park where charges apply (BH19 3EB) and there is a paid car park a five minute-walk from Swanage station (BH20 1PW).
By Boat: From April to October www.citycruises.com operate between Poole Quay and Swanage; the journey takes one hour each way.

Opening Times

Trains usually operate throughout the year, with daily services from late March until mid-October.

Line Mileage and Journey Time

0.00	Swanage
0.50	Herston Halt
3.00	Harmans Cross
5.00	Corfe Castle
5.50	Norden
11.00	Wareham

A return journey takes about one hour.

Stock List

Type	Number	Builder	Details
Steam	30053	LSWR	0-4-4T
Steam	31625	Southern Railway	2-6-0
Steam	31806	Southern Railway	2-6-0
Steam	31874	Southern Railway	2-6-0
Steam	80104	British Railways	2-6-4T
Steam	30120	LSWR	4-4-0
Steam	34072	British Railways	4-6-2
Steam	34010	Southern Railway	4-6-2
Steam	34028	Southern Railway	4-6-2
Diesel	4210132	Fowler	0-4-0
Diesel	Beryl	Hibberd	0-4-0
Diesel	08436	British Railways	Class 08
Diesel	D3591	British Railways	Class 08
Diesel	33111	BRCW	Class 33
Diesel	D6515	BRCW	Class 33
DMU	51356, 51388, 51392 & 59486	Pressed Steel	Class 117
DMU	55028	Pressed Steel	Class 121
EMU	70855, 76275, 76298 & 76322	British Railways	Class 491
EMU	70824	Metropolitan Cammell	Class 491

Attractions

The railway has a variety of main line locomotives, which are often joined by visiting examples for special events. There is a small railway museum at Corfe Castle station and Purbeck Mineral & Mining Museum can be found at Norden station. Corfe Castle is visible from the railway and can be reached by way of an uphill walk from its namesake station. There is plenty to see in the busy town of Swanage, the surrounding Isle of Purbeck and other well-known sites nearby, including Lulworth Cove, Durdle Door, Poole and the Jurassic Coast.

Special Events

17 May 2021: Sea Train Adventure.
10–12 September 2021: Classic Transport Rally.
From 1 October 2021: Taster Driving Experience.
Seasonal trains usually operate during December.

Swindon & Cricklade Railway

Introduction and History

The railway from Swindon Town to Cirencester Watermoor opened in 1883. Cricklade and Blunsdon were intermediate stations on the route and opened in 1883 and 1895 respectively. Blunsdon closed to passengers in 1924 and all passenger services were withdrawn in 1961. After this trains occasionally ran to Moredon Power Station, which was near the site of the present-day Taw Valley Halt, until 1969. The Swindon & Cricklade Railway Preservation Society formed in 1978 and took over the empty trackbed. Track laying began in 1980 and the first heritage steam trains used the route in 1984. In 2000 the railway reached Hayes Knoll and since then it has been extended in stages. It is currently being extended in both directions; to the south a new larger station at Moulsdon Country Park is being constructed. A 1.25-mile northern extension to a new station near the village of Cricklade is also in progress; track has been laid on part of the route and further lengths of rail recovered from the closed Didcot A Power Station are yet to be laid.

Contact Details

Website: www.swindon-cricklade-railway.org
Tel: 01793 771615
Email: Written enquiries can be made from the website.
Address: Swindon & Cricklade Railway, Blunsdon Station, Tadpole Lane, Swindon, SN25 2DA.

Transport Links

By Rail: Swindon railway station is five miles from Blunsdon.
By Road: Free car parking is available at Blunsdon station (SN25 2DA). At Mouldon Hill car park, which is a short walk from Taw Valley Halt (SN25 1WH), parking is provided by Swindon Borough Council. There is no road access at Hayes Knoll station.

Opening Times

The railway usually operates on Sundays for the majority of the year, on Saturdays from April to September and on selected weekdays.

Line Mileage and Journey Time

0.00	Taw Valley Halt
1.25	Blunsdon
1.75	Hayes Knoll

A return journey takes about one hour.

Stock List

Type	Number	Builder	Details
Steam	2354	Andrew Barclay	0-4-0ST
Steam	2138	Andrew Barclay	0-6-0ST
Steam	3135	Fablok	0-6-0T
Steam	1464	Hudswell Clarke	0-6-0T
Steam	6695	Armstrong Whitworth	0-6-2T
Steam	5637	GWR	0-6-2T

Steam	35011	Southern Railway	4-6-2
Diesel	4210137	Fowler	0-4-0DM
Diesel	4220031	Fowler	0-4-0DM
Diesel	21442 WOODBINE	Fowler	0-4-0
Diesel	D2022	British Railways	Class 03
Diesel	D2152	British Railways	Class 03
Diesel	D3261	British Railways	Class 08
Diesel	09004	British Railways	Class 09
Diesel	97651	Ruston & Hornsby	Class 97
Electro-Diesel	E6003	British Railways	Class 73
DMU	79978	AC Cars	Railbus
DMU	59514	Pressed Steel	Class 117
DMU	51074 & 51104	GRCW	Class 119
DEMU	60669 & 60822	British Railways	Class 205
DEMU	60127	British Railways	Class 207

Attractions

There are two museums at Blunsdon; one showcases the area's railway history and the other is a wartime museum run in connection with a re-enactment group, which has various exhibits including an air raid shelter. The railway's restoration and maintenance centre and a restored signal box are at Hayes Knoll. Train driver experience days are available. The nearby Cotswold Water Park consists of the largest amount of redundant gravel pits in the country, which have been converted for social uses including an inland beach resort, power boating and sailing.

Special Events

Events that usually take place on the railway include:

Mother's Day Event.
Steam, Diesel and Mixed Traffic Galas.
Military Weekend.
Santa Specials from late November.

▲ 33111 is one of the two Class 33s based at the Swanage Railway. On 21 July 2018, it was standing in for a steam locomotive and is seen passing Corfe Castle with the 14.40 Norden–Swanage.

Glen Batten

Tamar Belle Heritage Centre

Introduction and History

Bere Ferrers station opened in 1890, on the new railway between Devonport and Lydford, which completed the line across central Devon linking Exeter and Plymouth via Okehampton. During its first seven years the station was known as Beer Ferris, until it was given the spelling that it retains today, which was thought to be more sophisticated as it did not contain the word "beer"! Through services west of Okehampton were withdrawn in 1968, after which the line through Bere Ferrers continued to what became its terminus at Gunnislake. Beer Ferrers' station building then moved into private ownership and was first opened to the public when it celebrated its centenary in 1990. A section of standard gauge railway was laid and Bagnall 0-4-0ST "ALFRED" and a brake van were borrowed from the Bodmin & Wenford Railway, so that passenger rides could be provided to mark the occasion. Since then, the site has been developed into a heritage centre with a collection of railway exhibits, including on-site bed & breakfast accommodation within two ex-LNER teak corridor carriages.

Contact Details

Website: www.tamarbelle.co.uk
Tel: 07813 360066
Email: enquiries@tamarbelle.co.uk
Address: The Tamar Belle Heritage Centre, Bere Ferrers Station, Yelverton, Devon, PL20 7LT

Transport Links

By Rail: The Heritage Centre is on the site of Bere Ferrers station, which is approximately half way along the branch line between Plymouth and Gunnislake.
By Road: Free parking is available at the centre (PL20 7LT).

Opening Times

The railway operates on-demand and visitors should contact the owner in advance to make arrangements to travel on it. Open days are occasionally held and these are advertised in advance.

Line Mileage and Journey Time

The demonstration line is approximately 200 metres long and the journey time is relatively short.

Stock List

Type	Number	Builder	Details
Steam	HILDA	Peckett	0-4-0ST
Diesel	A.S. HARRIS	Hunslet	0-4-0DM
Diesel	EARL OF MOUNT EDGECUMBE	Hunslet	0-4-0DM
Diesel	LORD ST. LEVAN	Hunslet	0-4-0DM

Attractions

The Heritage Centre at Bere Ferrers has an exhibition coach and a visitor centre situated within a former sleeping coach. The original station building and various railway exhibits can be seen including a restored L&SWR signal box, a second signal box within a converted cattle wagon, a turntable, a yard crane and a collection of carriages. Signalling demonstrations are available and these should be arranged in advance. In addition to carrying passengers, the railway also operates demonstration freight and mixed traffic trains. Ex-LNER teak coaches 3132 & 1459 have been converted to bed and breakfast accommodation and the Tamar Belle dining coach is adjacent to these. The saloon car can be booked for meetings and social functions. There are several nearby heritage railways including the Plym Valley, the South Devon and the Dartmouth Steam Railway. Other nearby attractions include Dartmoor National Park, Dartmoor Prison Museum, the market town of Tavistock and the coastal city of Plymouth.

West Somerset Railway

Introduction and History

The broad gauge branch line from Taunton to Watchet opened in 1862; this was extended to Minehead in 1874 and converted to a standard gauge line in 1882. By the 1960s it was only profitable during the summer months, when it carried large volumes of seasonal passengers. British Rail closed the line in 1971, but unlike many other closed lines, the track was left in place. A society formed in 1971 to preserve the railway and the first stage of this aim was realised in 1973, when Somerset County Council purchased the line from BR and leased it back to the group. In 1975 vegetation was cleared to allow Class 25 25059 to make a trip to Minehead to collect LMS 6229 'Duchess of Hamilton' from the Butlins holiday camp. The first heritage passenger services operated between Minehead and Blue Anchor in 1976 and these were extended to Bishops Lydeard in 1979. When BR upgraded the signalling in the Taunton area in 1981, the rail connection to Bishops Lydeard was removed. The structure of the railway changed during the 1980s, utilising more volunteers which, along with support from Somerset County Council, triggered a growth in passenger revenues and infrastructure investment. The main line connection at Taunton has since been reinstated and this is used by occasional charter trains. The railway aims to return regular through passenger services to Taunton.

Contact Details

Website: www.west-somerset-railway.co.uk
Tel: 01643 704996
Email: info@wsrail.net
Address: West Somerset Railway, The Railway Station, Minehead, Somerset, TA24 5BG.

Transport Links

By Rail: The nearest station is Taunton, which is five miles from Bishops Lydeard.
By Road: There is a large free car park at Bishops Lydeard with a 2.1 metre height limit (TA4 3RU) and pay & display parking at Watchet (TA23 0AQ) and Minehead (TA24 5BG).

Opening Times

The railway usually operates at weekends and on the majority of weekdays from April to October, plus for Santa Expresses during December.

Line Mileage and Journey Time

0.00	Bishops Lydeard		0.00	Bishops Lydeard
4.00	Crowcombe Heathfield		2.25	Norton Fitzwarren
6.50	Stogumber		5.00	Taunton
9.75	Williton			
10.75	Doniford			
11.50	Watchet			
14.00	Washford			
16.25	Blue Anchor			
18.00	Dunster			
19.50	Minehead			

A return journey takes about 3 hours.

Stock List

Type	Number	Builder	Details
Steam	1984	Andrew Barclay	0-4-0F
Steam	CALEDONIA WORKS (1219)	Andrew Barclay	0-4-0ST
Steam	9351	GWR	2-6-0
Steam	4561	GWR	2-6-2T
Steam	5199	GWR	2-6-2T
Steam	7822	British Railways	4-6-0
Steam	7828	British Railways	4-6-0
Steam	4936	GWR	4-6-0
Steam	6024	GWR	4-6-0
Diesel	200793	Ruston & Hornsby	4wDM
Diesel	DH16	Sentinel	0-4-0
Diesel	1 (578)	Andrew Barclay	0-6-0

Diesel	2 (579)	Andrew Barclay	0-6-0
Diesel	D2133	British Railways	Class 03
Diesel	D4107	British Railways	Class 09
Diesel	D9518	British Railways	Class 14
Diesel	D9526	British Railways	Class 14
Diesel	D6566	BRCW	Class 33
Diesel	D6575	BRCW	Class 33
Diesel	D7017	Beyer Peacock	Class 35
Diesel	D7018	Beyer Peacock	Class 35
Diesel	47077	British Railways	Class 47
Diesel	D1010	British Railways	Class 52
DMU	51859, 51880, 51887 & 59678	British Railways	Class 115
DMU	51354 & 51396	Pressed Steel	Class 117

Attractions

The WSR is one of the longest heritage railways in Britain and one of the most popular attractions in the South-West. There are several museums on the railway; the Gauge Museum at Bishops Lydeard has exhibits of local and railway interest. The Great Western Railway Museum at Blue Anchor opens Sundays & Bank Holidays from Easter to September and during special events. The Somerset and Dorset Railway Trust have a museum at Washford. The Diesel & Electric Preservation Group's depot at Williton is usually open at weekends. There is a model railway at Bishops Lydeard and a bookshop and café at Minehead. Driving courses can be arranged, using either a steam or diesel locomotive. On some dates there is a bus link from Dunster station to Dunster Castle (National Trust). Bishops Lydeard is situated at the foot of the Quantock Hills, Watchet station is located next to the picturesque harbour and Minehead station is adjacent to the beach and town centre.

Special Events

Events that usually take place on the railway include:

A variety of themed trains, including Murder Mystery Specials, Steam & Cream Specials, Fish & Chip Specials and Cheese & Cider Specials.
Steam Gala.
Diesel Gala planned for 10-13 June 2021 (TBC).
1940s event.
Steam Express during December.

▲ The West Somerset Railway has a varied motive power fleet, which includes two Class 33s. D6566 and D6575 pass Cleave Hill near Watchet while working the 15.51 Bishops Lydeard–Minehead during the railway's summer Diesel Gala on 21 June 2019.   **Ken Davies**

Yeovil Railway Centre

Introduction and History

The Railway Centre is located within the sidings of the yard immediately south of Yeovil Junction station. The station opened in 1860 and the site which the centre occupies included a transfer shed, where goods were transferred between broad gauge and standard gauge railway wagons. Closure of Yeovil Junction station was proposed in 1964 and whilst local opposition prevented this, much of the freight traffic was lost and the railway was downgraded to a single track line during the 1960s. The first heritage railway group formed in 1994 and a lease for the site was agreed. A new engine shed was constructed, opening in 1999 and since then various steam and diesel locomotives have visited or been renovated at the centre.

Contact Details

Website: www.yeovilrailway.freeservers.com
Tel: 01935 410420
Email: yeovilrailway@hotmail.com
Address: Yeovil Railway Centre, Yeovil Junction Station, Stoford, Yeovil, BA22 9UU.

Transport Links

By Rail: The Railway Centre is adjacent to Yeovil Junction station.
By Road: There is free parking on-site, turn right under the railway bridge when approaching Yeovil Junction (BA22 9UU).

Opening Times

The shop opens 10.00–12.00 on Sundays and the railway usually operates on alternate Sundays from March until September and on selected dates during December. Trains are steam-hauled on most dates.

Line Mileage and Journey Time

The railway line runs for one third of a mile and the journey time is relatively short.

Stock List

Type	Number	Builder	Details
Steam	1398 LORD FISHER	Andrew Barclay	0-4-0ST
Steam	1579 PECTIN	Peckett	0-4-0ST
Diesel	DS1174	Ruston & Hornsby	4wDM
Diesel	44	Fowler	0-4-0DM
Diesel	22898	Fowler	0-4-0DM
Diesel	22900 SAM	Fowler	0-4-0DM
DMU	59515	Pressed Steel	Class 117

Attractions

The Centre has a 70-foot operational turntable, which is used when main line steam locomotives are serviced, as well as a model railway which is in use when the standard gauge railway operates. Steam locomotive driver experience courses are available. The visitor centre has various railway themed exhibits and serves light refreshments. Nearby attractions include Yeovil Country Park, several National Trust sites and various rural locations across Somerset and nearby Dorset.

Special Events

23 May 2021: Steam Train Day with "Lord Fisher" (subject to restrictions being eased). Santa Specials usually operate during December.

Proposed Heritage Railways

New heritage railways have opened almost every year since 1960 and as the chart in the Introduction shows, the years in which the sites in this book opened are spread over six decades and counting. It usually takes many years from the formation of a preservation group to the time when trains first operate, and the listings above summarise the 100+ such journeys that have already been made. This section showcases projects that are well-established and are advancing towards their aim of operating trains. It is by no means an exhaustive list, as there are plenty of other prospective heritage railways, where the preservation efforts are at an earlier stage. The Dolgarrog Railway in North Wales for example has taken "two steps forward and two steps back" recently, making good progress in clearing the trackbed and building a platform, but like some of its operational counterparts, it has suffered both vandalism and flood damage. As this and other similar schemes progress, it is hoped that they will be included in future editions of this book.

The criteria for inclusion in this section is most or all of the following:

- The organisation has been granted access to the railway line or trackbed. In most cases, this consists of an agreement with Network Rail or the land owner to lease or access the railway line.
- They are in possession of rolling stock for operating passenger carrying trains. This could be minimal, such as a brake van and small shunting locomotive or a DMU that requires renovation.
- The group have an online presence, with details of their activities, aims and any events which are open to the public.

The proposed heritage railway listings follow a similar format to their established relatives. Any readers considering visiting or volunteering with these organisations are encouraged to do so, making advance arrangements as necessary.

Invergarry & Fort Augustus Railway Museum, Scotland Region

Background

The original Invergarry & Fort Augustus Railway was a 23-mile branch line which ran from Spean Bridge, along the banks of Loch Lochy and Loch Oich, terminating at Fort Augustus at the southern end of Loch Ness. The railway opened in 1903 and was used by King George VII in 1905, when he took the royal train to Invergarry to visit Lord and Lady Burton at Glenquoich Lodge. As the line ran through a sparsely populated area, passenger numbers were low. Consequently, it was a short-lived venture and passenger services were withdrawn as early as 1933. Infrequent freight trains carrying coal and timber continued until 1946, when the line was closed. Part of the trackbed has since been converted to the Great Glen Way, which is a well-used footpath between Fort William and Inverness.

Heritage Railway Progress and Future Plans

In 2012 a group formed with the intention of preserving the remains of Invergarry station and establishing a museum there. Invergarry was one of four intermediate stations on the line and is approximately half way between Spean Bridge and Fort Augustus. A 150-metre section of standard gauge track was laid in 2015, running north-east from the station, enabling the first train rides to be provided that year. The line has since been extended to a length of one third of a mile. It is hoped that it will be further increased to half a mile during 2021 and that regular passenger rides can begin, using the diesel shunter and a restored brake van. A signal cabin has been built on the station platform and there are plans to construct a replica 1930s station building and a carriage shed. There is a visitor centre with information displays on the station and the railway's history. A Saxby & Farmer lever frame from Tyndrum Upper was donated by Network Rail and this will be installed and used on the site.

Contact Details

Website: www.invergarrystation.org.uk
Email: info@invergarrystation.org.uk
Address: Station Approach Road, South Laggan PH34 4EA.

Opening Times & Transport Links
Regular volunteer working days usually take place on most Tuesdays. The site also opens on the first Sunday of the month between May and September, when it may be possible to ride on a short section of the railway and a donation for this is suggested.

By Rail: Spean Bridge is the nearest railway station and this is 13 miles away.
By Road: Parking for up to 12 cars is available at Invergarry (PH34 4EA).
By Bike: Invergarry station is on Route 78 of the National Cycling Network.
By Water: From the Caledonian Canal and Loch Oich; alight at the Great Glen Water Park landing stage.

Stock List

Type	Number	Builder	Details
Diesel	236364	Ruston & Hornsby	4wDM

Local Attractions
Invergarry station is located on the banks of Loch Oich, on the route of the Great Glen Way and on Route 78 of the National Cycling Network. Many walks through the rugged Scottish landscape can be made within the area and Invergarry Castle is two miles away.

Poulton & Wyre Railway, Northern England Region

Background
The railway from Poulton-le-Fylde to Fleetwood opened in 1840 and was one of the first railways in the world to regularly carry holidaymakers. It also served the busy port at Fleetwood and was part of the fastest route between London and Glasgow until 1848, when a direct rail connection between Preston and Glasgow opened. Before then, trains ran from London to Fleetwood, where passengers continued north by steam ship to Ardrossan. In 1966 Fleetwood station closed and the line was cut back to a new terminus at Fleetwood Wyre Dock. Passenger services to Fleetwood ended in 1970 and the line was singled in 1973. Freight trains continued to use the route until 1999, when the final train to the chemical plant at Burn Naze ran. The track from Poulton-le-Fylde to Fleetwood remains in place; however, the main line connection at Poulton was removed in 2018, when the line between Preston and Blackpool North was electrified and resignalled. In November 2019, Prime Minister Boris Johnson visited Thornton-Cleveleys station, where he announced the £500 Restoring Your Railway Fund, for reopening disused lines.

Heritage Railway Progress and Future Plans
The Poulton & Wyre Railway Society (PWRS) formed in 2006 and Network Rail provided the group with a license to access the track, Thornton-Cleveleys and Burn Naze stations. The Society then began clearing vegetation, restoring the railway and the two stations. In 2010 a Fowler shunter was acquired, followed by a Class 108 DMU in 2016 which is now being restored at Thornton-Cleveleys. It was hoped that the heritage railway could connect with the main line at Poulton-le-Fylde, but this became less likely when Network Rail removed Poulton Junction. There are plans to operate trains on a short section of track soon; the long-term plan is for regular services between Poulton and a newly constructed Fleetwood South station.

Contact Details
Website: www.pwrs.org
Email: Written enquiries can be made from the railway's website.
Address: Poulton & Wyre Railway Society, The Print Room, Hillhouse Business Park, Thornton, Lancashire, FY5 4QD.

Opening Times & Transport Links
Volunteer working sessions usually take place on most Saturdays and Wednesdays at Thornton or Burn Naze. Membership of the PWRS is required to participate in these.

By Rail: Poulton-le-Fylde station is approximately two miles from Thornton.
By Road: Free parking is available near to Thornton station. There is no parking at Burn Naze station.

Stock List

Type	Number	Builder	Details
Diesel	4210108	Fowler	0-4-0
DMU	51937 & 56484	British Railways	Class 108

Local Attractions

The Wyre Way is a walking route which begins at Fleetwood, where it crosses the railway and continues along the Wyre estuary and to the Forest of Bowland in north-east Lancashire. Nearby attractions include Farmer Parr's Animal World and the coastal resorts of Fleetwood and Blackpool, which are home to many museums, theme parks and attractions.

Anglesey Central Railway, Wales Region

Background

The 17.5-mile branch line from Gaerwen, on the North Wales Coast main line, to Amlwch opened in stages between 1864 and 1867. In 1951 a one-mile extension was laid from a junction outside Amlwch station to the bromine works on the coast, beyond the town centre. Passenger services to Amlwch were withdrawn in 1964, after which the line was used to carry chemicals to and from the works site until 1993, when they were transferred to road haulage. Instead of being formally closed, the line was then mothballed and it has remained dormant since. The track remains in place, although the railway was severed in 2018, when a bridge in Llangefni was removed after being struck by a lorry.

Heritage Railway Progress and Future Plans

A preservation group formed in 1991, with the aim of restoring passenger services to the Amlwch branch. When freight traffic ended in 1993, there were calls for seasonal steam-hauled trains to operate on the line, but these didn't materialise. in 2011 Network Rail issued the group with a license to access the track and vegetation clearance began. The license also permits members to push a non-powered trolley on the railway. Members of the public are not currently permitted to access the line. A Fowler diesel 0-4-0 shunter is based at Llanerchymedd station, although this is not currently used. Before the coronavirus pandemic began in 2020, group members were working on the line on a twice-weekly basis and the working parties are due to resume during 2021. In 2011 the Welsh Assembly Government commissioned a feasibility study on reintroducing main line passenger trains to Llangefni, using the first 4.5 miles of the branch, but other than a 2020 Welsh Government request for funding to investigate this, this project has seen no further progress.

Contact Details

Website: www.leinamlwch.co.uk or search for "Lein Amlwch of Anglesey Central Railway" on Facebook.
Email: leinamlwch@gmail.com and written enquiries can be made from the Facebook page.

Opening Times & Transport Links

The railway across Anglesey is currently only accessible to members of the Anglesey Central Railway and therefore not currently open to the public.

Stock List

Type	Number	Builder	Details
Diesel	22753	Fowler	0-4-0DM

Local Attractions

Anglesey has many visitor attractions, including Amlwch Copper Kingdom, Oriel Mon museum & art gallery at Llangefni, South Stack Lighthouse, Pili Palas Nature World, Plas Newedd House & Gardens and Holyhead Maritime Museum.

Garw Valley Railway, Wales Region

Background
The railway from Tondu to Nantymoel opened in 1865 and the steeply graded branch from Brynmenyn Junction near Tondu to Blaengarw opened in 1876. The area's small population grew substantially after the railway opened, enabling the Garw Valley's rich coal resources to be exported via the ports of South Wales. Blaengarw lost its passenger services in 1953, although coal trains continued using the route until 1986, ending shortly after Ocean Colliery closed. The nearby line to Tondu and Maesteg was reopened to passenger trains in 1992 and trains briefly returned to Pontycymer during the 1990s to remove spoil tips. The northern-most section of the line between Pontycymer and Blaengarw was demolished in the 1990s, but the majority of the route from Tondu to Pontycymer has remained in situ since.

Heritage Railway Progress and Future Plans
The first preservation group formed in 1988, with the aim of creating a museum and heritage railway centre. Since then, a base and locomotive shed has been established at Pontycymer, where the heritage centre is to be built and the 4.75-mile line to Brynmenyn has been leased from Network Rail. In 2016, the first section of a new station at Pontycymer was built and a 200-metre section of track was laid. Work to increase the line's length to 600 metres is underway and it is hoped that this will be operational by the end of 2021. The next phase will be to extend the operational line to a length of approximately 1.25 miles and the long-term aim is for it to continue south to Tondu, where it would meet the Bridgend to Maesteg line.

Contact Details
Website: www.garwvalleyrailway.co.uk or www.facebook.com/garwvalleyrailway
Email: enquiries@garwvalleyrailway.co.uk
Address: Garw Valley Railway, Pontycymer Locomotive Works, Old Station Yard, Pontycymer, Bridgend, CF32 8AZ.

Opening Times & Transport Links
The locomotive shed at Pontycymer usually opens on Wednesdays and Saturdays, although visitors should check the website or contact the railway before travelling. Promotional open days are periodically held on Bank Holiday weekends, the next one likely to be during the August 2021 Bank Holiday weekend.

By Rail: The nearest railway station is Tondu, which is six miles away.
By Road: There is free parking at Pontycymer, which is shared with the leisure centre (CF32 8AZ).

Stock List

Type	Number	Builder	Details
Steam	7705	Robert Stephenson & Hawthorns	0-4-0ST
Steam	3840 PAMELA	Hunslet	0-6-0ST
Diesel	3890	Hibberd	0-4-0
Diesel	4006	Hibberd	0-4-0
Diesel	51919 & 52048	British Railways	Class 108

Local Attractions
Attractions in the area include Bryngarw Country Park, South Wales Miners Museum, Parc Slip Nature Reserve and Bridgend Miniature Railway.

180

Leiston Works Railway, Eastern Region

Background

Richard Garrett & Sons was established in 1778 and manufactured steam engines, traction engines and a variety of agricultural machinery across two sites in Leiston, Suffolk, which were known as The Works. Initially horse-drawn transport was used and when the railway from Saxmundham to Leiston opened in 1859 it connected to The Works, allowing products to be transported within and away from the two sites. In 1860 the railway was extended to Aldeburgh. By the early 20th Century, there was a comprehensive track network within Leiston linking the two sites and at its height the company employed over 3500 people. By the 1950s the industry was in decline, as road transport and motor vehicles were increasingly replacing steam traction. Passenger services on the railway from Saxmundham to Aldeburgh were withdrawn in 1966 and the line to The Works closed in 1968. After further decline, both sites of The Works closed in 1981. Much of the two sites were demolished and used for property development; however, some parts have been preserved and these can be seen in The Long Shop Museum. The railway track between Aldeburgh and Sizewell was lifted after passenger services ended, leaving a single line for nuclear fuel traffic from Saxmundham to Sizewell. This remains in the possession of Network Rail and has recently seen little traffic, although in August 2020 68026 and 66422 made a test run using a rake of 20 wagons, ahead of proposed construction traffic for a new reactor at Sizewell and the first nuclear flask train for a long time visited in April 2021.

Heritage Railway Progress and Future Plans

In 2011 a group of railway enthusiasts formed the Leiston Works Railway Trust with the aim of reopening a section of The Works railway. They purchased and cleared some of the trackbed and laid a 100-metre section of track to the north of the Long Shop Museum, using track panels from the former Ipswich Docks line. To celebrate the 160th anniversary of the railway reaching Leiston Works, in June 2019 the first preserved train ran. This consisted of a Ruston shunter making a series of light engine movements on the newly laid track. The next phase is to extend the line north to Buller Road, which is less than 100 metres from the Network Rail line to Sizewell Power Station, giving around 200 metres of operational track. Longer-term aims include reconnecting the railway to the former Garrett Works site at the Long Shop Museum and it is hoped that it may be possible to reconnect to the Sizewell branch, giving a much longer heritage railway. The group are also restoring vintage carriages and a brake van which will be used to carry passengers. The steam locomotive "Sirapite", which worked on the site until 1962, has been restored to operational condition and can be seen at the Long Shop Museum.

Contact Details

Website: www.lwr.org.uk
Tel: 07774 640708
Email: theleistonworksrailway@gmail.com
Address: Access is by prior arrangement. Please contact the railway.

Opening Times & Transport Links

Working parties for members usually meet weekly at the workshop. Membership is £10 per year; please contact the railway if you are interested in joining.

By Rail: Saxmundham is the nearest railway station and is four miles away.
By Road: Free car parking is available for Long Shop Museum visitors (IP16 4ES).

Stock List

Type	Number	Builder	Details
Steam	SIRAPITE	Aveling & Porter	0-4-0WT

Local Attractions

The Long Shop Museum is housed within the former works site at Leiston and showcases the town's industrial history. Other nearby attractions include RSPB Minsmere, Orford Ness National Nature Reserve and various coastal and rural sites across Suffolk.

North Dorset Railway, Shillingstone, South East Region

Background
The railway through Shillingstone opened in 1863, when the Templecombe to Blandford section of the recently formed Somerset & Dorset Railway was completed, creating a railway linking the Bristol Channel and the South Coast. Shillingstone station was closed when British Rail withdrew all traffic from the route in 1966 and the track was lifted the following year. Dorset Country Council then purchased the trackbed through Shillingstone, with the intention of building a bypass on it, but the project was later abandoned. The station site was then used by a number of commercial occupiers in the years that followed.

Heritage Railway Progress and Future Plans
A group of enthusiasts formed the North Dorset Railway Trust in 2001 and began negotiations with Dorset Country Council. A 99-year lease on Shillingstone station and part of the trackbed was granted in 2005. Restoration of the station commenced in 2006 and since then the down platform and signal box have been rebuilt. The site opened to the public in 2008 and 400 metres of track has been laid through the station. It is hoped that planning approval will be granted soon, allowing the railway to be extended north along the trackbed, crossing Lamb House Bridge and reaching the area known as Bere Marsh. There are long term aspirations to create an operational railway to Sturminster Newton, running alongside the North Dorset Trailway.

Contact Details
Website: www.northdorsetrailway.co.uk
Tel: 01258 860696
Email: info@northdorsetrailway.co.uk
Address: North Dorset Railway, Shillingstone Station, Station Road, Shillingstone, Blandford Forum, Dorset, DT11 0SA.

Opening Times & Transport Links
Shillingstone station is usually open on Saturdays and Sundays from 10.00 to 16.00.

By Rail: The nearest railway stations are Gillingham (12 miles) and Templecombe (13 miles).
By Road: There is limited parking at Shillingstone station.
By Bike: Shillingstone station is on the North Dorset Trailway, a 14-mile walking and cycling route between Sturminster Newton and Spetisbury, which predominantly follows the course of the former railway.

Stock List

Type	Number	Builder	Details
Steam	30075	Duro Dakovic	0-6-0T
Steam	30076	Duro Dakovic	0-6-0T
Diesel	D1186	Hudswell Clarke	0-6-0DM
Diesel	DS1169	Ruston & Hornsby	4wDM

Local Attractions
Shillingstone station has a museum, signal box, model railway and a collection of standard gauge rolling stock. The site also has a garden, shop and café. Nearby attractions include Shillingstone Hill, Sturminster Newton Mill, Hambledon Hill, Hod Hill and the traffic free North Dorset Trailway.

Rother Valley Railway, South East Region

Background
The railway between Robertsbridge on the Tonbridge–Hastings main line and Rolvenden opened in 1900. Details of the background and history of this route are given in the listing for the Kent & East Sussex Railway (K&ESR).

Heritage Railway Progress and Future Plans
The Rother Valley Railway (RVR) formed in 1991, with the intention of acquiring the trackbed and reinstating the disused railway between Robertsbridge and Bodiam, which is the western terminus of the K&ESR. Sections of trackbed at each end of the two and a half mile Rother Valley route were acquired and, starting in 2009, the railway relaid approximately three quarters of a mile of track near Bodiam. The first heritage trains operated in 2011. A further half mile of track was subsequently relaid at Robertsbridge and trains first used this in 2013. The RVR is in the process of acquiring the remainder of the route, which has been met with some local opposition. In 2017 Rother District Council issued planning permission for the line to be reinstated and when the Transport & Works Act Order has been approved, the remaining track can be relaid. Once the two sections have been joined, it is planned for the RVR to be absorbed into the K&ESR, which could then operate through trains from Tenterden to Robertsbridge.

Contact Details
Website: www.rvr.org.uk
Tel: 01580 881833
Email: reception@rvr.org.uk
Address: Rother Valley Railway, Robertsbridge Junction Station, Station Road, Robertsbridge, East Sussex, TN32 5DG.

Opening Times & Transport Links
There is a small shop and visitor centre at Robertsbridge, which usually opens 10.00–16.00 on Sundays. A model railway exhibition is planned for the weekend of 29–30 May 2021, with full details yet to be confirmed.

By Rail: The railway has a main line connection at Robertsbridge.
By Road: There is a pay & display car park at Robertsbridge station.

Line Mileage and Journey Time
There is currently half a mile of track, which runs north-east from Robertsbridge station.

Stock List

Type	Number	Builder	Details
Diesel	D77	Vulcan Foundry	0-4-0
Diesel	Titan (D140)	Vulcan Foundry	0-4-0
Diesel	D2112	British Railways	Class 03

Local Attractions
As well as the visitor centre at Robertsbridge, there is also a small collection of railway vehicles. The Kent & East Sussex Railway is nearby and details of other attractions in the area are given in the K&ESR listing.

▲ It usually takes years for the necessary legislative and engineering hurdles to be navigated before heritage railways can begin laying track. Before the Tarka Valley Railway could lay this initial section, the footpath of the Tarka Trail, as seen on the left, had to be realigned and a new fence erected. This view from 4 June 2020 shows the newly laid track panels that proceed from Torrington station, which is visible in the distance. **Phil Tarry**

▼ On 14 September 2020, Fowler 0-4-0 "PROGRESS" makes a test run along the Tarka Valley Railway's recently laid line which runs north-west from Torrington station. **Phil Tarry**

Tarka Valley Railway, South West Region

Background
The broad gauge railway from Barnstaple reached Bideford in 1855 and was extended to Torrington in 1872, where it initially terminated. The line was converted to standard gauge in 1877. In 1880 the three foot gauge Torrington & Marland Railway opened, travelling south from Torrington. This was converted to standard gauge in 1925 and extended south to Halwill, where it connected with the railway to Bude, creating a through route from Barnstaple to Bude. This closed to passenger traffic in 1965; however, milk traffic continued until 1978 and ball clay and occasional charter trains from Barnstaple to Torrington ran until 1982. The track was lifted in 1985 and Devon County Council purchased the trackbed from British Rail in order to create a traffic free walkway.

Heritage Railway Progress and Future Plans
The Tarka Valley Railway Group formed in 2008 to preserve the remaining traces of the railway at Torrington station and investigate the possibility of reinstating a railway line towards Bideford. A short length of track was laid alongside the platform of the former Torrington station in 2008 and in 2013 the group gained planning approval to extend this north by almost 300 metres to the first overbridge. Devon County Council granted a lease in 2018, enabling track laying to begin, including a further 100 metres for two sidings alongside the old coal loading bay. The Tarka Trail was then realigned slightly, to create space for the railway to run alongside the path and a dividing fence was erected. The line has now reached the overbridge and it is hoped that brake van rides can begin soon, using one of the railway's diesel shunters. The long-term aim is for the railway to operate between Torrington and Bideford, which is five miles to the north (see the listing for the Bideford Railway Heritage Centre). There are three small river bridges, a tunnel and a viaduct between Torrington and Bideford, all of which require engineering works before the railway beside the Tarka Trail can be completed.

Contact Details
Website: www.tarkavalleyrailway.co.uk or search for Tarka Valley Railway on Facebook
Email: tarkavalleyrailway@gmail.com
Address: TVR Membership Secretary, Puffing Billy, Torrington Station, Station Hill, Great Torrington, Devon, EX38 8JD.

Opening Times & Transport Links
The site and information centre open each Thursday (whatever the weather!) except at Christmas. Open days take place periodically and these are advertised in advance on the TVR website.

By Rail: The nearest railway station is Barnstaple, which is 11 miles away.
By Road: Car parking is available at the Torrington site (EX38 8JD).
By Bike: By way of the traffic-free Tarka Trail.

Stock List

Type	Number	Builder	Details
Diesel	PROGRESS	Fowler	0-4-0
Diesel	TORRINGTON CAVALIER	Ruston & Hornsby	0-4-0

Local Attractions
The Puffing Billy is a public house within the former Torrington station building, located directly on the Tarka Trail and this opens daily. Bicycle hire is available nearby, allowing visitors to explore the traffic-free Tarka Trail; this connects Torrington station with the Bideford Railway Heritage Centre, which is five miles to the north.

Vale of Berkeley Railway, South West Region

Background

The four mile branch line from Berkeley Road (between Bristol and Cheltenham) to Sharpness opened to freight in 1875 and to passengers in 1876. In 1879 it became a through route when the Severn Railway Bridge opened, connecting Sharpness to Lydney Town, which is now part of the Dean Forest Railway. The bridge was damaged beyond repair in 1960 and Sharpness was then relegated back to terminus status until passenger services ended in 1964. Shortly after this Sharpness and Berkeley station buildings were demolished. Network Rail owns the line from Berkeley Junction to Sharpness Docks and freight trains operated by Direct Rail Services use it to access the sidings on the site of the former Berkeley station. This is half way along the branch and is where radioactive waste is loaded onto trains. As there is no run-round facility at the sidings, trains have to proceed further along the branch to Oldminster Sidings on the outskirts of Sharpness Docks in order for the locomotives to run round. Consequently, almost the full length of the line remains in commercial use.

Heritage Railway Progress and Future Plans

The preservation group formed in 2013 and since 2015 it has leased the old engine shed at Sharpness Docks as a base. This is being used to restore various locomotives and other rolling stock. Discussions are in progress with the various stakeholders regarding the creation of a run-round loop at the Berkeley loading site, which would alleviate the need for main line trains to travel further along the branch to the run-round loop at Oldminster Sidings, Sharpness. The western half of the branch could then be freed-up for heritage use, with stations rebuilt at Berkeley and on the site of the original Sharpness station at Oldminster. After receiving a temporary licence from Network Rail in 2018, the group cleared the vegetation on the former Midland Railway Exchange Sidings, which occupy a four-acre site adjacent to Sharpness Docks. Negotiations are at an advanced stage to obtain a 25-year lease on the site, so that it can be developed as an operational base for the railway. The long-term aim is to create a heritage railway from Berkeley to Sharpness, using the main-line connection at Berkeley Road once the nuclear traffic has ceased.

Contact Details

Website: www.valeofberkeleyrailway.co.uk
Email: valeofberkeleyrailway@gmail.com
Address: Vale of Berkeley Railway, The Old Engine House, The Docks, Sharpness, Gloucestershire, GL13 9UD.

Opening Times & Transport Links

The Engine Shed usually opens 10.00–16.00 on Tuesdays, Wednesdays, Fridays and Saturdays. During these times visitors are welcome to look around the shed and meet volunteers.

By Rail: The nearest railway station is Cam and Dursley which is nine miles away.
By Road: Parking is available at The Old Engine House site (GL13 9UD).

Stock List

Type	Number	Builder	Details
Steam	CEGB (2126)	Andrew Barclay	0-4-0F
Steam	4027	LMS	0-6-0
Steam	15	Andrew Barclay	0-6-0ST
Steam	44901	LMS	4-6-0
Diesel	7069	LMS	0-6-0

Local Attractions

There are a number of locomotives, items of rolling stock, signalling and railway equipment which can be seen at the Old Engine House site in Sharpness. Attractions in the area include Wildfowl & Wetlands Trust Slimbridge Wetland Centre, Cattle Country Adventure Park, Dr Jenner's House and Berkeley Castle.

Appendix I: Locomotive and Multiple Unit Builders

Builder name used in listings	Builder's Full Name
82045 Steam Locomotive Trust	82045 Steam Locomotive Trust
AC Cars	AC Cars Ltd
AEG, Berlin	Allgemeine Elektricitäts-Gesellschaft, Berlin
Alan Keef	Alan Keef Ltd
Alexander	Walter Alexander Coachbuilders
American Locomotive Co.	American Locomotive Company
Andrew Barclay	Andrew Barclay Sons & Co.
Armstrong Whitworth	Armstrong Whitworth & Co
Aveling & Porter	Aveling & Porter
Avonside	Avonside Engine Company
B17 SLT	B17 Steam Locomotive Trust
Baby Deltic Project	Baby Deltic Project
Bagnall	W. G. Bagnall
Baguley	E. E. Baguley Ltd
Baldwin Locomotive Works	Baldwin Locomotive Works, USA
Beyer Peacock	Beyer, Peacock & Company
Black Hawthorn	Black, Hawthorn & Co.
Bluebell Railway SC2P	Bluebell Railway Standard Class 2 Project
Borrows	E Borrows & Sons
BRCW	Birmingham Railway Carriage & Wagon Co.
BREL	British Rail Engineering Limited
British Rail	British Rail
British Railways	British Railways
British Thompson Houston	British Thomson Houston
Brown Boveri	Brown, Boveri & Cie, Switzerland
Brush Traction	Brush Traction
Bury Curtis & Kennedy	Bury, Curtis & Kennedy
Caledonian Railway	Caledonian Railway
Clayton	Clayton Equipment Company
Cockerill	John Cockerill Company
Consett	Consett Iron Company
Cravens	Cravens
Danske Statsbaner	Danske Statsbaner, Denmark
DB, Germany	Deutsche Bahn, Germany
Dodman & Co	Dodman & Co.
Drewry	Drewry Car Co.
Dübs & Company	Dübs & Company
Duro Dakovic	Duro Dakovic, Yugoslavia
Electroputere	Electroputere S.A., Romania
English Electric	English Electric
Fablok	Fablok, Poland
Fairfield Shipbuilding & Engine Co.	Fairfield Shipbuilding & Engine Co.
Fire Fly Trust	The Fire Fly Trust
Fletcher Jennings	Fletcher, Jennings & Co.
Foster Rastrick	Foster Rastrick & Co
Fowler	John Fowler & Co.
Fox Walker	Fox, Walker & Company
GEC Traction Ltd	GEC Traction Ltd
George England	George England & Co.
George Stephenson	George Stephenson
GER	Great Eastern Railway
Gmeinder & Co.	Gmeinder & Co., Germany
GNR	Great Northern Railway
Grant Richie	Grant Richie & Company
GRCW	Gloucester Railway Carriage & Wagon Co. Ltd
Great Central Railway	Great Central Railway
Great Western Society	The Great Western Society
Greenwood & Batley	Greenwood & Batley Ltd
GWR	Great Western Railway
Hagglund and Soner	Hagglund and Soner, Sweden

Hartmann	Richard Hartmann, Germany
Hawthorne Leslie	Hawthorn Leslie & Company
Haydock	Haydock Foundry
Head Wrightson	Head Wrightson
Hibberd	F. C. Hibberd & Co.
Hitachi	Hitachi Ltd
Howard	J & F Howard
Hudswell Clarke	Hudswell Clarke
Hunslet	Hunslet Engine Company
ICI South Central Workshops	Imperian Chemical Industries, South Central Workshops
Kerr Stuart	Kerr, Stuart and Company
Kitson	Kitson and Company
L&NWR	London and North Western Railway
Lancashire & Yorkshire	Lancashire and Yorkshire Railway
LBSCR	London, Brighton and South Coast Railway
Leyland	Leyland Bus
Lima Locomotive Co	Lima Locomotive Corporation
Lister Blackstone	Lister Blackstone
Liverpool & Manchester	Liverpool and Manchester Railway
LMS	London, Midland and Scottish Railway
LMS-Patriot Project	LMS-Patriot Project
LNER	London and North Eastern Railway
LNWR	London and North Western Railway
Locomotion Enterprises	Locomotion Enterprises
LSWR	London and South Western Railway
LT&SR	London, Tilbury and Southend Railway
Manning Wardle	Manning Wardle
Markham & Co	Markham & Co Ltd
Metropliton Cammell	Metropolitan Cammell
Metropolitan Railway	Metropolitan Railway
Metropolitan Vickers	Metropolitan Vickers
Midland Railway	Midland Railway
Ministry of Defence	Mininstry of Defence
Motala Verkstad	Motala Verkstad, Sweden
Nasmyth Wilson	Nasmyth, Wilson & Co.
Neilson & Co.	Neilson & Co.
Neilson Reid	Neilson, Reid & Co.
NER	North Eastern Railway
North British	North British Locomotive Company
North London Railway	North London Railway
North Staffordshire Railway	North Staffordshire Railway
Norwegian State Railways	Norwegian State Railways (NSB)
Park Royal	Park Royal Vehicles Limited
Peckett	Peckett and Sons
Port Talbot Railway	Port Talbot Railway & Docks Company
Pressed Steel	Pressed Steel Company
R & W Hawthorn	R & W Hawthorn
Resco Railways	Resco (Railways) Ltd
Robert Heath	Robert Heath and Sons Ltd
Robert Stephenson & Co	Robert Stephenson & Company
Robert Stephenson & Hawthorns	Robert Stephenson & Hawthorns
Rolls Royce Sentinel	Rolls Royce Sentinel
Ruston & Hornsby	Ruston & Hornsby
Sara & Co	Sara & Co
SECR	South Eastern and Chatham Railway
Sentinel	Sentinel Waggon Works
Sharp Stewart	Sharp Stewart and Company
Siemans Harton	Siemans Harton
Simplex	Simplex (Motor Rail)
South Durham Steel & Iron	South Durham Steel & Iron Co
Southern Railway	Southern Railway
Stephen Lewin	Stephen Lewin
The Fire Fly Trust	The Fire Fly Trust
Thomas Hill	Thomas Hill (Rotherham) Ltd

▲ While visiting from the Gloucestershire Warwickshire Railway, Class 37 D6948 approaches Kentsford Farm Crossing near Watchet, while working the West Somerset Railway's 10.09 Bishops Lydeard–Minehead on 22 June 2019. **Ken Davies**

▼ 33035 passes Burrs on the rear of the 16.16 Rawtenstall–Bury Bolton Street on 5 July 2019 (classmate 33109 is on the front). **Tom McAtee**

Timothy Hackworth	Timothy Hackworth
Trevithick 200	Trevithick 200
USATC	United States Army Transportation Corps
Vulcan Foundry	Vulcan Foundry
Vulcan Iron Works	Vulcan Iron Works, USA
Waggon & Maschinenbau	Waggon & Maschinenbau, Germany
Wickham	D. Wickham and Company
Yorkshire Engine Co.	Yorkshire Engine Company

Appendix II: Abbreviations

Steam Locomotives Suffixes

T	Side Tank.
CT	Crane Tank.
PT	Pannier Tank.
ST	Saddle Tank.
WT	Well Tank.
VBT	Vertical Boiler Tank.
VBGT	Vertical Boiler Geared Tank.
F	Fireless.

Diesel & Petrol Locomotive Suffixes

DE	Diesel Electric.
DH	Diesel Hydraulic.
DM	Diesel Mechanical.
PM	Petrol Mechanical.

Other Abbreviations Used

DMU	Diesel Multiple Unit.
EMU	Electric Multiple Unit.
DEMU	Diesel-Electric Multiple Unit.
BR	British Railways; later British Rail.

Appendix III: Index of Heritage Railways

Name	Region	Page
Alderney Railway	South West	149
Aln Valley Railway	Northern England	28
Anglesey Central Railway	Proposed	178
Appleby Frodingham Railway	East Midlands	89
Avon Valley Railway	South West	150
Barrow Hill Roundhouse Railway Centre	East Midlands	90
Barry Tourist Railway	Wales	63
The Battlefield Line	East Midlands	92
Beamish: The Living Museum of the North	Northern England	29
Bideford Railway Heritage Centre	South West	152
Bluebell Railway	South East	128
Bodmin & Wenford Railway	South West	153
Bo'ness & Kinneil Railway	Scotland	14
Border Union Railway	Scotland	17
Bowes Railway	Northern England	31
Bressingham Steam and Gardens	Eastern	112
Bristol Harbour Railway	South West	154
Buckinghamshire Railway Centre	South East	130
Caledonian Railway	Scotland	18
Cambrian Heritage Railways	West Midlands	71
Chasewater Railway	West Midlands	72
Chatham Dockyard Railway	South East	132
Chinnor & Princes Risborough Railway	South East	133
Cholsey & Wallingford Railway	South East	134
Churnet Valley Railway	West Midlands	75
Colne Valley Railway	Eastern	114
Crewe Heritage Centre	Northern England	32
Dartmoor Railway	South West	156
Dartmouth Steam Railway	South West	157
Dean Forest Railway	South West	159
Derwent Valley Light Railway	Northern England	33
Didcot Railway Centre	South East	136
Doon Valley Railway	Scotland	20
East Anglian Railway Museum	Eastern	115
East Kent Railway	South East	137

East Lancashire Railway	Northern England	34
East Somerset Railway	South West	161
Ecclesbourne Valley Railway	East Midlands	94
Eden Valley Railway	Northern England	37
Elsecar Heritage Railway	Northern England	38
Embsay & Bolton Abbey Steam Railway	Northern England	39
Epping Ongar Railway	Eastern	116
Fawley Hill	South East	139
Fife Heritage Railway	Scotland	21
Foxfield Railway	West Midlands	77
Garw Valley Railway	Proposed	179
Gloucestershire Warwickshire Steam Railway	West Midlands	79
Great Central Railway	East Midlands	95
Great Central Railway–Nottingham	East Midlands	98
Gwili Railway	Wales	64
Helston Railway	South West	162
Invergarry & Fort Augustus Railway Museum	Proposed	176
Isle of Wight Steam Railway	South East	140
Keighley & Worth Valley Railway	Northern England	41
Keith & Dufftown Railway	Scotland	22
Kent & East Sussex Railway	South East	141
Lakeside & Haverthwaite Railway	Northern England	43
Lathalmond Railway Museum	Scotland	23
The Lavender Line	South East	143
Leiston Works Railway	Proposed	180
Lincolnshire Wolds Railway	East Midlands	99
Llanelli & Mynydd Mawr Railway	Wales	65
Llangollen Railway	Wales	67
Locomotion, Shildon	Northern England	44
Mangapps Railway Museum	Eastern	118
Mid Hants Railway	South East	144
Mid Norfolk Railway	Eastern	119
Mid Suffolk Light Railway	Eastern	121
Middleton Railway	Northern England	46
Midland Railway-Butterley	East Midlands	101
National Railway Museum	Northern England	47
Nene Valley Railway	Eastern	122
North Dorset Railway	Proposed	181
North Norfolk Railway	Eastern	124
North Yorkshire Moors Railway	Northern England	49
Northampton & Lamport Railway	East Midlands	103
Northamptonshire Ironstone Railway	East Midlands	104
Pallot Steam, Motor & General Museum	South West	163
Peak Rail	East Midlands	105
Plym Valley Railway	South West	164
Pontypool & Blaenavon Railway	Wales	68
Poulton & Wyre Railway	Proposed	177
Ribble Steam Railway	Northern England	51
Rocks by Rail	East Midlands	108
Rother Valley Railway	Proposed	182
Royal Deeside Railway	Scotland	24
Rushden Transport Museum & Railway	East Midlands	109
Severn Valley Railway	West Midlands	81
Somerset & Dorset Railway	South West	166
South Devon Railway	South West	167
Spa Valley Railway	South East	146
Stainmore Railway	Northern England	53
Stephenson Steam Railway	Northern England	54
Strathspey Railway	Scotland	25
Swanage Railway	South West	169
Swindon & Cricklade Railway	South West	170
Tamar Belle Heritage Centre	South West	172
Tanat Valley Light Railway	West Midlands	84
Tanfield Railway	Northern England	55

Tarka Valley Railway	Proposed	184
Telford Steam Railway	West Midlands	85
Tyseley Locomotive Works	West Midlands	86
Vale of Berkeley Railway	Proposed	185
Weardale Railway	Northern England	57
Wensleydale Railway	Northern England	58
West Somerset Railway	South West	173
Whitwell & Reepham Railway	Eastern	125
Yeovil Railway Centre	South West	175
Yorkshire Wolds Railway	Northern England	59

▲ On 5 April 2019, BR Class 4MT 2-6-0 76084 makes its way between Weybourne and Holt during the North Norfolk Railway's Spring Steam Gala. **Alisdair Anderson**